ARCHITECTURE
MYSTICISM & MYTH

ARCHITECTURE MYSTICISM AND MYTH

William R. Lethaby

with illustrations by the author

SOLOS PRESS

First published in 1891
this edition by
SOLOS PRESS 1994.

UK Distribution:
Ashgrove Publishers & Distribution,
7, Locksbrook Road Estate
Bath, Avon, BA1 3DZ.

US Distribution:
Atrium Publishers Group,
11270 Clayton Creek Road,
P.O. Box 108,
Lower Lake,
CA 95457.

ISBN   *Paper*   *1 873616 05 8*
         Cloth   *1 873616 06 6*

Set in 10.5 on 12 point Palatino
Printed and bound in Great Britain by
Cromwell Press Ltd., Broughton Gifford,
Melksham, Wiltshire, SN12 8PH.

Contents

Bigraphical Notes

William Lethaby occupies an unique position in the history of English architectural ideas. The son of a craftsman, he was born in Barnstaple in 1857. He attended the local grammar school and then at the age of fourteen became articled with a local architect, William Lauder. His skill as a draughtsman was soon recognised and he won a number of prizes including the R.I.B.A. Soane Medallion and the Pugin Travelling Scholarship.

In 1879 he moved to London and worked for Norman Shaw, one of the most successful architects of the day. He also became friends with William Morris and John Ruskin, leading lights in the new Arts and Crafts Movement. In 1889 he set up his own practice. Designing new buildings was not, however, to be his main occupation. Though an example of his work can be seen in the country church at Brockhampton, Ross-on Wye, he is better remembered for his writings and for his influence on the development of art education. In this connection he played a prominent part in the founding of both the Arts Workers Guild and the Arts and Crafts Exhibition Society. In 1896, when the Central School of Arts and Crafts was opened by the London County Council, he and George Frampton (who soon retired) were appointed as its first joint Principals. His role as a shaper of art education continued in 1900 when he became the first Professor of Design at the Royal College of Art.

As well as teaching and writing, he was also passionately interested in the care and preservation of old buildings. For nearly forty years he worked for the Society for the Protection of Ancient Buildings and in 1906 was appointed surveyor of Westminster Abbey with responsibility for the care of its ancient fabric. We have him to thank that this monument still retains so much of its ancient character, though he would probably have been rather concerned at the vigorous cleaning it and so many other London buildings have received in recent years.

Architecture, Mysticism and Myth was his first book and though it was received enthusiastically by the public and was reprinted within a year, the press was less keen. In an age that embraced the ideals of modernity based on the abstract notions of progress and evolution, his appeal to a more glorious and mystical past seemed curiously threatening. His book was, however, immensely influencial and stimulated the late 19th Century Byzantine Revival, typified by John Francis Bentley's Roman Catholic cathedral of Westminster. For us today, no longer enamoured with modernism in architecture, it makes fascinating reading.

Illustrations

PREFACE

In sending out this essay, I must ask for indulgence. In the first place, because this is, so far as known to me, the only attempt to set out, from an architect's point of view, the basis of certain ideas common in the architecture of many lands and religions, the purposes behind structure and form which may be called the esoteric principles of architecture.

And secondly, for an attempt to deal with a subject that could only be rightly handled by one having the equipments of a wide scholarship; while I can only claim that there should come of regular apprenticeship and long practice in any craft or art, a certain instinct of insight not possessed by mere outsiders though never so learned. 'the author who asks the question quoted on the title-page, says that Mr. Herbert Spencer's essay on the origin of the styles of architecture fails because he was not himself an architect, and no architect had prepared the way. I refer to this in the hope that writing thus, on my own art, may be sufficient excuse for any appearance of affectation and presumption in quoting unfamiliar matter at second hand; for I must say at once, what will be sufficiently apparent on any page, that my knowledge of books is only that of the general reader, and that I have made use of such inferior editions, translations, and chance extracts as have come in my way; venturing to suppose that, if the thought were clear, a passage originally in hieroglyphs, or on clay tablets, might be dealt with as readily as a paragraph from an evening paper.

In such a wide field I have thought it well to concentrate my attention on some few definite points, and I fear, in doing this, there may be some unnecessary insistence and repetition: a tendency to overprove, and an attempt to explain too much; on the one hand to burden with what is obvious, on the other to weaken by unfounded conjecture.

The main proposition occurred to me after collecting and comparing a large number of architectural legends, and it was not until I read definitely, for further confirmation, that I found statements, a sentence here and there, anticipating me on nearly every point. It is only since this has been in the publishers' hands that I have seen Dr. Warren's ' Paradise Found,' to find there several coincidences with my chapters iv. and v.

To clear the page of footnotes, and to strengthen the structure of the argument by expert evidence, I have generally preferred to transcribe my authorities directly rather than attempt, by paraphrasing them, to give an air of ease and unity to my own work. Equally by either method-
'Would you know the new, you must search the old.'

I have the pleasure of thanking friends who have helped me, especially Mr. Ernest Newton and Mr. E. S. Prior. The figures 22, 24, and 30 are from sketches kindly lent me by Mr. Brindley, Mr. Schultz, and Mr. Barnsley.

2 GRAY'S INN SQUARE.

'The prince Humayan fitted up seven houses of entertainment, and named them after the seven planets, ordering all the furniture, paintings, and also the dresses of those who waited upon him, to bear something that was an emblem of the tutelar star of the house. In the house of the Moon met foreign ambassadors, travellers and poets. Military men attended him in the house of Mars, and judges, lawgivers, and secretaries were received in that of Mercury'.

FERISHTA'S HISTORY OF INDIA.

ARCHITECTURE, MYSTICISM AND MYTH

INTRODUCTORY

> *'Invention, strictly speaking, is little more*
> *than a new combination of those images,*
> *that have been previously gathered and*
> *deposited in the memory: nothing can come*
> *of nothing: he who has laid up no materials*
> *can produce no combinations.'*
> —REYNOLDS, *Discourse II.*

THE history of architecture, as usually written, with its theory of utilitarian origins from the hut and the tumulus, and further developments in that way—the adjustment of forms to the conditions of local circumstance; the clay of Mesopotamia, the granite of Egypt, and marble of Greece—is rather the history of building: of 'Architecture' it may be, in the sense we so often use the word, but not the Architecture which is the synthesis of the fine arts, the commune of all the crafts.

As the pigments are but the vehicle of painting, so is building but the vehicle of architecture, which is the thought behind form, embodied and realised for the purpose of its manifestation and transmission. Architecture, then, interpenetrates building, not for satisfaction of the simple needs of the body, but the complex ones of the intellect. I do not mean that we can thus distinguish between architecture and building, in those qualities in which they meet and overlap, but that in the sum and polarity of them all; these point to the response of future thought, those to the satisfaction of present need; and so, although no hut or mound, however early or rude, but had something added to it for thought's sake, yet architecture and building are quite clear and distinct as ideas—the soul and the body.

Of the modes of this thought we must again distinguish; some were unconscious and instinctive, as the desire for symmetry, smoothness, sublimity, and the like merely aesthetic qualities, which properly enough belong to true architecture; and others were direct and didactic, speaking by a more or less perfect realisation, or through a code of symbols, accompanied by traditions which explained them. The main purpose and burthen of sacred architecture—and all architecture, temple, tomb, or palace, was sacred in the early days —is thus inextricably bound up with a people's thoughts about God and the universe.

Behind every style of architecture there is an earlier style, in which the germ of every form is to be found; except such alterations as may be traced to new conditions, or directly innovating thought in religion, all is the slow change of growth, and it is almost impossible to point to the time of invention of any custom or feature. As Herbert Spencer says of ceremonial generally: 'Adhering tenaciously to all his elders taught him, the primitive man deviates into novelty only through unintended modifications. Every one now knows that languages are not devised but evolve; and the same is true of usages.' It has, rightly, been the habit of historians of architecture to lay stress on the differences of the several styles and schools of successive ages, but, in the far larger sense, all architecture is one, when traced back through the stream of civilisations, as they followed or influenced one another. For instance, argue as archaeologists may, as to whether the columns at Beni Hassan are rightly called proto-Doric, it is a fact to be read as in an open book, that a Greek temple and an Egyptian temple are substantially at one, when we consider the infinite possibilities of form, if disassociated from tradition.

It has often been pointed out, how early examples of stone construction still repeat the forms of the manner of building in wood that went before, and so is it always. How long the steamship retained survivals of the sailing vessel, and how the vocabulary of the coachroad still answers for the railway.

What then, I want to ask, are the ultimate facts behind all architecture which has given it form? Mainly three: *First*, the similar needs and desires of men; *secondly*, on the side of structure, the necessities imposed by materials, and the physical laws of their erection and combination; and *thirdly*, on the side of style, nature. It is of this last that I propose to write; the influence of the known and imagined facts of the universe on architecture, the connection between the world as a structure, and the building, not of the mere details of nature and the ornaments of architecture, but of the whole—the Heavenly Temple and the Earthly Tabernacle. ' Has anyone,' says Mr Lillie in his "Buddhism in Christendom," 'puzzled over the fact, that the only modern representative of the initiates of the ancient mysteries should occupy themselves entirely with the business of the hodman and builder; what is the connection between the kingdom of heaven, and matter of fact mortar, tee-squares and trowels? Esoteric masonry occupied itself in reality, with a temple built without sound of hammer, axe, or tool of iron. It was the temple of the skies, the Macrocosmos, in point of fact.'

It will be necessary, not only to examine architecture in the monuments, but the contemporary statements which relate to them, the stories about buildings, and even the mythology of architecture, for such a mythology there is.

If we trace the artistic forms of things, made by man, to their origin, we find a direct imitation of nature. The thought behind a ship is the imitation of a fish. So to the Egyptians and Greeks the 'Black Ship' bore traces of this descent, and two eyes were painted at the prow. The custom still lingers on the Mediterranean and on the waters of China: the eyes are given, it is said, to enable the ship to see its way over the pathless sea. Tables and chairs, like the beasts are quadrupeds; the lion's leg and foot of modern furniture come to us from the Greeks, and, earlier, they were used in Assyria and Egypt. Thrones had beasts on either hand, a custom traditionally followed for thrones, Hittite, Chaldean, or Hindu, that of Solomon, the imperial throne at Constantinople, or our own Coronation chair. The Egyptian funeral bier seems like a joke, so frank and unmodified is the imitation: it looks, as shown on the mummy cases, like a long, flat-backed lion, tail and all; the example preserved in the Boulak Museum, has the ordinary parallelogram of a bed, each leg being a lion's leg; a head is attached to the middle of the front rail, and a tail, like a pump handle, projects far behind in a great sweeping curve.

Where else, indeed, should we go for the highest imagination? In the modern Greek folk stories, the hero usually has three marvellous robes; one embroidered with the heavens and its stars, the second with the sea and fish swimming there, the third with the earth in May and all its flowers. Could anyone produce finer designs?

The commonplaces of poetry, in which the world is likened to a building, 'heavenly vaults,' or 'azure domes,' 'gates of sunrise,' and the rest, are survivals of a time when the earth was not a tiny ball, projected at immeasurable speed through infinite space, one, among other fireflies of the night, but was stable and immovable, the centre of the universe, the floor on which the sky was built. The whole, a chamber lighted by the sun, moon, and stars.

The ceremonial of religion during the great building ages in Chaldea, Egypt, and India, was going through the phase of Nature worship, in which the sky, the sun, the sea were not so much veiled, as afterwards to the Greeks, until they became persons, not things; but open and understood, astronomical observation was closely associated as part of the cultus.

In all this there is enough to dispose us to receive evidence of a cosmical symbolism in the buildings of the younger world, and we shall find that the intention of the temple (speaking of the temple *idea*, as we understand it) was to set up a local reduplication of the temple not made with hands, the World Temple itself—a sort of model to scale, its form governed by the science of the time; it was a heaven, an observatory, and an almanack. Its foundation was a sacred ceremony, the time carefully chosen by augury, and its relation to the heavens defined by observation. Its place was exactly below the celestial prototype; like that it was sacred, like that strong, its foundations could not be moved, if they were placed foursquare to the walls of the firmament, as are still our churches—and was it not to be like the heavenly sanctuary, that Solomon built the temple without the sound of tool?

I do not necessarily claim that this was the origin of all structures set apart for a purpose in a sense sacred; nor possibly in every case was this the first interpretation of some of the symbols. Customs have many explanations. I claim that, given the idea of a universe and universe gods, the phase here set out was a necessary one; and as this stage certainly everywhere preceded the age, when works, worthy the name of architecture, were produced—buildings which enshrined ideas—it is here we shall find the formative factor in their design. And for this there is ample authority; De la Saussaye, in his comprehensive 'Manual of the Science of Religion ' (1891), says ' the symbolism of temple buildings sometimes seems to refer to the structure of the world, sometimes to the religious relationship of men to the gods.'

Beginning with the form of the world in the first chapter, the three or four which follow, deal with the relation of the building to it as a whole, and the rest with parts and details.

We need not suppose that temples were a sum of these symbols in all cases, if in any; but that from this common book of architecture, each took what he would, little or much, sometimes openly, sometimes with more or less translation, sometimes at first hand, often as a half-remembered tradition.

The ritual side of symbolism is entirely neglected here, but there is ample evidence that sacred ceremony, the state that surrounded a throne, and the pageant of war, all had reference to the ritual and pomp of nature; so that man might be one with her and share her invincible strength. Ridiculous as, at first, it may seem, the Throne, Crown, and Orb of Her Majesty Queen Victoria can only be explained in this way: they are all symbols of a God in his temple; and hereditary kingship has everywhere, as Mr Spencer has shown, claimed divinity, God descent, and afterwards God consent—the right divine. As is said in the old Chinese book, the Li Ki (Sac. Books of E. Vol. 28), 'all ceremonial usages, looked at in their general characteristics, are the embodiment of the ideas suggested by heaven and earth; take their laws from the changes of the four seasons; imitate the operation of the contracting and developing movements in nature, and are conformed to the feelings of men. It is on this account that they are called the Rules of Propriety; and when anyone finds fault with them, he only shows his ignorance of their origin.'

Old architecture lived because it had a purpose. Modern architecture, to be real, must not be a mere envelope without contents. As M. Cèsar Daly says in his *Hautes Etudes*, if we would have architecture excite an interest, real and general, we must have a symbolism, immediately comprehensible by the great majority of spectators. But this message cannot be that of the past—terror, mystery, splendour. Planets may not circle nor thunder roll in the temple of the future. No barbaric gold with ruddy bloom; no jewels; emeralds half a palm over, rubies like an egg, and crystal spheres, can again be used more for magic than for beauty. No terraced temples of Babylon to reach the skies; no gold-plated palaces of Ecbatana, seven-walled; no ivory palaces of Ahab; nor golden houses of Nero with corridors a mile long; no stupendous temples of Egypt at first all embracing, then court and chamber narrowing and becoming lower, closing in on the awed worshipper and crushing his imagination; these, all of them, can never be built again, for the manner and the materials are worked out to their final issue. Think of the Sociology and Religion of all this, and the stain across it, "each stone cemented in the blood of a human creature." Those colossal efforts of labour forced on by an implacable will, are of the past, and such an architecture is not for us, nor for the future.

What, then, will this art of the future be? The message will still be of nature and man, of order and beauty, but all will be sweetness, simplicity, freedom, confidence, and light; the other is past, and well is it, for its aim was to crush life: the new, the future, is to aid life and train it, ' so that beauty may flow into the soul like a breeze.'

CHAPTER I

THE WORLD FABRIC

'Tales of ages long-forgotten
Now the legends of creation
Once familiar to the children.'
—*KALEVALA.*

IF we erase from the mind absolutely all that science has laboriously spied out of the actual facts of the material universe, and ask ourselves what would have been the thoughts by which man attempted at first to explain and image forth the natural order, we may put ourselves in sympathy with notions that at first seem absurd. We may see that the progress of science is merely the framing and destruction one by one of a series of hypotheses, and that the early cosmogonies are one in kind with the widest generalisations of science—from certain appearances to frame a theory of explanation, from phenomena to generalise law.

In thus putting ourselves back into the early world, not only must we remember the limitations to the knowledge of phenomena, but also the inadequate means of expression. Not only must we ask ourselves what primitive man—to use the phrase for what it is worth, not letting it betray us—can have observed: we must ask at the same time; what images can he have had before him to which he might liken the wonder of the sky and the might of the sea? Or rather, these are two phases of the same question by which we may realise the early systems, for in these things at least concepts were immediately linked with words, words which were descriptive comparisons.

The unknown universe could then only be explained in terms of its known parts; the earth, shut in by the night sky, must have been thought of as a living creature, a tree, a tent, a building; and these each form the world system to peoples now living. 'Given the data,' says Herbert Spencer, 'as known to him, the inference drawn by the primitive man is the reasonable inference.'

A tree with wide over-arching branches must have formed an apt and satisfactory explanation, for legends of a world tree are so widely distributed; we meet with them at the dawn of record, and they still strike their roots where 'wild in woods' the savage runs.

The Chaldean inscriptions describe such a tree as growing at the centre of the world; its branches of crystal formed the sky and drooped to the sea. The Phoenicians thought the world like a revolving tree, over which was spread a vast tapestry of blue embroidered with stars. Traces of this scheme linger late into times of culture, and would account for a story in 'Apollonios of Tyana' that the people of Sardis doubted if the trees were not created before the earth; an idea exactly parallel to the controversy in the Talmud, as to the priority in creation of the heavens or the earth; one side maintaining that the object was made first and then the pedestal; the other, that the foundation is laid before the building is erected.

All the East knew of such a tree; in Japan the gods broke their swords against it in vain; in Greece its memory seems long to have survived as the olive of the forest of Colonas.

In the Norse system a vast tree, the world-ash rises in the centre of the earth, its branches forming the several heavens of the gods, its roots strike deep into hell, and there—

> '...A serpent evermore
> Lies deep asleep at the world's dark core.'

Maori science still represents such a tree as rising to the heavens, 'that dark nocturnal canopy which like a forest spreads its shade,' its mighty growth first forced asunder Heaven and Earth. Such an idea is probably very uniform at a certain early stage of civilisation—'The fundamental conception of these myths,' says Lenormant, 'which never appear in perfection except under their oldest forms, represents the universe as an enormous tree.' Its trunk transfixes the earth, projecting upwards into heaven and below into the abyss, the heavens revolve on this axis, and may be reached by climbing the stem.

An extract from Dr Tylor's *Early History of Mankind* will lead us to a later point of view. Man now surrounded by his own works sees in the universe a larger 'tent to dwell in,' a chamber, and ultimately a most elaborate structure, a conception which lasts long even in the direct line of descent of science. This idea it is children find so difficult to shake off—that there must be a brick wall somewhere circumscribing the universe, and we still recognise it in the phrase to 'make the welkin ring.'

'There are,' says Dr Tylor, 'other mythological ways besides the heaven-tree by which, in different parts of the world, it is possible to go up and down between the surface of the ground and the sky or the regions below.... Such tales belong to a rude and primitive state of knowledge of the earth's surface, and what lies above and below it. The earth is a flat plain surrounded by the sea, and the sky forms a roof on which the sun and moon and stars travel. The Polynesians who thought, like so many other people ancient and modern, that the sky descended at the horizon and enclosed the earth, still call foreigners " heaven bursters," as having broken in from another world outside. The sky is to most savages, what it is called in the South American language, "the earth on high," and we can quite understand the thought of some Paraguayans that at death their souls would go up to heaven by the tree which joins earth and sky. There are holes or windows through the sky-roof or firmament where the rain comes through; and if you climb high enough, you can get through and visit the dwellers above, who look and talk and live very much in the same way as the people upon earth. As above the flat earth, so below it, there are regions inhabited by men or manlike creatures, who sometimes come up to the surface, and sometimes are visited by the inhabitants of the upper earth. We live, as it were, upon the ground-floor of a great house, with upper storeys rising one over another above us, and cellars down below.'

This stage of thought lasted so long, embracing the great architectural ages in its span, that one cannot but see that there must have been a relation and reaction between such a world

structure and the buildings of man, especially the sacred buildings set apart, as they mostly were, for a worship that thought
it found its object in earth, sky, and stars.

It would appear generally that to the great civilising races a
square formed universe preceded the hemispherical; indeed, we
are much in the hemispherical age at present, it is just archaic
enough to furnish the poet with his similes, but an old poet like
Job found his comparisons in the chamber-form, a cubical box
with a lid on. In the centre of this vast box whose lid is the sky
rises the earth mountain, which is its prop and the pivot of its
revolutions. It was seen that the centre of this revolution is at a
point within the space guarded by the great bear, and that beyond this the stars dip under the earth of the northern horizon.
Thus the earth mountain in the North furnishes a most adequate
explanation of the apparent motions of the heavens; the crystal
or metal heaven of the fixed stars revolves about it, and consequently the stars are hidden behind it in every revolution. The
sun, moon, and planets issuing from a hole at the east, and sink-
ing into another at the west, move overhead and find their way
back by a subterranean path. The motive power was sometimes
given by active beings, as in the Book of Enoch, or by the winds;
thus the universe was like a great mill.

It is likely that the dome was the next step, although as yet
they were hard put to it to convey the idea, so a skull or half an
eggshell furnished the comparison for the whole. canopy of
heaven, as in the northern system of the Edda:—

Earth was not formed nor heaven above, a yawning gap there
was, but grass nowhere. The earth is made fast in the midst, the
sea round about it in a ring. The firmament in the form of a skull
was set up over the earth with four sides, and under each corner they set dwarfs. The earth, called Midgard, is round without, and beyond is the deep sea; in the midst of the world was
reared Asgard, where Odin is enthroned seeing over the whole
world and each man's doings. Without in the deep sea lies the
Midgard-worm, tail in mouth. The holiest seat of the gods is at
Yggdrasil's ash, its boughs spread over the whole world. Three
roots it has, one in heaven, one in hell, where is Nidhogg, one
where before was Yawning-gap, and there is the Spring of
Knowledge. A fair hall is there, and from it issue three maidens—Has-been, Being, and Will-be—who shape the lives of

men. On the boughs of the ash sits an eagle, wise in much, and between his eyes a hawk, while a squirrel runs up and down the tree bearing words of hate betwixt the eagle and the worm.

The following may serve as a general description of what we may call the chamber type, either square or round, with a ceiling or a dome. The earth is a mountain, and around its base flows the ocean, or it floats on the ocean; beyond is a high range of mountains which form the walls of the enclosure, and on these is either laid the ceiling in one great slab, or it is domed (sometimes the system is a compromise, the earth square, the sky circular, and they do not seem to have realised the difficulty of the pendentives !). The firmament is sustained by the earth mountain in the centre; as in the Esquimaux account given by Dr Rink 'the earth with the sea supported by it, rests upon pillars, and covers an under-world accessible by various entrances from the sea, as well as from mountain clefts. Above the earth an upper world is found, beyond which the blue sky, being of solid consistence, vaults itself like an outer shell, and, as some say, revolves around some high mountain top in the far north.' A man in a boat went 'to the border of ocean, where the sky comes down to meet it.' (H. Spencer, Sociology, I.) Man was created on the mountain top, where it is in contact with heaven, and all earthly vegetation springs from the seeds of the central tree. In the South Pacific, Mr Andrew Lang tells us, the sky is a solid vault of blue stone. In the beginning of things the sky pressed hard on the earth, and the god Ru was obliged to thrust the two asunder. Ru is now the Atlas of Mangaia, 'The sky-supporting Ru.'

Above the firmament is the Over-sea, and the rain falls from it through perforations; it serves as the floor of the upper regions, and flowing down the firmament, or down the sides of the mountain, supplies earthly seas; the stars are either attached to the firmament or float on this over-sea. There is an amusing story of this celestial sea as late as Gervase of Tilbury. Some people coming out of church were surprised to see an anchor dangling by a rope from the sky, which caught in the tombstones, presently a man was seen descending with the object of detaching it, but as he reached the earth he died as we should if drowned in water.

The Egyptian system would seem to have been of the square type. The Egyptian, says Champollion, 'compared the sky to the ceiling of an edifice;' illustrations which figure the Cosmos in personified forms are frequent on the temples and mummy cases. An example is given by Lenormant (*Histoire Ancienne*) showing Seb the Earth-Mountain, Tpe the firmament, and Nut the heavenly waters. In the Book of the Dead the soul passes through the gateway of this world into the other, 'the House of Osiris,' and that too was shut in by a wall with a great gateway for the sun at the east to reach our land; the dead had to be ferried over the waters which surrounded the earth, and so the river of death had purely a geographical import in its origin.

Renouf says that 'Ra is addressed as Lord of the great dwelling. The "great dwelling" is the universe, as the Hall of Seb is the earth, the Hall of Nut the heaven, and the Hall of the twofold Maat is the netherworld.'

Water was with them the primordial element in the formation of the universe, of which Maspero gives this account: 'For the astronomers of Egypt, as for the writer of the first chapter of Genesis, the sky was "fluid" (*une masse liquide*), and enclosed wholly the earth resting on the solid atmosphere; when the elemental chaos took form, the God Schou raised on high the waters and spread them out in space. It is on this celestial ocean, Nut, that the planets and stars float, the monuments show us them as genii of human or animal form navigating each his bark in the wake of Osiris. There was another widely known conception which presented the stars fixed like suspended lamps to the celestial vault, and they were lighted afresh each night by Divine power to give light to the nights of earth.'

The cosmogonic theories in the Veda have been abstracted by Mr Wallis and summarised in a review in the *Academy* (November 1887). 'The Rig Vedic hymns disclose three distinct lines of thought in regard to the creation of the world, yielding three separate views as to its construction. The simplest theory is that the building of the world was done very much as the building of a house, by architects and artificers.' 'What, indeed, was the wood? What, too, was that tree,' asks a hymn, 'from which they fashioned the heaven and the earth?' The space was laid out with the measuring rod of Varuna. This measuring-rod was the sun; and hence the measurers of the earth are the solar deities, especially Vishnu, 'who measured the regions of the earth, and made fast the dwelling-places on high, stepping forth the Mighty Strider in three steps.' The edifice had three stories or flats—the earth, the air, and the heavens—the measurement beginning from the front of the structure, or the East. 'Indra measured out as it were a house with measures from the front.' 'The Dawn shone with brilliance and opened for us the doors;' the doors that 'open high and wide with their frames.' The roofing of the house is referred to in the epithet of the sky as 'beamless or without rafters.' The firmness of the edifice is marvelled at and praised. While the design and general structure are assigned to the greater deities, and especially to Indra as their representative, the woodwork and other details are done by artificer gods. As the first act of the Indian peasant on taking possession of a new house is to bring in sacred fire, so, says Mr Wallis, 'the first act of the gods after the formation of the world was to produce the celestial Agni.'

In the Avesta the sky is said to be 'like a palace built of a heavenly substance firmly established with ends that lie far apart.' The idea of the temple of the sky is common to the classic poets, and becomes the palace or temple of glass of the Romancers.

The early system of Chaldea belongs to the hemispherical class, and it is an interesting fact that modern evidence goes to show that the dome was first known in the Land of the Plain. 'The Turanians of Chaldea represented the earth like a bark inverted and hollow underneath, not one of those oblong boats in use with us, but of a kind entirely round which the reliefs show, and which are still used on the Euphrates. In the interior hollow was concealed the abyss—the place of darkness and of death; upon the convex surface was spread the earth, properly so called, enveloped on all sides by the stream of Ocean.

Chaldea was regarded as the centre of the world, and far beyond the Tigris reposed the mountain of the east which united the heavens and the earth. The heavens were in the form of a vast hemisphere, of which the lower rim rested upon the extremity of the terrestrial bark beyond the river of ocean.'

'The firmament was spread out over the earth like a curtain; it turned, as if on a pivot, around the mountain of the east, and carried with it in its never resting course the fixed stars with which its vault was studded. Between the heavens and the earth circled about the seven planets like large animals full of life; then came the clouds, the winds, the thunder, the rains. The earth rested on the abyss, the sky upon the earth. The early Chaldeans had not yet asked themselves upon what rested the abyss' (Maspero).

It is delightfully appropriate that to the heroic age of Greece a shield (probably circular and convex with a central boss) figured the form of the earth. To Homer the land where appeared the phantoms of the dead is beyond the ocean. We may suppose that this was the lonely shore of the belt of mountains from which the firmament would spring. The abyss is Tartarus, as in Iliad VIII., 'gloomy Tartarus very far from hence (Olympus), where there is a very deep gulf beneath the earth, and iron portals and a brazen threshold as far below Hades as heaven is from earth.' Hesiod is more particular; in nine days would a brazen anvil fall from Heaven to Earth, and nine other days from earth to Tartarus.

Thus the Homeric scheme knew the earth as depicted by the shield of Achilles; it was surrounded by ocean, and was midway between the solid metal heavens and Tartarus, probably, like a disc in a spherical envelope. Many-peaked Olympus, where the gods assembled, is rather the celestial Olympus-the surface of the vault of heaven, than a mere earthly mountain. A good account of this is given in Duncker's 'History of Greece' (I. IX.), on its summit was the 'all-nourishing lake' from which flowed all the waters of the world; the earthly Olympus was but a symbol of the heavenly mount. Anaxagoras taught that the celestial vault was made of stone. Theophrastus said the milky way was the junction of the two halves of the solid dome so badly joined that the light came through; others said that it was a reflection of the sun's light on the vault of heaven (Flammarion, 'Astronomical Myths').

Later when Phoenician voyagers had explored the Western seas, and a knowledge of India opened up the East, it was evidently felt that the world extended east and west, and with the same climate, while north and south the range was inconsiderable and the climate changing; so that Herodotus says, 'I smile when I see many persons describing the circumference of the earth who have no sound reason to guide them; they describe ocean flowing round the earth, which is made circular as if by a lathe.' Certain, however, that it was planned on some simple geometrical form, the proportion of 2 to 1 was accepted. Mr Charles Elton, writing of the traveller Pytheas of Marseilles 330 B.C., and the extension of the estimate of size necessitated by his voyages, says, 'The world was thought to be twice as long as its own breadth; the total breadth from the spicy regions of Ceylon to the frozen shores of Scythia being taken at about 3400 miles; the length from Cape of St Vincent to the ocean east of India at about 6800 miles.' Pytheas increased the estimate, 'thus making the world 4700 miles wide, and being compelled by the accepted formula to extend its length to 9400 miles.'

The next step was to accept the spherical theory for the earth as well as for the heavens. We shall find a return to the Middle Ages to the proportion of the double square.

Pythagoras seems to have borrowed the fully-developed Eastern scheme; for the Babylonians had later arrived at a highly complex and carefully reasoned structure of several heavenly spheres; which apparently were elaborated in this way. The blue heaven of the fixed stars is seen to revolve around the pole at a constant rate, sweeping the whole of the stars with it. But the sun and moon and five other planets do not for long occupy their positions relative to the other bodies; it is seen that they have a motion through the signs proper to themselves from the thirty days of the moon to the thirty years of Saturn, and so the Chaldean astronomers assigned a revolving sphere to each of these: seven concentric spheres revolving at rates proportioned to their distance from the centre on a common axis through the pole star. 'The Chaldean astronomers,' says Lenormant (Magic), 'imagined a spherical heaven completely enveloping the earth; the periodical movements of the planets took place in the lower zone of the heavens underneath the firmament of the fixed stars; astrology afterwards ascribed to them seven concentric and successive spheres. The firmament supported the ocean of the celestial waters.' These seven spheres, forming as many regions above in the heavens or below in the underworld, were distinguished by colours such as Herodotus describes for the walls of Ecbatana of the Medes, 'a symbolism which,' continues Lenormant, 'was borrowed direct from the Babylonian religion—the colours of the seven planetary bodies.' It is necessary that this system should be firmly grasped; it is the perfected structure of astrology which for two thousand years solved the problem of the universe over the whole of civilisation; it is the system embodied in all Mysticism, Astrology, and Arts magic. It was by irresistible analogy that the earth also became a sphere.

In the Western world the scheme attributed to Pythagoras gives in all twelve spheres, which succeed each other in the following order, beginning from the remotest: (1) Sphere of the fixed stars; (2) of Saturn; (3) Jupiter; (4) Mars; (5) Venus; (6) Mercury; (7) Sun; (8) The Moon; (9) Sphere of Fire; (10) Sphere of Air; (11) Sphere of Water; (12) The Earth. 'The early Pythagoreans further conceived that the heavenly bodies, like other moving bodies, emitted a sound; these they supposed made up a harmonious symphony. Hence they established an analogy between the intervals of the seven planets and the musical scale' (Sir G. C. Lewis, '*Astronomy of the Ancients*').

The motive power in the Chaldean system was the energy of seven spirits who governed the several spheres; these, as angels of the stars, survived to the Middle Ages, and in their cabbalistic form—Zadkiel, Raphæl, and the like—are still familiar to those who put their trust in prophetic almanacks. We shall see what Dante says of the orders of angels.

The most picturesque prospect of these whirling spheres is that in Cicero's vision of Scipio.—'The globular bodies of the stars greatly exceeded the magnitude of the earth, which now to me appeared so small that I was grieved to see our empire contracted as it were into a very point. Which, while I was too eagerly gazing on, Africanus said: —"How long will your attention be fixed upon the earth? Do you not see into what temples you have entered? All things are connected by nine circles, or rather spheres; one of which (which is the outermost) is heaven, and comprehends all the rest, inhabited by the all-powerful God, who binds and controls the others; and in this sphere reside the original principles of those endless revolutions which the planets perform. Within this are contained seven other spheres that turn round backward; that is, in a contrary direction to that of the heaven. Of these, that planet which on earth you call Saturn occupies one sphere. That shining body which you see next is called Jupiter, and is friendly and salutary to mankind. Next, the lucid one, terrible to the earth, which you call Mars. The sun holds the next place, almost under the middle region; he is the chief, the leader, and the director of the other luminaries; he is the soul and guide of the world, and of such immense bulk, that he illuminates and fills all other objects with his light. He is followed by the orbit of Venus and that of Mercury as attendants, and the Moon rolls in the lowest sphere enlightened by the rays of the sun. Below this there is nothing but what is mortal and transitory, excepting those souls which are given to the human race by the goodness of the gods. Whatever lies above the moon is eternal. For the earth, which is the ninth sphere, and is placed in the centre of the whole system, is immovable, and below all the rest, and all bodies by their natural gravitation tend toward it." Which, as I was gazing at in amazement, I said as I recovered myself, "From whence proceed these sounds so strong and yet so sweet that fill my ears?" 'It is the melody of the spheres which human sensibility is too dulled by use to be conscious of hearing.

The distinction of above and below was not lost nor the solidity of the spherical heavens, as seen in this extract from the Astrologer Manilius:—

'Come, then, prepare your mind for learning the Meridians; they are four in number, their position in the firmament is fixed, and they modify the influence of the signs as these speed across them. One is placed where the heaven rises springing up to form its vault, and this one has the first view of the earth from the level. The second is placed facing it on the opposite border of the æther, and from this begins the falling-away of the firmament and its headlong sweep down to the Nether-world. The third marks the highest part of the heavens aloft, when Phoebus reaches this he is weary, and his horses out of breath; here, then, he rests a moment while he is giving the downward turn to the day and balancing the shadows of noon. The fourth holds the very bottom of all, and has the glory of being the foundation of the round world; on it the stars cease their sinkings and begin their upward course once more; it is equidistant from the setting and the rising.' The flatness of the earth was not necessarily affected in popular view. Strabo finds it necessary to argue that the earth must be of a spherical form, for if it was of an infinite depth it would transfix the planetary spheres and prevent them going round!

This seven-fold system came westward with Latin civilisation, and made the world-scheme for our Saxon forefathers.

From the fragments collected by Cory of the writings attributed to Zoroaster, it would appear that the Persian Universe was fashioned in the like form: 'For the Father congregated the *seven firmaments* of the world, circumscribing them of a convex figure.' These seven firmaments are conceived of in the old Persian writings as transparent 'mountains,' one without the other.

The ancient Hindus understood the universe to be formed by seven concentric envelopes around the central earth-mountain Meru, on which the waters of the celestial Ganges fell out of heaven, and circling it seven times in its descent, distributed its waters in four great streams to the whole earth. And the Mexicans had nine heavens distinguished by different colours one over the other.

The Arab system is clearly set forth by Lane:—

'According to the common opinion of the Arabs, there are seven heavens, one above another, and seven earths, one beneath another; the earth which we inhabit being the highest of the latter, and next below the lowest heaven. The upper surface of each heaven and of each earth are believed to be nearly plane, and are generally supposed to be circular. Thus is explained a passage of the Koran in which is said that God has created seven heavens and as many earths or storeys of the earth. Traditions differ respecting the fabric of the seven heavens. In the most credible account, according to a celebrated historian, the first is described as formed of emerald; the second of white silver; the third of large white pearls; the fourth of ruby; the fifth of red gold; the sixth of yellow jacinth; and the seventh of shining light. Some assert Paradise to be in the seventh heaven; indeed, I have found this to be the general opinion of my Muslim friends; but the author above quoted proceeds to describe, next above the seventh heaven seven seas of light, then an undefined number of veils or separations of different substances seven of each kind, and then Paradise, which consists of seven stages one above another (these are distinguished by the names of precious gems) canopied by the Throne of the Compassionate. These several regions of Paradise are described in some traditions as forming so many degrees, or stages ascended by steps.'

'The earth is believed by the Arabs to be surrounded by the ocean, which is described as bounded by a chain of mountains called Kaf, which encircles the whole as a ring, and confines and strengthens the entire fabric; these mountains are described as composed of green chrysolite like the green tint of the sky. Mecca, according to some, or Jerusalem, according to others, is exactly in the centre. The earth is supported by successive creations one beneath the other. The earth is upon water, the water upon the rock, the rock on the back of the bull, the bull on the bed of sand, the sand on the fish, the fish upon a still suffocating wind, the wind on a vale of darkness, the darkness on a mist, and what is beneath the mist is unknown. It is believed that beneath the earth and the seas of darkness is Jahennem, which consists of seven stages, one beneath another.'

Dante himself sums up in that culminating year 1300 of the Middle Ages all lore Classic and Oriental, and in the *Convito* gives the clearly reasoned system on which he constructs the world scheme of the 'Divine Comedy:'—

'I say, then, that concerning the number of the heavens and their site, different opinions are held by many, although the truth at last may be found. Aristotle believed, following merely the ancient foolishness of the Astrologers, that there might be only eight heavens, of which the last one, and which contained all, might be that where the *fixed* stars are ('fixed in the sense of attached) that is the eighth sphere, and that beyond it there could be no other. Ptolemy, then, perceiving that the eighth sphere is moved by many movements, seeing its circle to depart from the right circle, which turns from east to west, constrained by the principles of philosophy, of necessity desires a *Primum mobile*, a most simple one, supposing another heaven to be outside the heaven of the fixed stars, which might make that revolution from east to west, which I say is completed in twenty-four hours nearly, that is, twenty-three hours, fourteen parts of the fifteen of another, counting roughly. Therefore, according to him, and according to that which is held in Astrology and in Philosophy, since these movements were seen, there are nine movable heavens, the sight of which is evident and determined, according to an art which is termed Perspective, Arithmetical, and Geometrical, by which and by other sensible appearances it is visibly and reasonably seen, as in the eclipses of the sun it appears sen-

sibly that the moon is below the sun. And by the testimony of
Aristotle, who saw with his own eyes, according to what he says
in the second book on Heaven and the World, the Moon being
new, to enter below Mars, on the side not shining, and Mars to
remain concealed so long that he reappeared on the other bright
side of the Moon which was towards the west. And the order of
the houses is this, that the first that they enumerate is that where
the moon is; the second is that where Mercury is; the third is that
where Venus is; the fourth is that that is where the Sun is; the fifth is
that where Mars is; the sixth is that where Jupiter is; the seventh
is that where Saturn is; the eighth is that of the Stars; the ninth
is that which is not visible except by that movement which is
mentioned above, which they designate the great crystalline
sphere, diaphanous, or rather all transparent. Truly, beyond all
these the Catholics place the Empyrean Heaven, which is as
much as to say the Heaven of Flame, or rather the Luminous
Heaven, and they assign it to be immovable.'

'So, then, gathering together this which is discussed, it seems
that there may be ten heavens, and it is to be known that each
heaven below the crystalline has two firm poles as to itself; and
the ninth has them firm and fixed, and not mutable in any respect. And each one, the ninth even as the others, has a circle
which one may term the equator of its own heaven; and this circle has more swiftness in its movement than any other part of
its heaven. I say, then, that in proportion as the heaven is nearer
to the equatorial circle, so much the more noble is it in comparison to its poles; since it has more motion and more actual-
ity and more life and more form and more touch from that which
is above itself, and consequently has more virtue.... It is then to
be known, in the first place, that the movers thereof are substances apart from material that is intelligences, which the common people term angels; and of these creatures, as of the heavens, different persons have different ideas, although the truth
may be found. There were certain philosophers, of whom Aristotle appears to be one, who only believed these to be so many
as there are revolutions in the heavens, and no more; saying that
the others would have been eternally in vain, and without operation, which was impossible, inasmuch as their being is their
operation. There were others like Plato, a most excellent man,
who placed not only so many Intelligences as there are move-

ments in heaven, but even as there species of things, that is, manner of things; as of one species are all mankind, and of another all the gold, and of another all the silver, and so with all; and they are of the opinion that as the Intelligences of the heavens are generators of those movements each after his kind, so these were generators of the other things, each being a type of its species; and Plato calls them *Ideas*, which is as much as to say, so many universal forms and natures. The Gentiles call them gods and goddesses, although they could not understand these so philosophically as Plato did.'

He continues that as there are nine movable spheres, so are there nine orders of Angels divided into three Hierarchies: ' The first is that of the Angels, the second of the Archangels, the third of the Thrones. Then there are the Dominations; after them the Virtues; then the Principalities. Above these are the Powers, and the Cherubim, and above all are the Seraphim.'

As an abstract of the early Jewish system, we will condense the substance of the article 'Firmament' in Dr Smith's Bible Dictionary. 'The word translated firmament is the Hebrew word *rakia*. The verb *raka* means to expand by beating, and is especially used of beating out metals into thin plates, and it is in this sense that the word is applied to the heaven in Job xxxvii. 18: "Hast thou spread [rather hammered] out the sky, which is strong, and as a molten looking glass?" The mirrors to which he refers being made of metal. The sense of solidity, therefore, is combined with the ideas of expansion and tenuity.... Further, the office of the *rakia* in the economy of the world demanded strength and substance; it was to serve as a division between the waters above and the waters below, being supported at the edge of the earth's disc by the mountains. In keeping with this view the *rakia* was provided with windows and doors through which the rain and the snow might descend. A secondary purpose of the *rakia* was to support the heavenly bodies—sun, moon and stars—in which they were fixed as nails, and from which, consequently, they might be said to drop off.'

Philo and Josephus state that there was a relation between the design of the Temple and the world; and the early Fathers set forth the scheme with much fullness, as shown by Letronne in the '*Revue des deux Mondes*.' Clement of Alexandria is one of these, writing in the beginning of the third century; and

Severianus, Bishop of Gabala in Syria, compares the world to a house of which the earth is the ground floor, the lower sky (the firmament) the ceiling, and the over-sky the roof. Dioderus, Bishop of Tarsus, about the same time compares the world to a two-staged tent. Theophilus of Antioch in the second century sets out a similar view. The light shining as in an enclosed chamber lit up all that was under heaven; a second heaven is to us invisible, after which this heaven we see has been called firmament, and to which half the water was taken up that it might serve for rains, and showers, and dews to mankind; and half the water was left on earth for rivers, and fountains, and seas. In the 'Recognitions of Clement,' there is an account of the creation. 'In the beginning when God had made the heaven and the earth as one house, the shadow which was cast by the mundane bodies involved in darkness those things which were enclosed in it,' i.e. the world before the sun was a *camera obscura*, 'then at length light is appointed for the day and darkness for the night. And now the water which was within the world, in the middle space of that first heaven and earth, congealed as if by frost, and solid as crystal, is distended; and the middle spaces of the heaven and earth are separated as by a firmament of this sort; and that firmament the Creator called heaven, so called by the name of that previously made; and so He divided into two portions that fabric of the universe although it was only one house!' The waters that remained below flowed away to the abyss exposing the land. And so all things were prepared for the men who were to dwell in it.

The next writer claims also to follow the teaching of an Eastern bishop as to the world fabric, and reverts to the symbolism of the Tabernacle. This is Cosmas, a merchant of Alexandria and traveller into India and the far East, in the first half of the sixth century, who wrote a treatise on the subject.

In this work, 'Christian Topography,' he attempted to demonstrate that it was necessary for all Christians to believe the universe to be of the form of a travelling trunk with a rounded lid; the tabernacle of Moses being its true image, the whole enclosing the sun, moon, and stars in a sort of immense coffer of oblong form, of which the upper part forms a double ceiling. He thinks the Babylonians were led away to believe in the spheri-

cal form of the earth after the building of the tower of Babel, but
he demolishes 'very easily all these fables for the figure and composition of the universe.'

'God in creating the world supported it on nothing; according to the word of Job, "He has suspended the earth in the void."
God therefore having created the earth, united the extremity of
the sky to the extremity of the earth, supporting the firmament
on four sides by the sky, as a wall which raised itself aloft, forming so a sort of house entirely enclosed, or a long vaulted chamber; for, as saith the Prophet Isaiah, "He has disposed the heavens in form of a vault;" and Job speaks thus of the earth and the
heavens: "He has spread out the sky which is strong, and like a
molten looking glass. Whereupon are the foundations thereof
fashioned? Or who laid the corner stone thereof?" How can such
words be applied to a sphere? Moses, speaking of the Tabernacle—that is, the image of the world—says that it was twice as
long as wide. We say, therefore, with the Prophet Isaiah, that the
form of the heavens that embraces the universe is that of a vault,
with Job that it was joined to the earth, and with Moses that the
earth is more long than large. The second day of creation God
made a second sky, that which we see, like in appearance, but
not in reality, to the first; this second sky is placed in the midst
of the space which separates the earth from the outer heavens,
and it extends like a second roof or ceiling all over the earth,
dividing in two the waters, those that are above the firmament
from those below on the earth, and so of one house was two
made, the one above, the other below. The length of the earth is
from east to west, the sea we call ocean divides the part we inhabit from that beyond, to which is joined the sky.'

Some drawings, given in Charton's *Voyageurs Anciens*,' accompany the original manuscript. The earth rises like a mountain, around which circle the sun and moon, alternately hidden
and revealed; at the base is the ocean, and beyond are the mountains which take the vertical sides of the sky; from the lateral
walls rises a semicircular barrel vault, at the spring of which is
the flat firmament supporting the waters like a floor.

He then considers the Tabernacle in detail. The candlestick represented the seven planets, the veil with its tissue of hyacinth, purple, scarlet, and fine linen, recalled the elements, and divided the outer temple from the sanctuary, as the earth is divided from the heavens.

'Thus,' says Cosmas, 'were all the phenomena of the universe represented in the Tabernacle.'

CHAPTER II

THE MICROCOSMOS

The altar cell was a dome low-lit
And a veil hung in the midst of it:
At the pole points of its circling girth
Four symbols stood of the world's first birth
Air and water and fire and earth.'
—ROSSETTI, Rose Mary.

WE cannot think of a time when Man had not asked, Where am I? Nor, when he had arrived at an explanation, that it was not set forth by representation; not a definition in a book, or by carefully chosen speech, but dramatically by that *parler aux yeux* which is an increasing factor in speech as you go backwards in the history of intelligent communication.

If we remember that 'old means not old in chronology, but in structure: that is most archaic which lies nearest to the beginning of human progress considered as a development,' we may roughly put as the beginning of graphic and descriptive astronomy the dance and the story. The dance, on the one hand, becomes a part of ritual, and the story passes into mythology.

Every key applied to custom and mythology unlocks some of their secrets; and Mr Max Muller, Mr Andrew Lang, and Dr Tylor are certainly agreed that to a large extent what is now mythology was once an explanation of nature. In this view the Odyssey itself is an old and artistic geography, and the stories of Hercules, Theseus, and Jason, astronomy for the young.

We ought at this point to examine rites and ceremonies, savage dances, priestly observance, courtly ceremony, and the pomp of war, the great festivals and games; and in all these things we should find that man, after a certain stage was reached, was ever trying to conform himself to the ritual of nature, so that, like it in some respects, he might share its power and permanence.

But ritual is too wide a subject merely to glance at; we must limit ourselves to things made, or poets' views of how they should be made. In these the tendency has been universal to embody the natural order: not a plan of the world for science, but as a religious mystery and symbol; as magic amulet, charm, fetish.

Such was the shield of Achilles; and Mr Gladstone, so well is this understood, bases his inquiry as to the Homeric Geography on the description in the Iliad of this work of Hephæstos, the fabricator God. ' On it he formed earth, sky, and sea, the unwearied sun, full moon, and all the signs with which the sky is crowned—Pleiades, Hyades, the might of Orion, and the Bear (which men also call the Wain) it turns there and watches Orion, nor dips it into ocean.' And so on with the whole lovely description comprising the entire Cosmos.

I. The sun, moon, and revolving signs of the heavens.

2. The earth, two cities—one at peace, the other at war; the life of the fields in the round of the year; ploughing, reaping and the vintage, herding of cattle and sheep folds.

3. The dancing place that Dædalus built for fairhaired Ariadne, where they imitated in the circling dance the tortuous way of the labyrinth—a hint on the shield of the under-world.

4. Ocean which flowed round the world beside the outer edge of the thick-made shield.

This making the shield a map of things celestial is followed by Æschylus in the 'Seven against Thebes.' Before the first gate Tydeus bore a shield—

> 'With this proud argument. A sable sky
> Burning with stars, and in the midst full orbed
> A silver moon, the eye of night ...'

And Nonnos gives Bacchus a shield blazoned with the whole celestial system (*Dupuis*).

In Temple pageantry the sky was often represented by a veil or mantle of purple tissue scintillating with stars, either robing the God, hung before the sanctuary, or covering artificial erections, *Asherim*, 'The Groves' of Scripture.

Lenormant in his *'Origines,'* remarking that a winged oak with a veil thrown over it, 'the tree and the peplos,' was the image by which the Phœnicians figured the universe, citing Pausanias for an actual temple veil of this kind at Gabala in Syria; quotes from Nonnos the description of Harmonia weaving the magnificent web patterned with the images of the whole natural order-

'Bent over Athene's cunning loom, Harmonia wove a peplos with the shuttle; in the stuff which she wove, she first represented the earth with its *omphalos* in the centre; around the earth she spread out the sphere of heaven, varied by the figures of the stars. She harmoniously accompanied the earth with the sea that is associated with it, and she painted thereon the rivers, under their image of bulls with men's faces furnished with horns. Lastly, all along the exterior edge of the well-woven vestment she represented the ocean in a circle enveloping the Universe in its course.'

Josephus states that the veil of Herod's temple was blue, scarlet, white, and purple, embroidered with the constellations of heaven.

The well-known practice of renewing these temple veils yearly agrees with their astronomical significance. The annual procession with the new covering to the Caaba at Mecca, still continues this practice.

> '....Which of the deities
> Shall we have as a patron ?
> We must weave our mantle,
> Our sacred mantle of course....
> The yearly mantle
> To one or other of them.'
>
> —*ARISTOPHANES*, Birds.

When the world was a tree, every tree was in some sort its representation; when a tent or a building, every tent or building: but when the relation was firmly established, there was action and reaction between the symbol and the reality, and ideas taken

from one were transferred to the other, until the symbolism became complicated, and only particular buildings would be selected for the symbolic purpose: certain forms were reasoned
from the building to the world, and conversely certain thoughts
of the universe were expressed in the structure thus set apart as
a little world for the House of God—a Temple.

To the Teutonic nations trees were the first temples, as resembling the universe tree, the shelter of the gods: with them, according to Grimm, temple and tree were convertible words.

Pliny says 'trees were the first temples; even at this day the
simple rustic of ancient custom dedicates his noblest tree to God;'
and in 'Outlines of Primitive Belief' (Keary) it is said, 'Certain
it is that, among people who live in woody lands, we find long
continuing the habit of using a tree trunk for the main pillar of
the house, of building circular walls round that tree, and sloping the roof down to them from it. Of such kind was the house
of our Northern ancestors.... All this is mere prosaic fact, but
soon we pass on to the region of belief and mythology. The
Norseman on the image of his own house fashioned his picture
of the entire world. The earth with the heaven for a roof, was to
him but a mighty chamber, and likewise had its great supporting tree, passing through the midst and branching far upwards
among the clouds.' The general accuracy of this view would
seem to be confirmed by the Japanese story given by Sir H. Reid,
in which the first home of newly created man was built round
the heavenly spear, which formed at once its roof tree and the
world axis.

Berosos describes the paintings in the Temple of Belus at
Babylon; chaotic rather than cosmic it may be said, but having
not any the less a direct reference to the framing of the
world:—'There was a time when all was water and darkness, in
which monstrous animals were spontaneously engendered:
men with two wings, and some with four; with two faces and
two heads, the one male and the other female, and with the other
features of both sexes united in their single bodies; men with the
legs and horns of a goat and the feet of a horse; others with the
hind quarters of a horse and the other part a man like the hippo-
centaurs. There were also bulls with human heads, dogs with
four bodies and fishes' tails, and other quadrupeds, in which

various animal forms were blended, fishes, reptiles, serpents, and all kinds of monsters with the greatest rariety in their forms, monsters whose images we see in the paintings of the temple of Bel at Babylon.'

These composite figures, says Perrot, 'were not a caprice of the artists who made them, but were suggested by a cosmic theory of which they formed, as it were, a plastic embodiment and illustration.' The description of the abominations done in Jerusalem (Ezekiel viii. 10, 11) is a close parallel and confirmation.

Other descriptions of Babylonian temples lead us to see a cosmical symbolism in their structure; that by Apollonius is quoted in a later chapter, and another in an Arab translation of the Nabathean agriculture, relates how the images of the gods throughout the world betook themselves to Babylon, to the temple of the sun, 'to the great golden image suspended between heaven and earth. The sun image stood, they say, in the midst of the temple surrounded by all the images of the world; next to it stood the images of the sun in all countries; then those of the moon; next those of Mars; after them the images of Mercury; then those of Jupiter; after them those of Venus; and last of all, of Saturn.' (Baring Gould, 'Curious Myths.') This was evidently a temple with a dome like the firmament, from which golden sun and planets were suspended, and agrees entirely with the account by Apollonius.

But the buildings of Babylon and their more or less lineal descendants in Persia, all of well-defined planetary symbolism, are considered in later chapters, so we will pass them for the present with just an extract from that old mine, Maurice's 'Antiquities of India:'—

'Porphyry states that the Mithraic caverns represented the world. According to Eubulus, Zoroaster first of all, among the neighbouring mountains of Persia, consecrated a natural cell, adorned with flowers and watered with fountains, in honour of Mithra, the father of the universe. For he thought a cavern an emblem of the world fabricated by Mithra; and in this cave were many geographical symbols arranged with the most perfect symmetry and at certain distances, which shadowed out the elements and climates of the world.'

'In Persia's hallowed caves the Lord of Day
Pours through the central gloom his fervid ray;
High wrought in burnished gold the Zodiac shines,
And Mithra toils through all the blazing signs.'

—*STATIUS.*

Not to elaborate an interpretation of the Pyramids, which have already had far too many ingenious theories built with their silent stones, and it is better to keep clear of conjecture lest the whole argument becomes a sort of pyramid-inverted. Can we believe that the greatest works ever accomplished by man, with infinite toil and laborious accuracy, in an age when almost every act had a religious significance and a mystical reason, carried no symbol—had no thought and message embodied in their design? And this in a tomb the dwelling of no mere man, but the Pharaoh, son of Ra the Sun. Moreover, there is hardly a sepulchral tablet but has expanded on its top edge the sign of the sky, at times painted blue and dotted with stars. Mr R. Proctor thinks it proved that they had an astrological significance in addition to their use as tombs.

According to Brugsch, the Sun temple at Heliopolis had a sacred sealed chamber in form of a pyramid, called 'Ben-Ben,' in which were kept the two barks of the sun; an inscription gives an account of the visit of a king:—' The arrangement of the House of Stars was completed, the fillets were put on, he was purified with balsam and holy water, and the flowers were presented to him for the house of the obelisk. He took the flowers, and ascended the stairs to the great window to look upon the Sun god Ra in the house of the obelisk. Thus the king himself stood there. The prince was alone. He drew back the bolt and opened the doors, and beheld his father Ra in the exalted house of the obelisk, and the morning bark of Ra, and the evening bark of Tum. The doors were then shut, the sealing clay was laid on, and the King himself impressed his seal.'

The imagery of the temples and many inscriptions make clear that their intention was to localise their great prototype, the temple of the heavens. The dedicator of an inscription speaks thus of the temple of Neith, the mother of the Sun god Ra: 'Moreover, I informed him (Cambyses) also of the high consequence of the habitation of Neith; it is such as a heaven in all its quarters ('a heaven in its whole plan,' Renouf translates).... Moreover, of the high importance of the south chamber, and of the north chamber, of the chamber of the morning Sun Ra, and of the chamber of the evening Sun Tum. These are the mysterious places of all the gods' (Brugsch).

Maspero in his recent book 'Egyptian Archeology' considers at length the constructive and decorative symbolism of the Egyptian temple. 'The temple was built in the likeness of the world, as the world was known to the Egyptians. The earth, as they believed, was a flat and shallow plane, longer than its width; the sky, according to some, extended overhead like an immense iron ceiling, and, according to others, like a shallow vault. As it could not remain suspended in space, without some support, they imagined it to be held in place by four immense props or pillars. The floor of the temple naturally represented the earth. The columns, and if needful, the four corners of the chambers stood for the pillars. The roof vaulted at Abydos, flat elsewhere, corresponded exactly with the Egyptian idea of the sky. Each of these parts was therefore decorated in consonance with its meaning; those next to the ground were clothed with vegetation. The bases of the columns were surrounded by leaves, and the lower part of the walls were adorned with long stems of lotos or papyrus, in the midst of which animals were occasionally depicted. Bouquets of water plants, emerging from the water, enliven the bottom of the wall space in certain chambers. Elsewhere we find full-blown flowers interspersed with buds or tied together with cords.... The ceiling was painted blue, and spangled with five pointed stars painted yellow, occasionally interspersed with the cartouches of the royal founder. The vultures of Nekheb and Uati, the godesses of the south and north, crowned and armed with divine emblems, hovered above the central nave of the hypostyle halls and on the underside of the lintels of the front doors, above the head of the Great King as he passed through on his way to the sanctuary.'

'At the Ramessium, at Edfou, at Philæ, at Denderah, at Ombos, at Esnah, the depths of the firmament seemed to open to the eyes of the faithful, revealing the dwellers therein. There the celestial ocean poured forth its floods, navigated by the sun and moon, with their attendant escort of planets, constellations, and decans; there also the genii of the months and days passed in long procession. In the Ptolemaic age zodiacs fashioned af-

ter Greek models were sculptured side by side with astronomical tables of purely native origin. Finally, the decoration of the
lowest part of the walls and of the ceiling were restricted to a
small number of subjects, which were always similar, the most
important and varied scenes being suspended as it were between earth and heaven on the sides of the chambers and the
Pylons. These scenes illustrated the official relations which sub-
sisted between Egypt and the gods.... The sun, travelling from
east to west, divided the universe into two worlds—the world
of the north and the world of the south. The Temple, like the
universe, was double, and an imaginary line, passing through
the axis of the sanctuary, divided it into two temples—the temple of the south on the right hand, and the temple of the north
on the left. Each chamber was divided, in imitation of the temple, into two halves.'

To pass to the Semitic peoples. Philo Judæus states that the
Temple of Solomon was built in imitation of the world fabric,
and Josephus gives the same explanation of the symbolism of
the Tabernacle. It has been seen in the first chapter how the
Tabernacle was the pattern of the universe in small to the early
Christian Fathers; and the text of the Psalms would seem to
prove that this was the Psalmist's own view: 'And he built his
sanctuary like high (palaces), like the earth, which he hath established for ever' (Ps. lviii.).

Often it is not so much the actual earth and visible heavens
that were symbolised, as the original celestial world of the
golden age—Paradise; but a real, substantial, and geographical
Paradise.

Of the Caaba of Mecca—an early Arab temple still preserved
in continued use—the story is told, that after Adam and Eve
were cast out of Paradise, they came together again near to
Mecca. Adam prayed for a shrine 'similar to that at which he had
worshipped when in Paradise. The supplication of Adam was
effectual. A tabernacle or temple, formed of radiant clouds, was
lowered down by the hands of angels, and placed immediately
below its prototype in the celestial paradise. Towards the
heaven-descended shrine Adam thenceforth turned in prayer,
and round it he daily made seven circuits, in imitation of the rites
of the adoring angels.' So much for the symbolism of the
Caaba—'the Cube'—of Mecca. Other allied Semitic structures,

the small buildings found by Renan in Syria, have this cubical form. So also have later buildings of Roman date, described by Count de Vogue as 'Kalybes': these are surmounted by cupolas. This accomplished archæologist says: 'The cube is essentially a mystical form, which is found in the cellæ of Egyptian temples and that of Jerusalem; the hemisphere is the image of the celestial vault. We know that the cella of a temple was regarded as the dwelling of the god represented by the statue—a mystic symbol, or an invisible oracle. Originally the sacred edifice was the image of the celestial dwelling, as the symbol which inhabited it was the image of the divine personage. The Etruscan priest who built a sanctuary, traced above in the sky with his wand the foundations which he re-produced on earth—he transported, so to say, upon the earth a part of the sky to make a dwelling for his God. This idea is found in all countries, although it may not be so formally expressed' (*La Syrze Centrale*).

To the early European races, in the same way, 'the most magnificent temple which the ancients imagined, and which preceded all their notions of buildings made with hands, was the vault of Olympus, in which they supposed the great Jove to reside.' More particularly was this symbolism preserved in later time in the circular structures, the *Tholos* of Hestia in Greece, and of Vesta in Rome: a form which is allowed by the latest authorities to represent the heavenly vault.

Plutarch in 'Isis and Osiris' describes a temple of Vesta:—'Numa built a temple of an orbicular form, for the preservation of the sacred fire; intending by the fashion of the edifice to shadow out not so much the earth, or Vesta considered in that character, as the whole universe, in the centre of which the Pythagoreans placed fire, which they called Vesta and Unity.' Ovid in the 'Fasti' gives the same explanation; the temple represented the round earth, 'a reason for its figure worthy of our approval.'

The great rotunda at Rome, the Pantheon, is, of course, the most superb temple in this manner, 143 feet in diameter, with a simple aperture in the dome thirty feet across, through which streams the great beam of the sun. The height to the zenith, from the floor is equal to the diameter, so that it would just contain a sphere. Of this vast domed expanse, Pliny says, 'quod forma ejus convexa fastigiatum caeli similitudinem ostenderet.' It has been

suggested for the plan, a circle with eight great niches, one of
which is occupied by the door to the north, that the south niche
was intended to be occupied by Phœbus Apollo, and the rest by
the Moon and five other planets—Diana, Mercury, Venus, Mars,
Jupiter, and Saturn.

The ancient Latin custom at the foundation of sacred buildings, in relating them to the heavens, is thus described:
'Templum is the same word as the Greek temenos; for the
templum, according to Servius, was any place which was circumscribed and separated by the augurs from the rest of the land
by a certain solemn formula. A place thus set apart and hallowed
by the augurs was always intended to serve religious purposes,
but chiefly for taliing the auguria. The place in the heavens
within which the observations were to be made was likewise
called templum, as it was marked out and separated from the
rest by the staff of the augur. When the augur had defined the
templum within which he intended to make his observations,
he fixed his tent (tabernaculum), in it, and this tent was likewise
called templum or, more accurately, templum minus' (Dr
Smith's Dict.).

The Druids had, as a rite, yearly to pull down and rebuild the
roof of their temple, 'as a symbol of the destruction and reno-
vation of the world.' The yearly veil, or the rekindled fire, is a
much less serious form of the renewal, type and guarantee of the
world's continuance.

The poets and romance writers have preserved the tradition
of buildings like the world temple even to the Renaissance; the
central temple in the Hypnerotomachia is circular, with a dome
from which hangs one great orbicular lamp; and the town and
temple in Campanella's 'Civitas Solis' is elaborately symbolical.
The town was divided into seven great rings named from the
seven planets, with four main streets and gateways looking to
the points of the compass; the temple in the centre was also circular, and domed. Above the altar, a large globe represented the
earth; on the dome were all the stars of heaven from the first to
the sixth magnitude, with their names and influences marked,
and the meridians and great circles in relation to the altar. The
pavement was of precious stones. Seven golden, everburning
lamps bore the names of the seven planets. Louis XIV seems to

have tried to realise something of this sort at Marley; and according to Mr H. Melville, 'Royal Arch Mason.' in a book entitled ' Veritas,' even the modern ritual of Masonic Lodges is cosmical.

But we have not done with the East and the beginning of history. 'It has ever been accepted as a physical axiom in China that heaven is round and earth is square; and among the relics of Nature worship of old. we find the altar of heaven at Pekin round, while the altar of earth is square.' The former is described farther on in Chapter VI. According to Professor Legge, it dates from the twelfth century B.C, and is thus primitive Chinese before Confucius. 'The sovereigns of the Chan dynasty (1152-250 B.C.) worshipped in a building which they called the Hall of Light, which also served the purpose of an audience and council chamber. It was 112 feet square, and surmounted by a dome typical of heaven above and earth beneath' (Giles' 'Historic China').

In the old Chinese book the Li-Ki (Sacred Books of the East) there is a long account of the 'Hall of Distinction,' accompanied by a native plan. In it the Emperor as 'Son of Heaven' has to go through an elaborate solar ritual, passing from room to room as the sun passes into the several solar mansions. A large square enclosure surrounds the whole, with four ceremonial gateways (*Pailoos*) opening to the cardinal points. The building is perfectly square, and divided into three each way, making in all nine apartments, the middle one being called the hall of the centre. The exterior wall of each apartment—three facing each of the four quarters of the heavens—is dedicated to one of the months, the angle rooms being named twice over. The 'hall of the centre is only occupied for a time between the sixth and seventh month. The 'Son of Heaven's' progress is also marked by dress and symbolism appropriate to the season.

If we compare this with the Buddhist plan of the world given in Bock's 'Siam,' the reproduction of the pattern of the world will be apparent. The diagram of the twelve heavenly houses used by astrologers is very similar (see figures).

The first emperor of United China in the third century B.C. —a Caligula for cruelty, a Nero for splendour—is said in Chinese history to have built a gorgeous country palace. 'The most remarkable feature of the whole was the plan on which it was arranged. The various edifices were so disposed as to correspond

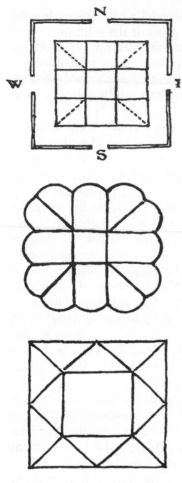

with and otherwise represent that part of the heavens which lies between the North Star, the Milky Way, and the Constellation Aquila, the vacant spaces being denoted by courts, corridors, and winding paths. This, it is said, was partly intended as an acknowledgment of the benign celestial influences to which the emperor ascribed the brilliant success that had always attended him, and partly as a monument of the vastness of his dominions, which could only be symbolised by an imitation of the starry vault on high' (Balfour, '(Chinese Scrap Book'.)

Sir W. Chambers, in his account of Chinese gardens, with their summer-houses and pavilions, says: ' Some of these are called *Mian Ting*, or Halls of the Moon, being of prodigious size, and composed each of a vaulted room made in the shape of a hemisphere, the concave of which is artfully painted in imitation of a nocturnal sky, and pierced with an infinite number of little windows, made to represent the moon and stars, being filled with tinted glass that admits the light in the quantities necessary to spread over the whole interior fabric the pleasing gloom of a fine summer's night. The pavements of these rooms are sometimes laid out in parterres of flowers; but oftenest the bottom is full of clear running water, which falls in rills from the sides of a rock in the centre; many little islands float upon its surface, and move around as the current directs, some of them covered with tables for the banquet, seats, and other objects.'

Of the Taouist temples, Dr Edkins tells us: ' The endeavour is made in these to represent the gods of the religion in their celestial abodes seated on their thrones.' In India the rock-cut caves of Ellora are said to be complete representations of the paradise of Siva; the great props left to support the roof are called 'Sumeru,' after the sky-supporting mountain, the 'Beautiful Meru.'

The Buddhist Stupas or Topes—those nearly solid masses of the form of a bubble floating on water, as an old author has it, or of a bell on a platform, surmounted by umbrella-shaped canopies—would more properly, perhaps, be classed with the solid structures of Babylon and Mexico in Chapter VI., as representing the heavenly regions from without as the mount of heaven, instead of from within, as a dwelling for deity. Asoka, according to the legend, had eightyfour thousand constructed simultaneously: on them every splendour was lavished—gilding, great glass jewels, golden bells; statues of elephants with real tusks guarded the enclosures, and at festivals they were buried in a profusion of flowers. Fa-Hian speaks of one as 700 feet high; but some were only a foot or two in diameter. Mr A. Lillie, in his 'Buddhism in Christendom,' gives a diagram of a stupa representing the successive zones of the heavens. Professor Beal in the 'Journal of the Royal Asiatic Society,' vol. v., states that the great tope at Sanchi represents heaven and earth, and points out how even the curious Buddhist railing, which surrounds some of these structures, is of a chessboard pattern, as the enclosing walls of Paradise are described to be; the four great gates in these enclosures are called Torana, which means an ornamental gate or door to the abode of the celestials.

The same author in his little book on Chinese Buddhism remarks: 'Whether it be true or not that a simple idea underlies all rightly-directed efforts of man to raise a building fit for the worship of God, in this particular Buddhism illustrates the supposed rule. The symbolism of the tope or stupa from the crowning spire of which the (Chinese) pagoda originates, is, like that of all other sacred edifices, intended to figure out an idea of the world or universe ruled over or occupied by one supreme Spirit or Being. This certainly was the meaning of the figure and furniture of the Jewish tabernacle and of the temple. As Josephus says in his 'Antiquities,' Solomon rose up and said, 'O Lord!

Thou hast an eternal house, and such as Thou hast created for Thyself out of Thine own work, we know it to be the heaven, and the air, and the earth, and the sea:' it was a symbol of this that Solomon built, so Philo tells us, and Cosmas labours at length to show the same thing. The stupa is a high solid structure based on a square foundation or platform, from which rises into the air a semicircular dome, which is crowned by a square railing, or sometimes a solid cube with eyes on every side. The square platform represents earth, the semicircular dome figures out the air, the railed structure on the top denotes the heaven, where watch the four gods (indicated by eyes). This was the first great effort to describe in stone the idea of the world, or the three worlds, over which the supreme presence of Buddha was supposed to rule; in this stupa were his relics denoting his presence, the only authorised substitute for himself As the system grew the idea of the universe expanded also, and it was not only earth and air and heaven that had to be represented, but the towering

worlds above the heaven, and after that the platforms or pla-
teaux (it is the only word we can use) of heavens extending
upwards and towards the eight points of space; hence the symbolism expanded also, and above the cubical structure was
erected a high staff with rings or umbrellas to denote world soar-
ing above world to the uppermost empyrean. Now it is this
crowning pole with its rings or umbrellas that originated the
idea of the pagoda. Each platform in this structure denotes a
world; as they tower upwards in beautifully decreasing size,
they offer to the eye an effort of the mind of man to represent
the idea of the infinite. On each side of these platforms there are
bells and tinkling copper leaves to denote the eternal 'music of
the spheres,' and the beautifully carved balustrades and projecting eaves are ever described as proper emblems of the happy
beings who enjoy the presence of the Buddhas dwelling in these
supreme regions. This is the origin of the pagodas, and there is
nothing which gives China its distinctive architectural character so much as these Buddhist structures not used for worship,
but to figure out the illimitable nature of the space in which
dwells the spiritual essence of all the Buddhas' (Beal).

In the modern Chinese ritual of Buddhism Dr Edkins says,
'Kan (heaven) is the covering let down over an idol, as in the
phrase Fo-Kan (a shrine for Buddha), and it here represents the
sky as a canopy stretched over the world. Yu (the earth) is the
chariot in which the idol sits.' The tooth of Buddha in Ceylon is
preserved under nine of these bell-shaped gold and jewelled
canopies representing the nine heavens. Buddhist bells in China
and Japan are usually ornamented with meridian lines, the sun,
and the stars.

In China the tombstones are often the well-known composite symbol consisting of a cube as a base, on it a sphere, then a
cone, a crescent, and an inverted pear-shaped apex; on each of
the solids are characters signifying earth, air, fire, water, and
ether, in the order in which the elements were supposed to be
superimposed. And even the coinage, circular with a square
hole, is well-understood as symbolising heaven and earth.

In Christian architecture it is still said at times that the nave and the chancel, divided by the screen, symbolise earth and heaven; and Curzon gives it as the acknowledged significance of the Byzantine Churches with the Bema shut off by the Iconastasis.

Didron tells us that the two or three thousand sculptures of one of the greater French cathedrals of the thirteenth century are stone encyclopadias comprising nature, science, ethics, and history. 'These sculptures, then, are, in the fullest sense of the word, what in the language of the Middle Ages was called the "Image or Mirror of the Universe." 'But it is rather the universe of religious ideas than the actual solid built world. The Byzantine scheme preserved more of the original thought: Christ was enthroned at the zenith of the central dome, then zone below zone, were the heavenly powers, the saints, and all nature, one great chorus of praise.

A Byzantine church in Athens, the *Magale Panagia*, is described in 'Archaologia' (Vol. I., New Series), and photographs are given of the paintings now destroyed. High in the centre of the dome is the Christ enthroned, with His feet on the mystic wheels, the whole expanse being a deep blue, next comes a series of nine semicircles containing representations of the Orders of the Hierarchy—the Seraphim, the Cherubim, the Thrones, the Dominions, the Virtues, the Powers, the Principalities, the Archangels, the Angels—which respectively rule the nine heavenly zones; the *primum mobile*, sphere of the fixed stars, and the seven planets. Below these a belt circles the dome, blue of the firmament, set all over with stars and the twelve signs of the zodiac; to the east is the sun, and to the west the moon; still below these on the walls are the winds, hail, and snow; and still lower mountains, and trees, and the life on the earth, and with all is interwoven passages from the last three Psalms:—

'O praise the Lord of heaven; praise Him in the height. Praise Him, all ye angels of His; praise Him, all His host. Praise Him, sun and moon; praise Him, all ye stars and light. Praise Him, all ye heavens; and ye waters that are above the heavens. Let them praise the Name of the Lord.'

CHAPTER III
FOUR SQUARE

'A tower of strength that stood
Four Square to all the winds that blow.'
—TENNYSON.

THE perfect temple should stand at the centre of the world, a microcosm of the universe fabric, its walls built four square with the walls of heaven. And thus they stand the world over, be they Egyptian, Buddhist, Mexican, Greek, or Christian, with the greatest uniformity and exactitude. When the world has become circular and spherical, the squareness is retained almost universally as a characteristic of the celestial earth, the four-square enclosure on the top of the world mountain, where the polar tree or column stands, and whence issue the four rivers. From the thought of such an enclosure we get, Lenormant states, our word 'Paradise.'

The significance of the direction of buildings is much wider than is understood by Orientation, a looking to the rising sun; for the pyramids, and the Babylonian and Mexican stepped temples, or rather altars, are square, and the Buddhist topes circular in a square enclosure, with no sanctuary to define direction. When, however, there is a major axis, it agrees (with some exceptions in Egypt) with the sun's path through the heavens.

The universal early use in temples was to have the entrance at the east, facing the sunrise, and the more sacred part of the sanctuary to the west, where was the throne of the presence. It was the god or the altar that thus fronted the sun as it rose through the eastern door, and the reversal of this later seems to have been the result of the temple becoming a place for congregation rather than a local habitation of the god.

Egypt furnishes some exceptions in temples, which have their axes at various angles. In a recent lecture (May 1891) before the Society of Antiquaries, Mr Norman Lockyer explained some conclusions he had reached as to complicated temple groups like that at Karnak. Starting with Mariette's dates obtained from the inscriptions, and searching the star-lists for each angle, he found that the temples were directed to watch certain important stars, such as Gamma Draconis, Canopus, and Vega. When, owing to the precession of the equinoxes, the star no longer rose or set through the open portal as viewed from the remote and dark sanctuary which was specially contrived like a great stone telescope for the purpose of receiving pure light, another temple was built at an angle with the first, and possibly across its 'fairway' to the horizon, for it was no longer required. This is evidently a refined and complicated system, and therefore comparatively late.

The pyramids, however, are set out with the greatest accuracy. Mr Petrie's careful survey shows that the Great Pyramid deviated only 5', and he says that it is the world that has shifted rather than the structure—no fault to its builders! The group of three, moreover, stand *en echelon*, so that each has its four sides clear to the four quarters to which Mariette says they were dedicated. On the east side of each was a small isolated temple with its door eastward. One of these is the so-called temple of the Sphinx. 'It is to be noticed,' Mr Proctor says, 'that the peculiar figure and position of the pyramids will bring about the following relations. Between the autumn and the spring equinoxes the rays of the rising and setting sun illuminated the southern face of the pyramids; whereas during the rest of the year, that is, the six months between the spring and autumn equinoxes, the rays of the rising and setting sun illuminated the northern face.' The slanting passage appears to have pointed directly to the pole star.

'Like the house of the living, the tomb was strictly oriented, but after a mystic principle of its own. In the necropolis of Memphis the door of nearly every tomb is turned to the east, and there is not a single stele which does not face in that direction. In the necropolis of Abydos both door and stele are more often turned

towards the south; that is, towards the sun at its zenith. But neither at Memphis, at Abydos, nor at Thebes is there a tomb which
is lighted from the west, or presents its inscription to the setting
sun. Thus, from the shadowy depths where they dwell, the dead
have their eyes turned to the quarter of the heavens where the
life-giving flame is each day rekindled, and seem to be waiting
for the ray which is to destroy their night, and to rouse them
from their long repose' (Perrot and Chipiez). 'The major axis of
the rectangle upon which these structures (tombs) are planned
always runs due north and south; and at Gizeh, the necropolis
of the west, they are arranged upon a symmetrical plan, so as
to resemble a chessboard, on which all the squares are strictly
oriented. The principal face of the tomb is turned to the east. In
four cases out of five the entrance to its chambers, when there
is one, is found upon this face. Next after the eastern face in relative importance comes that which is turned towards the north '
(Mariette).

That orientation in a limited sense was not the object to the
Egyptians, but rather a desire to make their building square with
the cardinal sides of earth and sky, is again and again expressed
in the inscriptions. That of Thothmes III. on the foundations of
Karnack says that 'after the position of the building had been
fixed according to the position of the four quarters the great
stone gates were erected ' (Brugsch). This laying out the lines to
square with the world is a part of ceremonial at foundations in
all countries at all times; we see it again and again repeated, as
also the thought that there was a magic influence in it, the magic
of correspondence; for, as the foundations of heaven and earth
are firm, 'not to be moved for ever,' so the building imitating
them would share their stability. In Egypt it is expressed in a
regular formula—'It is such as a heaven in all its quarters,' 'firm
as the heavens.' In the Psalms, as also in the Vedas, the firmness
of the world temple is extolled.

The Buddhist buildings are strictly related to the heavens.
The circular tope is surrounded by an enclosure exactly square,
with a gateway to the north and to the south, to the east and to
the west; the east gate being the chief entrance, the west the exit.
The temples containing statues of Buddha were entered at the
east—'Statue of Buddha facing the east,' Fa-Hian reiterates. The
Hindu temple of Jagannatha follows the same rule. In the tem-

ples of Japan, a mirror hangs at the far end; and in the old temples of Peru a golden disc of the sun, over the altar, fronted
through the open door the dawn of day.

The Greek temples were entered at the east. Mr Penrose finds
that, like the Egyptian temples, the axis through the open door
was directed to the point of rising of some star which appeared
above the horizon before dawn. The Syrian and Persian temples
were also entered at the eastern end.

In Western Asia (again to quote from Perrot) 'the inhabitants
of Mesopotamia were so much impressed by celestial phenomena, and believed so firmly in the influence of the stars over
human destiny, that they were sure to establish some connection between those heavenly bodies and the arrangement of their
edifices. All the buildings of Chaldea and Assyria are oriented;
the principle is everywhere observed, but it is not always understood in the same fashion. Mesopotamian buildings were always rectangular and often square on plan, and it is sometimes
the angles and sometimes the centres of each face that are directed to the four cardinal points. The earlier Chaldean structures, as Warka, follow the former method, as do the remains at
Nineveh.' 'On the other hand, in those ruins at Nimroud that
have been identified with the ancient Calah, it is the sides of the
mound and of the buildings upon it that face the four cardinal
points. The first of these two methods of orientation had the
advantage of establishing a more exact and well-defined relation between the disposition of the building and those celestial
points to which a peculiar importance was attached.' The two
small temples excavated at Nimroud by Layard were entered at
the east, and had their sanctuaries to the west. The inscriptions
repeat very much the thoughts which we have seen were present
to the Egyptian builders. In the inscription on the great bulls at
the entrance gates of the square enclosure at Korsabad the
founder says, 'I placed the lintels in the four heavenly directions,
I opened eight gates in the direction of the four cardinal points.
Towards the four regions of the sun I disposed the cornices and
the door posts' (Inscription of Sargon, B.C. 710, 'Records of the
Past').

Of this four-sided world, each quarter had a 'regent,' apparently in their origin the winds. These four guardians of the regions play a part in many systems, and generally under the symbols of amorphous persons or beasts.

That this was the case in Egypt we have the word of Mariette; they are the 'four powers of the Amenti,' whose heads, three animal and one human, surmount the four funereal vases in the burial ceremonies.

In the northern system of the Edda the heavens, which were set up with four sides, have a dwarf supporting every corner.

In the myths of ancient America these creatures play a large part, and are defined clearly as the four winds. ' In the mythology of Yucatan the four gods Bacab were supposed to stand one at each corner of the world, supporting like gigantic caryatides, the overhanging firmament. When at the general deluge the other gods and men were swallowed by the waters, they alone escaped to people the earth anew.

The East was distinguished by yellow, the South by red, the West by black, the North by white, and these colours appear again in different parts of the world with the same meaning, as representing the four quarters of the world' (M. Muller, Gifford Lect. 1890).

All over the East these four kings of the regions are known. In the Avesta and other Persian writings they are described as 'four chieftains appointed on the four sides.' They are the four Maharajas of the Buddhists. 'Great champions of the earth and the heavens against the demons. These four are represented in full armour with drawn swords' (Sir M. Williams). In a mystical form they enter into Jewish tradition. They appear as the four composite creatures of Ezekiel's vision, full of eyes, that support the firmament, 'the colour of the terrible crystal which stretched forth over their heads above,' with faces of a man, a lion, an ox, and an eagle. They seem to stand at the four cardinal points, the lion on the right side (south), and the ox on the left (north).

The pseudo Enoch writes: 'I also beheld the four winds which bear up the earth, and the firmament of heaven,' and in his vision of heaven he 'heard the voices of those upon the four sides magnifying the Lord of Glory.' He asks whose were the four voices of the four sides, and is told that they are Michael, Raphael, Gabriel, and the fourth Phanuel.

In the Apocalypse, it is these, the beast symbols of the North, South, East, and West, round about the throne, who 'cease not day nor night, saying, Holy, holy, holy.' The ' four winds of the four corners of the earth' are also mentioned in Revelation vii. I.

Compare the like forms of the protecting genii of the Chaldeans given by Lenormant (Magic, p. 121). The four riders in the Revelation on horses white, red, black, and pale resemble the four chariots with horses, red, black, white, and grisled in Zechariah (chap. vi.). ' These are the four spirits (or winds) of the heavens.' Renan thinks the riders of the Apocalypse are planets, but see how each is associated with one of the four beasts, and how they had power over a fourth part of the earth. Lenormant tells us (Contemp. Rev. Sept. 1881) that the four rivers spouted out from their fount on Meru through the mouths of four symbolic animals of four colours and metals. E. white or silver, S. red or copper, W. yellow or gold, N. brown or iron. These are the colours of the four castes and of all kindred who set out from Meru to people the world.

Then there are the four ages 'of the gradual degeneracy of successive ages, which is expressed by the metals the names of which are applied to them; gold, silver, bronze, and iron ' (Lenormant). Remark also how in Daniel vii., 'Four great beasts diverse from one another,' symbolise the coming of four great kingdoms.

These four symbols we find present in our microcosm the temple. In the Buddhist temples of China, 'two colossal wooden statues meet the eye on each side, these are the four great Kings of Devas; they govern the continents lying in the direction of the four cardinal points from mount Sumeru.' They are called *Tein-Wang*, 'the Princes of Heaven.' Miss Bird saw them in Japanese temples painted in bright colours, and trampling demons under foot. The 'Celestial' army, according to directions in the ancient books, was to be marshalled under the banners of these four regents of the quarters; to the East a blue Dragon, West a white tiger, a red bird to the South, and to the North a black warrior.

The celestial mount Meru was of different colours on the four sides. In the temple to the Spirits of Land and Grain at Pekin, 'the terrace is laid with earth of five colours arranged according to the ordinary Chinese distribution of the five colours among the cardinal points: blue is east, red is south, black is north, white is west, and yellow is central. The inner wall is built with different coloured bricks on each of its four sides, according to position ' (Edkins, in Williamson's Journeys).

If we rearranged these colours for ourselves, white might reasonably stand for the east as the point of light, red for the meridian sun of south, blue for the west of evening, and black for north.

Sometimes there appears to have been eight regents, who thus guarded the angles as well as the sides of the square, just as the four winds became eight. In the *Ramayana* the City of Ayodhya is described: 'Every gate of the city was guarded by mighty heroes who were as strong as the eight gods who rule the eight points of the universe.' These eight giant porters are sculptured in pairs on the side posts of each of the four gates at the Sanchi tope.

The guardians of the corners of the world stand at the four angles of the Egyptian sepulchral chamber shown in the papyrus of Ani, published by the British Museum: and as the four powers of the Amenti they always accompany the throned Osiris. Under the form of the four beast-symbols of the Evangelists they rightly fill the pendentives of the domed heavens of Byzantine churches, as at the Mausoleum of Galla Placidia. At St. Mark's the four Evangelists stand over the four heavenly rivers, which pour out their waters one in each angle; and we seem still to preserve in the nursery the tradition of these watchers—

> 'Matthew, Mark, Luke, and John,
> Bless the bed that I lie on,
> Two to foot, and two to head,
> Four to carry me when I'm dead.'

In Chaldea there were powers, not beneficent guardians, but to be guarded against. 'From the four cardinal points the impetuosity of their invasion burns like fire. They violently attack the dwellings of man' (Chaldean Magic).

They were legion, but certain spirits of the winds seem to have had distinct forms according to the quarters from which they approached. These demons had horrible compound forms made up of lion, eagle, bull, scorpion, and whatever beast bites, thrusts, and stings, and Lenormant remarks how the talisman consisted of the form of the power to be combated placed to face the quarter from which each one acted; for so terrible was each of them in appearance, that it was affrighted by its own image, like a Gorgon slain by a mirror. Besides the great bulls and lions guarding the doors, there were sculptured on the walls of the facade a combat between the Chaldean Hercules, Gilgames (Gizdhubar), 'Patrol of the four regions,' and one of these creatures.

At Persepolis there are four colossal sculptures of this kind, of which fine photographs are given in Dieulafoy's great work, and they are described by Sir R. K. Porter as—(1) A compound of lion with head of eagle; (2) a winged lion with eagle's claws; (3) a horned lion; and (4) a unicorn bull. All these the hero, in this case Cyrus the King, calmly slays with the sword, a token to the demons what they were to expect.

The world walls made a vast square, the type of all perfect gardens and cloisters, the enclosure four-square, in which, according to the Avesta, man was first placed. The square paradise of Yima, where men were saved from the flood. The word Yard (garth) is but the Scandinavian Garth, the world.

The Sacred Court, the Temenos of the Greeks, the Haram or Mosque of the Arabs, preceded the temple; the steps probably being—(1) The Sacred Site; (2) the Enclosure delimiting this; (3) the Altar; (4) the Shrine by the Altar in the Court, the dwelling of the Deity worshipped from without by procession and prostration; (5) the Altar is brought within the building; and (6) the temple becomes a place for congregation, the orientation being changed.

The Book of Enoch, after describing the rising and setting of sun and moon, proceeds to account for the winds: 'I beheld twelve gates open for all the winds; three of them are open in the front of heaven, three in the west, three on the right side of

heaven, and three on the left. The first three are those which are towards the east.'

This is the perfect type of the Temple enclosure, or the City wall; 'on the east three gates; on the north three gates; on the south three gates; and on the west three gates.'

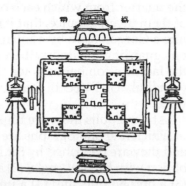

Compare Ezekiel's vision (c. 48) of the ideal city 4500 measures square, and three gates to each quarter, with the plan of an Assyrian, or a Hindu enclosure, or with the walls of the City of Pekin (Taidu), as described by Marco Polo: 'The wall of the city has twelve gates, three on each side of the square.' The modern town of Mandalay, the Burmese Capital City, is likewise walled square, a mile and an eighth long on every face, and there are twelve gates, three on every side. The palace is in the midst, and in the exact centre of the palace and of the city rises the seven-roofed spire, which the Burmese look upon as the centre of Burma, and therefore of creation (Scott, 'Burma').

The perfect type of these cities is the Chinese square enclosure, with twelve gates of the 'Hall of Distinction,' as figured in Dr Morrison's Dictionary,' or of the Temple of Earth at Pekin given by Du Halde. That the gates should face the cardinal aspects is quite universal. Was it not on issuing from the four gates of the city in succession, beginning at the east, that Buddha saw the sights which made him enter on 'the path'? The towns in England of Roman foundation still have north, south, east, and west gates, following the camps and the Etruscan cities. The east gate was reserved for the prince as directed by Ezekiel. When there are three gates together, the central one is the Royal Gate, 'and kept shut, except when the Khan passes that way,' as Marco Polo says; just as in the great churches from Constantinople to Chartres, the middle door is the King's. From the triple eastern gate the main avenue ran westward, as at Alexandria. At Palmyra, over fifteen hundred columns, sixty feet high, were disposed in four rows. At Damascus 'the street called Straight' started from the east gate, and had two rows of Corinthian pillars.' Every great city of the East had a *via recta*—a "straight street," or high street, somewhat similar in plan and ornament to that at Palmyra' (Porter, 'Bashan').

This four squareness was a talismanic assurance of permanence and stability. The thought that, as the heavens were stable upon the earth, so any building four square with them would be immovable, seems, as we have seen, a natural analogy. Fa-Hian says of a Buddhist monastery, 'The side is forty paces square; though heaven should quake and the earth open, this spot would not move.' Professor Beal in a note compares this with the Egyptian treasure city of Rameses, 'solid upon the earth like the four pillars of the firmament.' In the Talmud the Temple of Jerusalem is called the 'immovable house; ' and it is surely the same symbol of indestructibility that is taken by St. John in the cubical city of the Apocalypse.

The most ancient form of Rome, 'the City of Romulus,' was called *Roma Quadrata*; it was built on the Palatine Hill, and enclosed by a wall, around which the sacred pomœrium was marked out by a plough furrow, a religious ceremony in the foundation of towns by the Etruscans. 'Within the area of Apollo (temple on the Palatine) was also a mysterious object which appears to have symbolised the ancient *Roma Quadrata*. This sacred object, which was probably a cubical block of stone used as an altar, was called *Roma Quadrata*, and was surrounded by a circular trench, the *Mundus*, a symbol of the mystic plough turned furrow, by which the pomœrium or sacred circuit line was marked in accordance with the primitive religious ceremonies performed while founding a new city' (Middleton, 'Ancient Rome').

Of all forms, the cube and the hemisphere are the most sacred; the first was that of the Sanctuary at Jerusalem, and that chosen by St John as the type of the Holy City; 'its length, breadth, and height were equal.' Mr Fergusson tells us that the temple of Herod was 100 cubits long in the body 100 cubits high, and 100 cubits broad on the facade, 'so as to make it practically a cube, or at least a building of three equal dimensions.' The cube was the form of the shrine of one stone forty cubits every way that Herodotus saw in Egypt; the Phoenician shrines found by Renan at Amrit; and the Caaba, 'the cube,' of Mecca. The temples of Janus Quadrifrons were 'built with four equal sides, with a door and three windows on each side. The hemisphere is the form of the Buddhist topes. To combine the two has been the builder's problem in all ages.

Another form is also persistent—the double-square; Vitruvius, indeed, says, 'The length of a temple must be twice its width;' and, roughly, this is the proportion to which classic examples conform. Plato makes the temple that surmounted his ideal city one stadium long by half a stadium wide. The King's chamber in the great Pyramid is exactly of this proportion, as was the Cella of the Temple of the Jews. We have seen the classic geographers of the fourth century, B.C., amongst whom is Pytheas, making the earth of precisely this form, and a reason has been suggested sufficient to account for it. Another, however, which must strongly have confirmed their view is to be found in the range of the sun along the horizon from the winter to the summer solstice. Symmetrical both on the rising and setting horizons, and subtending an angle which seemed just within the ends of a parallelogram of which the width was equal to half its length.

Now to the Hindus east to west is 'lengthways,' north to south is 'crossways.' In the Persian *Bundahish* it is said, 'From where the sun comes in on the longest day to where it comes in on the shortest day is the East; from where it comes in on the shortest day to where it goes off on the shortest day is South; where it goes in on the shortest to where it goes in on the longest day is the West; from where it comes in on the longest to where it goes off on the longest day is the North.' In the Talmud an exactly similar account is given. The sun rages up and down the eastern and western horizon like a mighty beast prisoned in a cage; it cannot go farther because of the enclosing sides of the firmament. The gates for it to pass to the lower world and rise again are only found in the ends of the box.

We need barely refer to the actual use of the Temple as a calendar; the sun ray entering at the eastern door at the moment of its appearance above the horizon was certainly registered, and so gave in a long series an accurate observation of the solar year; once a year more especially it exactly fell on the altar. Even now

in some of the French cathedrals—Bourges and Nevers, for instance—diagonal lines may be seen right across the floor gradu-
ated into a scale of months and days.

The observations and ceremony connected with determining
the orientation, and laying the foundation stone, were of the
greatest importance. Brugsch gives an inscription recording the
foundation of Abydos: 'I gave the order,' says the King, 'to prepare the cords and pegs for the laying of the foundation in my
presence. The advent of the day of the new moon was fixed for
the festival of the laying the foundation stone.'

Accordingto Berosos, the gods taught the Chaldeans the rules
for the foundation of towns and building of temples. Of the
modern Buddhist custom, Bock gives us an instance from Siam:
'The site being duly dedicated to the purpose, eight round stones
are taken, and a parallelogram marked out with them, one being placed at each of the eight points of the compass.' In the old
Latin rites (quoting the French Dictionary of Antiquities) one of
the chief duties of the augurs was to set out the new temple
foundation from the heavens. The usage 'appears to have been
to direct the *Cardo* according to the meridian when the observer
faced the south, and had at his left the east, "the happy side,"
later they adopted the Etruscan practice, and turned towards the
west, with the view of combining the ideas of the Etruscans, who
placed the seat of the gods to the north—therefore the happy
side—and the Roman custom which had placed the north to the
left in turning to the east. It has been thought that at times the
Cardo was not the axis, but the diagonal of a square, and that the
augur stationed at the centre directed his vision to the angles.'

To the late Romans of the time of Vitruvius the aspect seems
to have been opposed to what had been the universal earlier
practice. He tells us, 'If there be nothing to prevent it, and the use
of the edifice allow it, the temples of the immortal gods should
have such an aspect that the statue in the Cella may have its face
towards the west, so that those who enter to sacrifice, or to make
offerings, may have their faces to the east as well as to the statue
in the temple. Thus suppliants and those performing their vows
seem to have the temple, the East, and the Deity, as it were, looking on them at the same moment. Hence all the altars of the gods
should be placed towards the east.' In another place he explains

how the true north may be obtained. In a marble slab or a level
space a gnomon is placed upright. The shadow cast by the gnomon is to be marked about the fifth hour before the meridian,
the extreme point being accurately determined, and from the
centre of the gnomon a circle is described equal in radius to the
length of the shadow just obtained. After the sun has passed the
meridian watch the shadow until the moment when it touches
the circle again at another point; a line drawn from the centre
bisecting the arc thus obtained will indicate the north.

Christian buildings at first followed the old westward direction of the Jewish temple; for instance, the Church of the Holy
Sepulchre in Jerusalem built by Constantine. So also early
churches in Italy, and even here in England, were 'occidented '
rather than oriented. This ultimately gave way to the eastward
direction; all Justinian's churches have their prospect towards
the east, and it becomes of interest to determine if this is with
the object of their being directed towards Jerusalem, or of con-
forming to orientation. The great church built by Constantine at
Bethlehem, which is directly south of Jerusalem, and only a few
miles off, lies east and west, not north and south, as it would if
directed to the Holy City. Still further south the Coptic Churches
of Egypt are described by Mr Butler as having the entrance 'almost invariably towards, if not in the western side, while the
sanctuaries lie always on the eastern.' Far south in Abyssinia the
curious excavated monolithic churches follow the same axis
west to east.

A passage in Procopius gives a clear statement of the purpose
in the orientation of Sta Sophia, the great Church of Christendom. He says, 'The part where the sacred mysteries are performed in honour of God is built towards the rising sun.' And
of the Church of the Apostles, rebuilt by Justinian, in Constantinople, he gives this interesting relation: 'The lines were drawn
in the form of a cross, joining one another in the middle, the
upright one pointing to the rising and the setting sun, and the
other cross line towards the north and the south wind. These
were surrounded by a circuit of walls, and within by columns
placed both above and below; at the crossing of the two straight
lines, that is, about the middle point of them, there is a place set
apart that may not be entered except by the priests, and which
is consequently termed the sanctuary. The transepts which lie

on each side of this about the cross line are of equal length; but that part of the upright line towards the setting sun is built so much longer than the other part as to form the figure of the Cross.'

The old Antiquary Stukeley gave a very clear account of orientation anticipating the points here set out. 'Ever since the world began, in building temples or places of religious worship, men have been studious in setting them according to the quarters of the heavens; since they considered the world as the general temple, or house of God, and that all particular temples should be regulated according to that idea. The east naturally claims a prerogative, where the sun and all the planets and stars rise. The east they therefore considered the face and front of the universal temple.'

CHAPTER IV
AT THE CENTRE OF THE EARTH

> . . . *That stellar concave spreading*
> *overhead, softly absorbed into me, rising so*
> *free interminably high, stretching east,*
> *west, north, south—and I thought but a*
> *point in the centre below embodying all.*
> —WALT WHITMAN.

THERE would seem to be delight and mystery inherent to the ideas of a boundary or a centre. Children show this by standing in two counties or parishes at the same time, and being much comforted thereby—only disappointed, like the little girl in *Punch*, that there are not pretty colours at the division, as on the maps. Do you not remember being told that the Town Hall 'at home' was the centre of the mileage of the diverging roads, and being much impressed by this, the middle of the world, which should have been specially marked by a 'golden milestone.' Paris, London, or Boston is the 'hub' of the universe to their several inhabitants. 'All roads lead to Rome.'

'Ah! Messer Greco,' George Eliot makes her cultured Barber, Nello, say of his shop 'Apollo and the Razor,' 'if you want to know the flavour of our scholarship, you must frequent my shop; it is the focus of Florentine intellect, and in that sense the navel of the earth, as my great predecessor Burchieilo said of *his* shop, on the more frivolous pretension that his street of the Calimara was the centre of our city.'

When the earth was a plane surface with boundaries which were certain in form, if unknown in extent, 'the centre is with us' would be a claim advanced in a much more definite form by different countries or rival cities. On an Arab fountain in Sicily was the inscription, 'I am in the centre of the garden; this garden is the centre of Sicily, and Sicily of the whole world.'

The Mediterranean still preserves its name of the world's central sea. Maspero tells us the Chaldeans considered themselves better than their neighbours, and the centre of the world; and Professor Sayce that in the forest of Eridu—into the heart whereof man had not penetrated—was the 'centre of the earth' and the 'holy house of the gods.' The Egyptians, too considered they were the only true centre. 'The Egyptians were particularly remarkable for their great love for their country, which is also inherited by their successors. They considered it to be under the immediate protection of the gods and the centre of the world; they even called it the world itself; and it was thought to be the favoured spot where all created beings were first generated, while the rest of the earth was barren and uninhabited' (Wilkinson). Bunsen mentions a map of the world under the form of a human figure in which Egypt was the heart.

In 'Voyageurs Anciens' Charton says, 'Chaque peuple repondait avec une assurance naive. "Le centre est chez moi"— For the Egyptians the centre was Thebes; for the Assyrians, Babylon; for the Hindus, Mount Meru; for the Jews, Jerusalem; for the Greeks, Olympus or the temple of Delphi, and later, in the time of Herodotus, Rhodes.' In the same collection of travels a modern Arab view as to the form and centre of the world is given. God created the earth square, and covered with stones; and from the top of Mount Sinai which is the centre of the world, traced a great circle whose circumference touched the four sides of the square. He then commanded the angels to throw all the stones into the corners, which correspond with the four cardinal points. The circle thus cleared was given to the Arabs, who are the children best beloved; then he called the four angles France, Italy, England, and Russia.

An inscription of a king of Susa (B.C. 710, 'Records of the Past') makes this claim for the 'Susian land, which is the first of the earth, and the centre of all mankind.'

It was the same with Persia— 'The country of Iran is better than other places, for it is in the middle.'

China also has always been a specially favoured country, and its position is marked in its very name —the 'Middle Kingdom.' In the letter from the Emperor of China to the King of England in 1817 he claims that he has received from heaven the government of the world, and that China is 'the flourishing and central empire,' the source of good influences. The Hindus also have a name implying that their country is the centre, and the old Japanese poems call theirs the Middle Kingdom.

A confusion was likely to arise at once in regard to this centre, for the centre of the heavenly revolutions is seen to be in the north; hence the world mountain, the pivot of these revolutions also rose in the north. For instance, according to the 'Encyclopædia of India,' 'The Hindus at Bikanir Rajputana taught that the mountain Meru is in the centre surrounded by concentric circles of land and sea. Some Hindus regard Mount Meru as the north pole. The astronomical views of the Puranas make the heavenly bodies turn round it.'

This world-mountain was Nizir to the Chaldeans, Olympus to the Greeks, Hara Berezaiti to the Persians of the Avesta, the later Alborz and Elburz; a transfer, as says Mme. Ragozin, of 'mythical heavenly geography to the earth.' This mountain—the solar hill of the Egyptians—we shall again refer to in the next two or three chapters. At its apex springs, the heaven tree on which the solar bird is perched. From its roots spring the waters of life—the celestial sea, which, rushing adown the firmament, supplies the ocean which circumscribes the earth or falls directly in rain. At their fountain these springs are guarded by a goddess. In Egypt Nut, the goddess of the oversea, leans from the branches of the heavenly *persea* and pours forth the celestial water. In the Vedas, Yama, lord of the waters, sits in the highest heaven in the midst of the heavenly ocean under the tree of life, which drops the nectar Soma, and here, on the 'navel of the waters,' matter first took form. In the Norse, the central tree Yggdrasil has at its roots the spring of knowledge guarded by the Norns, the northern Fates; two swans the parents of all those of earth, float there. In Chaldea the mighty tree of Eridu, centre of the world, springs by the waters. The Avesta gives a very complete picture —Iran is at the centre of the seven countries of the world; it was the first created, and so beautiful, that were it

not that God has implanted in all men a love for their own land,
all nations would crowd into this the loveliest land. To the east
somewhere, but still at the centre of the world, rises the 'Lofty
Mountain,' from which all the mountains of the earth have
grown, 'High Haraiti;' at its summit is the gathering place of
waters, out of which spring the two trees, the heavenly Haoma
(Soma), and another tree which bears all the seeds that germi-
nate on earth. This heavenly mountain is called '*Navel of Waters*,'
for the fountain of all waters springs there, guarded by a majestic
and beneficent goddess. In Buddhist accounts, the waters issue
in four streams like the rivers of Eden from this reservoir, and
flow to the cardinal points, each making one complete circuit in
its descent. In the Persian *Bundahish* there are two of these heavenly rivers flowing east and west. To the Hindus the Ganges is
such a heavenly stream. 'The stream of heaven was called by the
Greeks Achelous.' The Nile in Egypt, the Hoang-Ho in China,
and the Jordan to the Jews, seem to have been celestial rivers.
This mountain of heaven is often figured in Christian art with
the four rivers issuing from under the Throne of God.

Sir John Maundeville gives an account of the earthly Paradise
quite perfect in its detailed scheme. It is the highest place on
earth, nearly reaching to the circle of the moon (as in Dante), and
the flood did not reach it. '*And
in the highest place, exactly in the
middle*, is a well that casts out
the four streams —Ganges,
Nile, Tigris, and Euphrates.
'And men there beyond say
that all the sweet waters of the
world above and beneath take
their beginning from the well
of Paradise, and out of that well
all waters come and go.' The illustration is from the Hereford
Map.

In the Odyssey—which appears to be a voyage to the three
worlds by a Greek Dante, and parallel, as Mr Andrew Lang has
remarked, to an old Indian tale in which the hero sets off to find
the city of gold—Ulysses, after visiting the country of Cyclops
and other lands evidently beyond the verge of civilisation, law,

and order, goes to the isle of Æolus, King of the winds, and to the island of Circe, where is the 'dancing place of the dawn.' He descends to the underworld and explores it; returning, he passes the gates of the firmament, the clashing mountains, and comes to the isle of the Sun, and shipwrecked, he alone reaches the isle of Calypso, and remains eight years; but then leaving her, comes at last to divine Scheria, paradise, and city of gold, 'far off from men that live by bread.' Then asleep in a magic bark he is conveyed to earth and home.

This island of the lone goddess Calypso is Ogygia, *'where is the navel of the sea,'* far removed on a 'wondrous space of brine whereby is no city of mortals;' 'and, lo, there about the hollow cave trailed a gadding garden vine all rich with clusters. *And fountains four set orderly were running with clear water hard by one another, turned each to his own course.* And all around soft meadows bloomed of violets and parsley.' Can we doubt that Calypso is the guardian goddess of the heavenly spring, of the four streams that supply the earth? Can we doubt that this 'outer zone' of Ulysses' voyages is on the oversea, thus making a complete pendant to the underworld. As a parallel let us remark how closely Lucian follows all this in his Satire, reaching upperworld and lower world in a ship. The heavenly spring is, of course, the fountain of the water of life, and Ulysses ought certainly to have drunk of it like the traveller of the Egyptian Ritual of the Dead. What did the hero of the Odyssey go there for if not to bring back a true report of such a remarkable place? Duncker says of Athene, 'She is the spirit of this fountain itself'

All the scheme is rational enough; men wanting to explain the rain, the moving tides and flowing rivers of earth, supposed a perennial fountain rose in the heavens, four streams from which flowed down the heavenly vault, and entering by certain openings, circled round the ocean stream, and then fell into the abyss: Acheron, Pyriphlegethon, Cocytus, and Styx, probably have their origin in this thought.

To return to the Middleworld. Sung-Yun, the Chinese traveller in India to collect Buddhist records (518 A.D.), speaking of the great mountain country, the watershed of the Indus and Oxus, still called the Roof of the World, says: 'After entering the Tsung-Ling mountains step by step, we crept upwards for four days, and reached the highest point of the range. From this point as a centre, looking downwards, it seemed just as though we were poised in mid-air. Men say that this is the middle point of heaven and earth. The people of this region use the water of the rivers for irrigating their lands; and when they were told that in the *Middle Kingdom* (China) the fields were watered by the rain, they laughed and said, 'How could heaven produce enough for all ?' Hiuen Tsiang (A.D. 629) says that at the central point of the world, in the mountains of Pamir, there was a lake blue and bottomless; out of it flowed two streams to east and west, supplying the waters of the world.

When China received Buddhism there arose a difficulty as to the Middle Kingdom; for the orthodox said that India, where Buddha lived, was the middleland, 'as shown *by the gnomon which at the summer solstice in that latitude casts no shadow*. China, they say, cannot so well be called the central kingdom, because there is a shadow on the day mentioned' (Edkins). Fa-Hian was disliked by his countrymen for admitting the superior claim of India. It shows how the human mind works in fixed grooves to find Sir John Maundeville giving the same 'proof' of the gnomon for the central position of Jerusalem.

The Greeks seem to have attached great mystic and ritual importance to the centre. Delphi was the navel of all Greece, but Crete had an omphalos, and a story was attached regarding the birth of Jupiter. Pausanias mentions an omphalos at Phlius marking the centre of the Peloponnese. In Sicily the modern Castro Giovanni occupies the site of Enna, *Umbilicus Siciliae*, and this was the place where Persephone was carried away from the upper world. In Babylon also it was at the world's centre that Tammuz made his descent, for here is the lid stone of the lower world. Each separate worship appears to have its 'Kibleh,' Delos for Apollo, Paphos for Venus, and Delphi the ancient hearth of Hestia. At Megara the altar was the omphalos.

Mount Cronios in Olympia, Lenormant says, 'was the omphalos of the sacred city of Elis, the primitive centre of worship.' It is easy to see that this 'centre of worship,' this 'centre of the earth where is the holy house of the gods,' was likely to become identified with a building, the ancient mother temple of a people, be it at Babylon, at Delphi, or at Mecca. Brugsch says,

'The Egyptians, like the ancients in general, commenced the foundation of their towns by the construction of a temple, which formed the centre of the town that was to be built.'

Delphi to the Greeks was pre-eminently the centre of the world; here was the famous and ancient temple of Apollo, the god who, as Plato has it, 'sits in the centre on the navel of the earth.'

Has Delphi taken over this tradition as being seated on Parnassus, the mountain of the flood of Deucalion? And do the other stories of Parnassus and the spring of poesy arise from its being associated with another tradition of the earthly paradise?

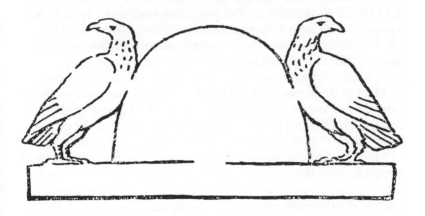

In the description before given of the peplos representing the universe woven by Harmonia, we have seen how 'she first represented the earth with its omphalos in the centre:' but this centre of the world is not only to be found in ideal poet-made designs, it was realised in architecture. On the floor of the temple of Delphi was a stone 'called by the Delphians the Navel, according to their tradition, the centre of the world (Pausanias). The story was told, that to determine the true centre of the earth, Jupiter sent out two eagles, one from the east, the other from the west, and they met at this spot.

According to Strabo, two gold eagles were placed at the sides of the omphalos. This composition is preserved to us by a marble found in Sparta. As early as Pindar these golden birds of Zeus are mentioned, but later marble sculpture or mosaic represented

them. On the vases we have many contemporary drawings of this composition (see T. H. Middleton in Jour. Hellenic Soc., vol. ix.): in most of these the sacred stone is shown of the form of half an egg, raised on a step on which the birds stood 'affronted;' other representations show the egg form complete: it was decorated by fillets, leafy branches, and netted work.

This centre stone of the whole world seems to have profoundly touched the Greek imagination; and among the multitude of references to it, it has a part in the tragedies of Æschylus, Sophocles, and Euripides. The first scene of the 'Eumenides ' takes place in the outer court of the oracle—A priestess passes into the Adytum, but returns crouching with fear supporting herself against the walls:-

> 'Lo ! Into yon recess
> With garlands hung I go, and there I see
> Upon the central stone a God-loathed man
> Sitting as suppliant, and with hands that dripped
> Blood drops, and holding sword but newly drawn.'
> —*Plumpire.*

Orestes, pursued by the Furies, has taken sanctuary in the temple of Apollo, and the matricide is thus discovered on the centre-stone of the world, of the universe, a 'God-loathed man,' while his sword still drips with his mother's blood.

We may see embodied in this myth of the centre stone the result of the general direction of thought; as each people were certainly 'the people' first born and best beloved of the gods, so their country occupied the centre of the world. It would be related how the oldest and most sacred city, or rather temple, was erected exactly on the navel. A story like this told of a temple

would lead to the marking in the centre of its area the true middle point by a circular stone, a stone which would become most
sacred and ceremonial in its import. Such a tendency seems to
lie close to the root of ideas; Professor Smyth in his interpretation of the great Pyramid thought that it marked in a special way
the world's centre.

In the rites of Greece and Rome it was the hearth that was
specially identified with the omphalos and so in Latin we have
'focus,' and in French 'foyer,' at once hearth and centre.

'According to Pythagoras, the fire of Hestia (*foyer du monde*)
was at the centre of the earth and the world.'

'In this sanctuary of Apollo at Delphi (formerly dedicated to
Hestia), near the stone omphalos was the altar of the sacred fire
of Hestia, the goddess who symbolised the stability of the earth.
In the primitive Greek houses of a circular form the hearth was
at the centre, and the smoke found its way out at the apex. Each
Greek city had its prytaneum in form of a rotunda (tholos), an
edifice consecrated to Hestia; and the hearth sacred to the city
was placed under the centre of the vault, in the same way that
the foyer of Delphi—foyer common to all Greeks—was under
the summit of the heavenly vault' (*Dictionnaire des Antiquités*).

The Prytaneum was the civic hall, the pole of the city life, and
here, on the focus of the town, was kept alight the undying fire
of Hestia; for just as the family life centred around the hearth,
so political life surrounded the city hearth, from which colonists
going from the mother town took of the sacred central fire to
establish their own prytaneum; and if in after time it ceased to
burn, the metropolis was again the source of new fire. So it was
that, according to tradition, Æneas brought from Troy the sacred
fire, which was maintained by the Vestals in the circular temple
of the Forum.

A mystery still clings to the hearth, and it still is the centre
of the world. It seems a part of the Aryan inheritance; for while
the nations were as yet unseparated, 'the hearth was in the midst
of the dwelling; that hearth was to each member of the house-
hold, as it were, an umbilicus orbus or navel of the earth. . . .
Hearth being only another form of earth, as in the German *erde*

and *herde'* (Keary, 'Dawn of History'). It has been suggested that this early home was a circular roofed hut, and thus a sky-like canopy to the central fire.

A central circle was found in the palace at Tiryns. Dr Schliemann writes: 'In the exact centre of the hall, and therefore within the square enclosed by the four pillars, there is found in the floor a circle of about 3.30 m. diameter. There can be little doubt that this circle indicates the position of the hearth in the centre of the megaron. The hearth was in all antiquity the centre of the house, about which the family assembled, at which food was prepared, and where the guest received the place of honour. Hence it is frequently indicated by poets and philosophers as the navel or centre of the house. In the oldest time it was not only symbolically, but actually the centre of the house, and especially of the megaron. It was only in later days, in the great palaces of the Romans, that it was removed from the chief rooms and established in a small by-room.... It is hardly an accidental circumstance that, in the middle of the largest hall in the pergamos of the Homeric Troy, a large circle is to be seen in the centre of the floor. . . . There can be no doubt that at Troy too the spacious hall, with its vestibule, was the megaron, and the circle in its centre marked the place of the hearth.'

The imperial palace at Constantinople, which must have been the topstone of the worldly art in building—embodying as it did all knowledge and tradition, Classic and Christian, and gathering for material all the splendours of the earth—had on the floors of those wonderful rooms, the design of which we can still follow in the descriptions collated by Labarte (*Palais Imp. Cons.*), sacred hearth or navel stones. 'The floor of *Chalce* was composed of beautiful marble mosaic; below the dome in the pavement was a large slab of porphyry, of circular form, to which they gave the name of Omphalion.' The Emperor, after having bought back for a large sum certain bonds, to which citizens of Constantinople had put their hands, burnt these bonds upon the omphalion of porphyry in Chalce. We also find an omphalion encased in the pavement of the grand triclinium of Justinian; they existed in other rooms of the palace, and notably in front of the thrones. The Emperor stood on these slabs of porphyry at certain ceremonies, and his passing over or pausing on them seems to have been the occasion for those present to prostrate themselves before him.

On the floor of St Peter's, in Rome, there is a circular slab of antique porphyry, 8 ft. 6 in. in diameter, on which, tradition says, every emperor since Charlemagne stood at coronation. The Popes also on it performed certain official acts. Ducange mentions an omphalos in Sancta Sophia; it was directly under the dome,and called meso-naos, omphalos, ormes-omphalos.

Whether the temple of Vesta in Rome, close to the Forum, was or was not at any time actually a geographical centre, it is certain that the Forum contained such an one in the *Milliarum aureum Umbilicus Urbis*, which had on it the names and distances of the towns on the roads which here met at a centre from all Italy. As some late writers speak of the omphalos as distinct from the golden milestone, and as the foundations of two circular structures have been discovered in the Forum, Mr. Middleton is inclined to look on one as the milestone, and the other as the omphalos. The sacred stone on the Palatine, mentioned in the last chapter, would seem to have been the omphalos of primitive Rome, 'the city of Romulus.' Mr Gomme tells us a stone was always set up at the establishment of primitive villages, and that London Stone is an example.

If we go to the west, the centre is there. 'The historian of Yucatan describes a celebrated sanctuary known as "the centre and foundation of heaven," which was the object of great veneration' (Charnay); and M. Reville quotes Garcilasso, the native historian of Peru, who says that Cuzco, the sacred city, was founded by the gods, and 'its name signifies navel.' 'Splendid roads stretched from Cuzco towards the four quarters of the heavens.' And again, 'The great Teocalli of Mexico commanded the four chief roads that parted from its base to unite the capital to all the countries beneath the sceptre of its rulers. It was the palladium of the empire.' The roads diverge in this way from the great Lamassary of the holy city of Thibet, which is also a world centre. The 'four cross roads' of old English customs were probably of so much consequence, because such a situation established a sympathetic magic with the universe.

If we go to the far East, the stone of foundation is there. In Japan the world is carried on an enormous leviathan the Earthquake fish (*Jishin-uwo*), and when it moves there is an earthquake; one god only can then quiet it, and this he does 'by pinning it down with the *Kaua-mi-ishi*, or 'rivet rock of the world.' As every Japanese knows, this stone is in the province of Hitachi' (The 'Century,' Jan. 1890). Two temples at Ise form the kibleh of Shintoism, toward which the people turn in prayer.

There appears from Grimm (*Teut. Myth.*) to have been such a stone known to the Northern nations as the 'Dille-Stein,' or Lid of Hell; he compares it with the *lapis manalis* that closed the mouth of the Etruscan Mundus. In the Talmud there was access to the lower world at Jerusalem, although the whole world was but a 'pot-lid' to hell.

In India the great iron pillar of Delhi, standing amidst the ruins of the old capital, was set up in the fourth century; later, in the twelfth century, the great Mohammedan Mosque of the Imperial City was built round it as the exact middle point of its vast court. The pillar commemorated the power of a Raja who, as the inscription reads, 'obtained with his own arm an undivided sovereignty over the earth.' A Holy Braman assured a Raja of the eighth century that the pillar had been driven so deeply into the earth that it rested on the head of Vasuki, the serpent king, who supports the world, and consequently had become immovable, whereby the dominion was insured forever to the dynasty of its founder as long as the pillar stood. The incredulous Raja ordered the monument to be dug up, when it was found to be reddened with the blood of the serpent king (Hunter's Gaz. of India). We have here probably a Braman centre in opposition to the sacred site of the Buddhists. In Southern India the Temple of Mandura is the centre of the Tamil people; here in the inmost sanctuary a rock, symbol of Siva, crops out of the floor. 'Its roots are said to be in the centre of the earth, and to have been there since the Creation.' Here the kings were taken when about to die (Clements Markham).

In China, the centre of the ancient royal cult is the altar or temple of heaven, in the old city of Pekin. One stone circular and flawless forms the centre of zone after zone of marble steps and terraces. 'Here the Emperor kneels, and is surrounded first by the circles of the terraces and their enclosing walls, and then by the circle of the horizon. He thus seems to himself and his court to be in the centre of the universe, and, turning to the north, assuming the attitude of a subject, he acknowledges in prayer that he is inferior to heaven and to heaven alone' (Edkins. see Williamson's Journeys).

Gaya is the great Holy Place of Buddhism, the Mecca of its sites; here Buddha sat under the Bodhi tree when he reached complete enlightenment. While he was yet seeking there came to him a voice saying that he was to find a Pipal tree, under which was a 'diamond throne.' All the past Buddhas seated on this throne have obtained true enlightenment (Beal).

The Bodhi tree itself as described by Hiuen Tsiang was surrounded by an enclosure which was long east and west, and narrow north and south, with four gates to the cardinal points. 'In the middle of the enclosure is the diamond throne, when the great earth arose this also appeared. It is the middle of the great *Chiliocosm*; it goes down to the limits of the golden wheel, and upwards it is flush with the ground. It is composed of diamonds; in circuit it is a hundred paces or so. . . . It is the place where the Buddhas attain the sacred path of Buddahood. When the great earth is shaken this spot alone is unmoved. Therefore when Tathagata was about to reach the condition of enlightenment, and he went successively to the four angles of this enclosure, the earth shook and quaked; but afterwards coming to this spot, all was still and at rest. When the true law decays and dies it will be no longer visible.'

The Chiliocosm is not this world alone, but the whole assemblage of worlds—the universe. Sir M. Williams tells us a stone marked with nine concentric circles is still shown at Gaya as the Diamond Throne.

Jerusalem has been to Jews and Christians the centre of the world, 'beautiful for situation, joy of the whole earth.' What the Temple was as a centre of worship is shown by Solomon's dedicatory prayer and by Daniel's open window toward Zion. The following is the direction as to prayer in the Talmud: 'Those who are in foreign countries beyond the borders of Palestine ought in praying to turn their faces towards the sacred land as it is written, "They shall address their prayer to Thee by the way of the land which Thou hast given to their ancestors" (I Kings viii.

48). Those who dwell in Palestine direct their countenance towards Jerusalem, for it is written, "They shall pray unto Thee towards the city which Thou hast chosen." Those who make their prayer in Jerusalem turn towards the mount of the Temple, as it is said in the same verse, "And the house which I have builded in Thy name." Those who are upon the mount of the temple turn towards the Holy of Holies. "They shall address their prayer to Thee in this place, and Thou wilt hear it in heaven Thy dwelling-place, Thou wilt hear it and will pardon." Hence it follows that those of the north should turn towards the south, those of the south towards the north, the men of the east towards the west, the men of the west towards the east, so that all Israel shall turn in the act of prayer.'

But not only was it a ceremonial centre; it was geographically the midst of the earth; and the following from the Talmud (Hershon) shows that to the Rabbis the Temple had an omphalion stone, and that it was built not only on *a* rock, but on *the* rock.

'The world is like the eyeball of man; the white is the ocean that surrounds the world, the black is the world itself, and the pupil is Jerusalem, and the image in the pupil is the Temple.'

'The world's "foundation stone" sank to the depths under the Temple of the Lord, and upon this the sons of Korah used to stand and pray.'

'The land of Israel is situated in the centre of the world, and Jerusalem in the centre of the land of Israel, and the Temple in the centre of Jerusalem, and the Holy of Holies in the centre of the Temple, and *the foundation stone on which the world was grounded is situated in front of the ark.*'

'When the ark was removed a stone was there from the days of the first prophets; it was called *Foundation*. It was three digits high above the earth.'

The great temple of Bel, the most ancient, most sacred temple at Babylon, was called, Professor Sayce tells us, in his Hibbert Lectures, 'the house of *the foundation stone of heaven and earth.*' In Jerusalem the 'Dome of the Rock,' *El Sakhrah*, occupying the traditional site of the temple sanctuary, surrounds a mass of the living rock, the bare summit of Mount Moriah, which for about sixty by forty feet crops out of the beautiful paving; under it is the 'Well of Souls;' and the Turkish Pacha told Sir Charles Warren 'it lay on the top leaves of a palm tree, from the roots of which

spring all the rivers of the world.' Nusir-i-Khusran, who visited
the sites in 1003 AD., says that God commanded Moses to make
this stone the kibleh, and later Solomon built the temple about
it as a centre. From it the four doors open, as an early pilgrim
says, to the four quarters of the world. In Mohammedan tradition this rock is the world's foundation stone. It is known to
them as the *kibleh* (point of adoration, centre) of Moses. Mahomet
thought at first of adopting it in the place of the old Arab centre
of Mecca, well understanding the religious need of such an
omphalos to Eastern thought, as in it the idea of separation from
others is most forcibly expressed. The Prophet says, 'Verily although thou shouldest show unto those to whom the Scripture

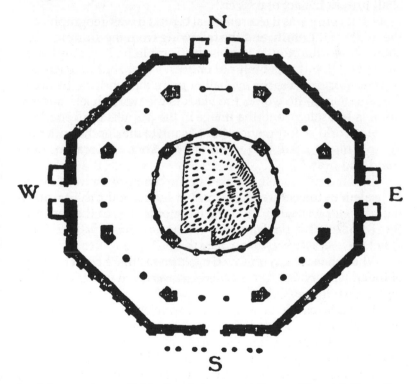

hath been given all kinds of signs, yet they will not follow thy
kibleh, neither shalt thou follow their kibleh; nor will one part
of them follow the kibleh of the other.' At the last day, however,
even the black stone of Mecca will come as a bride to the rock of

Jerusalem, and thus arises any confusion there may be as to the world centre of Islam. The late Professor Palmer tells us what the rock is to those in Jerusalem: ' This Sakhrah is the centre of the world, and on the day of resurrection the angel Israfil will stand upon it to blow the last trumpet; it is also eighteen miles nearer heaven than any other place in the world; and beneath it is the source of every drop of sweet water that flows on the face of the earth; it is supposed to be suspended miraculously between heaven and earth. The effect upon the spectators was, however, so startling that it was found necessary to place a building round it and conceal the marvel.'

The Samaritans still look to Gerizim as their holy mountain. 'This is their kibleh, to which they turn in prayer wherever they maybe' (Warren). 'Our fathers worshipped in this mountain, and ye say that in Jerusalem is the place where men ought to worship.'

Of Hermon Miss Beaufort wrote: 'It is remarkable that Hermon was anciently encompassed by a circle of temples all facing the summit. Can it be that this mountain was the great sanctuary of Baal, and that it was to the old Syrians what Jerusalem was to the Jews, and what Mecca is to the Moslems?' One of these temples has sculptured on the side towards the mountain a huge watching face. Another Syrian temple, that of Mabog (Hierapolis), seems to have been a world centre and well of the abyss; this city occupied the site of Carchemish, the capital of the Hittites, and it is probably their rites and legends that were continued here. The temple stood in the very centre of the 'Holy City,' and it was built (so went the legend) by their Noah directly over the chasm where the waters of the Deluge had been swallowed up (Sayce Hittites). 'At Jerusalem also there was a cleft in which the waters of the flood disappeared ' (Robertson Smith, Semites). Pausanias says there was a cavity in the precincts of the temple of Olympia where the waters of the deluge escaped.

To the Mohammedans generally the Caaba at Mecca is the true centre, lowered as it was directly from Paradise under which it stands, and to it all Islam turns in prayer, 'Turn thy face towards the temple of Mecca, and whenever ye pray, turn your faces towards that place' (*Koran*). In an account of modern schools in Cairo, Mr Loftie says, 'The children learn that it takes five hundred years of travelling to get round the mighty plain,

while perhaps a few yards from the school door hangs one of
Mr Cook's placards offering to do the whole business in ninety
days. The one important fact which the children retain is, that
Mecca is the centre of the earth.' All mosques look to this kibleh.

To the early Christians and throughout the Middle Ages Jerusalem was the centre. Jerome calls it the navel of the world,
and Clement of Alexandria remarks that the outer court of the
Tabernacle was, 'they say,' the middlemost point of heaven and
earth. Arculf in 670 A.D. tells us that Jerusalem being in the
middle, was called the 'navel of the earth,' and he gives the proof
of the shadowless pillar. In the time of Abbot Daniel's visit
(1106) the centre was canopied by a small dome on pillars. The
Hereford map of the thirteenth century shows the world as a
plane circle surrounded by ocean, round whose borders are the
eaters of men and the one-eyed, the half men and those 'whose
heads do grow beneath their shoulders.' Within this border we
find everything that heart could desire, the red sea is very red,
the pillars of Hercules are pillars indeed; there is the terrestial
paradise enclosed by a battlemented wall; and unicorns,
manticoras, salamanders, and other beasts of fascinating habits
are clearly shown on the lands where they live. The centre of all
is Jerusalem, a circular walled town, within which again is a
smaller circle, the Church of the Holy Sepulchre. The central position of Jerusalem was not given up when it became accepted
as a fact that the earth was a sphere. Dante holds both for true,
and this is how Sir John Maundeville reconciles any difficulty:
'In going from Scotland or from England towards Jerusalem,
men go always upwards, for our land is in the low part of the
earth, towards the west; and the land of Prester John is in the low
part of the world towards the east; and they have the day when
we have the night, and, on the contrary, they have the night
when we have the day; for the earth and sea are of a round form,
as I have said before; and as men go upward towards one part,
they go downward to another. Also you have heard me say that
Jerusalem is in the middle of the world; and that may be proved
and shown there by a spear which is fixed in the earth at the hour
of mid-day, when it is equinoctial, which gives no shadow on
any side.'

The Greek Church still accepts Jerusalem as the middle of the world, and in their portion of the Holy Sepulchre point it out to unbelieving tourists to-day.

'The Greeks,' says Curzon, ' have possession of the choir of the church which is opposite the door. This part of the building is of great size, and is magnificently decorated with gold and carving and stiff pictures of the saints. In the centre is a globe of black marble on a pedestal, under which they say the head of Adam was found; and you are told also that this is the exact centre of the globe.'

His plan shows this by the sign

'THE CENTRE OF THE WORLD.'

CHAPTER V

THE JEWEL-BEARING TREE

> 'Impious! the trees of vegetable gold Such
> as in Eden's groves Yet innocent it grew;
> Impious! he made his boast though Heaven
> had hid
> So deep the baneful ore,
> That they should branch and bud for him
> That art should force their blossoms and
> their fruit And recreate for him whate'er
> Was lost in Paradise.
> Therefore at Shedad's voice
> Here towered the palm, a silver trunk The
> fine gold network growing out Loose from
> its rugged boughs.
> Tall as thc cedar of the mountain, here
> Rose the gold branches hung with emerald
> leaves,Blossomed with pearls, and rich with
> ruby fruit.'
> —SOUTHEY, Thalaba.

OF all the wonders of the Palace at Constantinople as described
in 'Count Robert of Paris,' the most wonderful is the golden tree
that stood near the throne, with the singing birds that moved by
mechanical art. Such a tree is indispensable to the palace of Romance.

In the 'Gest Hystoriale' of the destruction of Troy, Englished in the fourteenth century, the writer does his utmost for the splendours of Troy town and its palace. During a truce Ulysses—

'He was the fairest by ferre of all the felle Grekes,
And falsest in his fare, and full of disseit '—

and Diomedes visit the palace called Ylion, 'made all of marbyll with mason devyse.' They are astonished at its splendour, especially the great hall, in the midst of which 'was a tre that was tried all of tru gold.' It was larger than a laurel, twelve cubits high; its boughs made the circuit of the whole hall, some of gold, some of silver; with leaves, buds, and fair fruit 'that shemert as shire as any shene stonys.'

Lydgate, in the 'Warre of Troy,' brings forward, without discount, the description of such desirable properties when he tells

'Of a tree that Amyddes stode,
On which to loke they thought it did them good,
Musing where it were Artifyciall,
Erect or sette by magyke natirall,
Or by engyne of workmen curyous,
Through subtyll craftes supersticious
Or other worke of Nycromancye
Or profounde castynge of Philosophye,
By apparaunce or Yllusyion
Outher by crafte of incantacion.'

The genealogy of this tree probably descends through the romance of Alexander. Alexander having in India jousted with a Sultan for a kingdom, finds in the palace so won, along with other treasures, a vine of gold, with leaves of emeralds, and fruit of other precious gems. Just such a tree as is described by Sir John Maundeville, 'Of the great Chan of Cathay, of the royalty of his palace, and how he sits at meat.' 'Within the palace, in the hall, there are twenty-four pillars of fine gold; and all the walls are covered within with red skins of animals called panthers, fair beasts, and well smelling; so that for the sweet odour of the skins no evil air may enter into the palace. The skins are as red as blood, and shine so bright against the sun that a man may scarcely look on them. And many people worship the beasts when they meet them first in a morning, for their great virtue, and for the good smell that they have. . . . The hall of the palace is full nobly arrayed and full marvellously attired on all parts, in all things that men apparel any hall with. And first, at the head of the hall, is the emperor's throne, very high, where he sits at meat; it is of fine precious stones, bordered all about with purified gold and precious stones, and great pearls. And the steps up to the table are of precious stones, mixed with gold; and at the left side of the emperor's seat is the seat of his first wife, one step lower than the emperor, and it is of jasper bordered with gold and precious stones. And the sea of his second wife is lower than his first wife, and is also of jasper bordered with gold, as that other is. And the seat of the third wife is still lower by a step than the second wife—for he has always three wives with him wherever he is. And, after his wives, on the same side, sit the ladies of his lineage, still lower, according to their ranks, and all those that are married have a counterfeit, made like a man's foot, upon their heads, a cubit long, all wrought with great, fine, and orient pearls, and above made with peacock's feathers, and of other shining feathers; and that stands upon their heads like a crest, in token that they are under man's foot and under subjection of man; and they that are unmarried have none such.

'And after, at the right side of the emperor, first sits his eldest son, who shall reign after him, one step lower than the emperor, in such manner of seats as do the empresses; and after him other great lords of his lineage, each of them a step lower than the other, according to their rank. The emperor has his table alone by himself, which is of gold and precious stones; or of crystal bordered with gold and full of precious stones; or of amethysts, or of lignum aloes that comes out of Paradise; or of ivory bound and bordered with gold; and each of his wives has also her table by herself, and his eldest son, and the other lords also; and the ladies and all that sit with the emperor have very rich tables alone by themselves; and under the emperor's table sit four clerks, who write all that the emperor says, be it good or evil, for all that he says must be held good; for he may not change his word nor revoke it.

'At great feasts men bring before the emperor's table great tables of gold, and thereon are peacocks of gold, and many other kinds of different fowls, all of gold, and richly wrought and enamelled; and they make them dance and sing, clapping their wings together, and making great noise; and whether it be by craft or by necromancy, I know not, but it is a goodly sight to behold. But I have the less marvel, because they are the most skilful men in the world in all sciences and in all crafts; for in subtilty, malice, and forethought they surpass all men under heaven; and therefore they say themselves that they see with two eyes, and the Christians see but with one, because they are more subtle than they. I busied myself much to learn that craft; but the master told me that he had made a vow to his god to teach it to no creature, but only to his eldest son.

'Also above the emperor's table and the other tables, and above a great part of the hall, *is a vine made of fine gold*, which spreads all about the hall; and it has many clusters of grapes, some white, some green, some yellow, some red, and some black, all of precious stones; the white are of crystal, beryl, and iris; the yellow of topazes; the red of rubies, grenaz, and alabraundines; the green of emeralds, of perydoz, and of chrysolites; and the black of onyx and garnets. And they are all so properly made that it appears a real vine bearing natural grapes.

'And before the emperor's table stand great lords and rich barons, and others that serve the emperor at meat; and no man is so bold as to speak a word unless the emperor speak to him, except minstrels that sing songs and tell jests, or other disports, to solace the emperor. And all the vessels that men are served with in the hall or in chambers are in precious stones, and especially at great tables, either of jasper, or of crystal, or of amethyst, or of fine gold, and the cups are of emeralds, and sapphires, or topazes, of perydoz, and of many other precious stones. Vessel of silver is there none, for they set no value on it to make vessels of; but they make therewith steps, and pillars, and pavements to halls and chambers. . . . This emperor hath in his chamber, in one of the pillars of gold, a ruby and a carbuncle of half a foot long, which in the night gives so great light and shining that it is as light as day.'

This is quoted at length, because it is such a very well-furnished hall, 'marvellously attired on all parts,' as Sir John has it, and typical of architectural ideas here in England in the fourteenth century. It was only poverty of resource made them content with stone, and oak, and glass; marble, ebon-tree, and beryl-stone would have pleased them better. But all this glory almost dims beside the imperial palace at Constantinople under the later emperors, of which there is preserved sufficient account by contemporary writers of authority.

So vast was this palace that it was divided into different regions, known by several names, as Chalce, Daphne, Cathisma. In the middle of the atrium of the last was a great basin of bronze and silver, with a vase of gold, on certain occasions filled with fruit, which 'all the world' might take. Beyond this atrium was a peristyle of the most precious marbles in the form of an arc, and called the *Sigma*. Amongst the imperial apartments was the chrysotriclinium; this, the very sanctuary of the imperial cult, was of octagonal form, covered by a cupola. From each of the eight sides opened an apse, that opposite the entrance being closed by doors covered with plates of silver. At great receptions these doors remained closed until all had taken their places; then, when everything was still, two officers threw back the silver valves, and the emperor was discovered on his throne, before whom all prostrated themselves. In the apse of another chamber was placed the throne called 'Solomon's.' It was of gold, purfled with precious gems, and on it mechanical golden birds warbled songs; above shone an immense cross encrusted with precious stones; around were golden seats for the imperial family. On the steps were two lions of gold, which rose to their feet roaring. Thereby were golden trees, on the branches of which birds of different kinds imitated the songs of those in the wild wood.

This account is taken from Labarte's *Le Palais imperial de Constantinople*. Much the same may be found in Gibbon, who gives a description of an audience that Liutprand, Bishop of Cremona, had with the emperor: 'When he approached the throne, the birds of the golden tree began to warble their notes, which were accompanied by the roarings of the two lions of gold. With his two companions Liutprand was compelled to bow and fall prostrate; thrice he touched the ground with his forehead; he arose, but in the short interval the throne had been hoisted by an engine from the floor to the ceiling: the imperial figure appeared in new and more gorgeous apparel, and the interview was concluded in haughty and majestic silence.'

This palace, it is said, was built on the model of that of the Caliph of Baghdad, brought back by an ambassador to that court, and there also we shall find the golden tree. An Arab writer quoted by Gibbon gives the following account of the reception of a Greek embassy in the year 917: 'The porters or doorkeepers were in number seven hundred. Barges and boats with the most superb decoration were seen swimming on the Tigris, nor was the palace itself less splendid, in which were hung up thirty-eight thousand pieces of tapestry, twelve thousand five hundred of which were of silk embroidered with gold. The carpets on the floor were twenty-two thousand. A hundred lions were brought out, with a keeper to each lion. Among the other spectacles of rare and stupendous luxury was a tree of gold and silver spreading into eighteen large branches, on which and on the lesser boughs sat a variety of birds made of the same precious metals, as well as the leaves of the tree. While the machinery affected spontaneous motions, the several birds warbled their natural harmony. Through this scene of magnificence the Greek ambassador was led by the vizier to the foot of the Caliph's throne.' Lane says the tree rose from a pond which was surrounded by the ' Palace of the Tree.' Without doubt it represents the vegetation of Paradise, and probably it formed a part of the treasure taken from Chosroes, as Baghdad was built about a hundred years after the Conquest. A story of a king who built a false paradise seems always to have been current in this region of Western Asia. Here Marco Polo places the paradise of the King of the Assassins.

The East is the true soil to produce trees like this; there, indeed, they seem to flourish. Permit an extract describing a tree that may not properly belong to the present subject. The monk Rubruquis, sent on a mission from St Louis to Central Asia in quest of Prester John, found in the service of the Tartar Khan a goldsmith of Paris who had just fabricated what he considered his masterpiece:—

'In the Khan's palace,' says Rubruquis, 'because it was unseemly to carry about bottles of milk and other drinks there, Master William made him a great silver tree, at the root whereof were four silver lions, having each one pipe, through which flowed pure cow's milk, and four other pipes were conveyed within the body of the tree unto the top thereof, and the tops spread back again downwards; and upon every one of them was a golden serpent, whose tails twined about the body of the tree, and one of these pipes ran with wine, another with koumis, another with "ball "—a drink made of honey, and another of drink made of rice. Between the pipes, at the top of the tree, he made an angel holding a trumpet, and under the tree a hollow vault, wherein a man might be hid, and a pipe ascended from this vault through the tree to the angel. He first made bellows, but they gave not wind enough. Without the palace walls there was a chamber wherein the several drinks were brought, and there were servants there ready to pour them out when they, heard the angel sounding his trumpet. And the boughs of the tree were of silver, and the leaves of the fruit. When, therefore, they want drink the master butler crieth to the angel that he sound the trumpet. Then he, hearing (who is hid in the vault), bloweth the pipe strongly, which goeth to the angel, and the angel sets his trumpet to his mouth, and the trumpet soundeth very shrill. Then the servants hearing, which are in the chamber; each of them poureth forth his drink into the proper pipe, and all the pipes pour them forth from above, and they are received below in vessels prepared for that purpose.'

It may be remarked that these mechanical movements were within the range of legitimate art in the Middle Ages, for Villars de Honecourt, a contemporary of Rubruquais, describes how angels might be made to bow the head at the holy name.

In the seventeenth century, Tavernier, another French traveller, saw a golden gem-bearing tree made for the Great Mogul's palace at Agra; and as he was an expert in gems, there is no doubt of his testimony. In this palace, 'on the side that looks towards the river, there is a divan, or a kind of outjutting balcony, where the king sits to see his elephants fight. Before the divan, is a gallery that serves for a portico, which Cha-Jehan had a design to have adorned all over with a kind of lattice-work of emeralds and rubies that should have represented to the life grapes when they are green and when they begin to grow red; but this design, which made such a noise in the world, and required more riches than all the world could afford to perfect, remains unfinished; there being only three stocks of a vine in gold, with their leaves like the rest ought to have been; and enamelled in their natural colours with emeralds, rubies, and garnets wrought into the fashion of grapes.'

In such collections of Hindu Folk-stories as 'Old Deccan Days,' we find these trees; indeed, in India they appear to be realised even to this day. Sir George Birdwood says: 'Trees of solid gold and silver representing the mango or any other tree, and of all sizes, are common decorations in Hindu houses. Often they are made of silk and feathers and tinsel, and they always recall to mind the terpole or golden vine made in ancient times by the goldsmiths of Jerusalem.'

One of these golden vines of Jerusalem decorated the entrance to Herod's Temple. The gate, Josephus says, with the wall about it, was all covered with gold. 'It also had golden vines upon it, from which clusters of grapes hung down equal in height to that of a man.' This appears to have been carried on the beams of the Toran or isolated gate, and 'whoever vowed a leaf, or grape, or bunch of grapes, suspended it from the vine.' Thus adorned, the gate of sunrise must have surpassed all imagination in splendour, as the rising sun shone on the precious metal. Another vine of the value of five hundred talents called Terpole, 'the delight,' was sent to Pompey, which seems to have much impressed the people of Rome when carried in the triumph, as it is mentioned by Pliny and Tacitus.

In Mediæval and Eastern traditions there existed somewhere, difficult, but mayhap not impossible of access, the terrestrial Paradise, and there such trees expanded, their branches swaying in the perfumed air. After the discovery of America and the riches of Peru, the hope of finding this golden land seems to have revived. Even men like Raleigh appear to have been moved by the illusion; in his account of the discovery of Guiana he quotes with approval the description by the Spanish historian of the Indies, Lopez, of the state and magnificence of the Emperor who had his seat at Manoa, which the Spaniards call El Dorado. All the vessels of the kitchen were of gold, and he had the images of all beasts, birds, and trees in their due proportion and bigness all of gold. 'Yea, and they say the Ingas had a garden of pleasure in an island near Puna, where they went to recreate themselves when they would take the air of the sea, which had all kind of garden herbs, flowers, and trees of gold and silver, an invention and magnificence till then never seen.' This agrees with the native accounts of the temple of the sun and its gardens at Cuzco, where the animals, insects, and trees were of gold (Nadaillac). Such gardens wherever found are set imitations of Paradise.

One of the rulers of Cairo, the son of Ibn-Tulun, who succeeded him in 883, seems to have set himself to rival the garden of delights in a 'paradise,' 'which was filled with lilies, gilliflowers, saffron; with palms and trees of all sorts, the trunks of which he coated with copper gilt, behind which leaden pipes supplied fountains which gushed forth to water the garden. Peacocks, guinea-fowls, doves, and pigeons with rare birds from Nubia, had their home in the garden and aviary. There was also a menagerie, and especially a blue-eyed lion, who crouched beside his master when he sat at table, and guarded him when he slept. But the chief wonder remains to be described. It was a lake of quicksilver; on the surface of this lake lay a leather bed inflated with air, fastened by silk bands to four silver supports at the corners; here alone the insomnolent sovereign could take his rest ' (S. Lane-Poole).

We remember the garden in which Aladdin gathered from the trees the precious stones they bore, tall of the largest size, and the most perfect ever seen in the whole world.' To the Mohammedan such a garden still exists, but hidden from human eyes. It is said that Sheddad, the third or fourth in descent from Noah, built in 'Irim of many columns' a palace, and enclosed a garden in imitation of Paradise. Southey gives the following in his notes to 'Thalaba:' 'A pleasant and elevated spot being fixed upon, Sheddad despatched a hundred chiefs to collect skilled artists and workmen from all countries. He also commanded the monarchs of Syria and Ormus to send him all their jewels and precious stones. Forty camel-loads of gold, silver, and jewels were daily used in the building, which contained a thousand spacious quadrangles of many thousand rooms. In the areas were artificial trees of gold and silver, whose leaves were emeralds, and fruit clusters of jewels and pearls. The ground was strewed with ambergris, musk, and saffron. Between every two of the artificial trees was planted one of delicious fruit. This romantic abode took up five hundred years in the completion. When finished,

Sheddad marched to view it, and when arrived near, divided two hundred thousand youthful slaves whom he had brought with him from Damascus into four detachments, which were stationed in cantonments prepared for their reception on each side of the garden, towards which he proceeded with his favourite courtiers. Suddenly was heard in the air a voice like thunder, and Sheddad, looking up, beheld a personage of majestic figure and stern aspect, who said, "I am the angel of death, commissioned to seize thy impure soul." Sheddad exclaimed, "Give me leisure to enter the garden," and was descending from his horse, when the seizer of life snatched away his impure spirit, and he fell dead upon the ground. At the same time, lightnings flashed and destroyed the whole army of the infidel, and the rose garden of Irim became concealed from the sight of man.'

The gold trees of Paradise may be found even to-day. Lady Dufferin tells us how the colossal gilt stupa of Rangoon stands on a raised plateau; all round it there is an enclosure of small topes: 'outside these is a row of gilt trees bearing glass fruits.' The whole is symbolic of the celestial mountain of the gods.

Quintus Curtius, in the 'History of Alexander,' describes the state and splendour of the Indian monarch Musicanus: 'Golden vines twined round the silver columns of the palace, amidst whose branches artificial birds of silver in imitation of those most esteemed in India were disposed by the nicest art by the curious designer' (Maurice).

The Greeks told of a tree of gold, the handiwork; of the somewhat mythical artist Theodorus of Samos, who is said to have been the first to cast bronze statues. Heredotus tells us that Pythias, a Lydian of enormous wealth, made Darius a present of a golden vine and a plane tree. Athenæus describes the vine as having clusters of jewels in form and colour of grapes, the whole spread like a rich canopy over the golden bed of that monarch.

Philostratus says that Apollonius saw the golden tree, with fruit of olives represented by emeralds, which was given by Pygmalion King of Tyre to the Tyrian temple of Hercules at Gades.

In the last resort such great achievements are 'works of fairy,' or of the immortal crafts-gods. Hephæstos who formed the shield of Achilles like the world in shape, who wrought the gold and silver dogs at the Palace gate of Alcinous like the guardians of the gate of the west, made also such a tree. 'Zeus after carrying off Ganymede to be his cupbearer, made atonement to the royal family of Troy by the present of a vine of gold fashioned by Hephæstos' (A. Lang, Myth, Ritual, and Religion).

The transition from a tree made by supernatural art to a 'natural' golden tree is but slight; such was the tree from which Æneas had to pluck the bough before he could pass on the way to the underworld.

> 'A branch held sacred to the Stygian Juno,
> Whose leafage and whose twigs are flexile gold:
> The subterranean kingdom none may enter
> Who doth not gather first the golden foil.'

An Indian historian, quoted by Orme, says of Mamud of Gazna, that in the course of his conquests he found a tree growing out of the earth to an enormous size, of which the substance was pure gold; this would seem an Eastern version of the incident quoted later from the 'Romance of Alexander,' where the tree foretells his death.

In Greek stories, too, we have trees which bear golden fruit or flowers connected with the land of the blissful west, as in Pindar—' But the ocean breezes blow around the blessed islands, and golden flowers burn on their bright trees for evermore; ' or Hesiod-'The Hesperian maids who guard the golden fruit beyond the ocean's sound.' And just as Hercules goes to this garden, so does the Babylonian hero Gilgames, in his wanderings beyond the gates of the sun, see a tree, which—

> 'To the forest of the trees of the gods in appearance was equal,
> Emeralds it carried as its fruit,
> The branch refuses not to support a canopy,
> Crystal they carried as shoots,
> Fruit they carry, and to the sight it is glistening.'

Count d'Alviella, in an exhaustive article, 'Les Arbres Paradiseaques,' speaks of this conception as that of 'a celestial tree carrying for fruit the planets, stars, and all the gems of heaven.' Fire and thunder were produced in its branches which cloud the sky, and drop the heavenly ambrosia. Professor Sayce and

Lenormant agree in this view. The fruit of this tree, says the latter, is fire. It can hardly be doubted that it is this same tree whose many branches we have been tracing to a common stem. The golden gem-bearing tree is the natural growth of traditions of that all-embracing world tree which carries the stars for its fruit in the dark heaven of night. Dr Terrien de Lacouperie has also devoted a special study to this cosmic tree. He sees it represented in the Tat pillar of Egypt as well as in the star-bearing tree of Hindus and Iranians, the calendar tree of China, and many others.

A similar conception is plainly expressed in the *Kalevala* where Wainamoinen—

> 'Sang aloft a wondrous pine tree
> Till it pierced the clouds in growing
> With its golden top and branches,
> Till it touched the very heavens
> Spread its branches in the ether,
> Sings the moon to shine for ever.
> In the fir tree's emerald branches,
> In its top he sings the Great Bear.'

The bear was in a cradle, and the tree stood on the summit of the Gold Hill; and, as in our nursery song,

> '. . . The winds and sacred branches
> Rock him to his lasting slumber,
> To the pleasure of the hunter.'

Sir William Drummond says of the tree of the Cabbalists: 'Though called a tree, it was a type of the mundane system, and in Œdipus Judaicus a fruit tree was certainly a symbol of the starry heavens, and the fruits typified the constellations. The Arabians typify the zodiac by a fruit tree, and on the twelve branches of this tree the stars are depicted as fruits. The Cabbalists represent the tree of life as marked with the emblems of the zodiac, and as bearing twelve fruits,' etc., and concludes: 'We shall hardly doubt that trees, *and especially fruit trees* were symbols of the starry heavens' (Landseer). This, may we not say, becomes certainty when the trees are golden and bear gems as fruit.

The planets were co-related to the several precious stones, as is shown in the next chapter. The fitness of the comparison between a gem and a star is at once apparent to the child, 'like a diamond in the sky.' It is curious here to remember that gold and precious stones were always thought of as self-lustrous; Homer's palaces give out a radiance like moonlight; and Cupid's palace in Apuleius was plated over with gold, so that 'even were the sun to withhold his light the palace could make a day for its own.' The columns of gold and emeralds seen by Herodotus at Tyre gave out light, and the imperial crown hanging over the throne at Constantinople, as seen by Benjamin of Tudela, lighted up the whole chamber with its brilliance. The well-designed palace of romance is always lighted, like Prester John's, externally by a carbuncle on every gable; and inside as in the Folk tale ' Childe Rowland,' where a huge carbuncle was suspended from the dome, 'spinning round and round, and this is what gave light by its rays to the whole hall.'

Many avenues lead us to the one gem-bearing tree; its branches may be said to stretch over all the earth. The story of Jason and the golden fleece is strictly parallel to that of Theseus—the imposed task, the help of the princess, the flight, and the parting. But the scene is the northern hemisphere of the heavens, not the underworld of the south pole. The golden treasure is guarded by a serpent, doubtless the cloud dragon of darkness, who winds about that tree whose stem is the axis of the heavenly revolution, just as Draco still coils about the pole.

The tree of the golden fruit of the Hesperides grows on Mount Atlas, the sky-sustaining mountain, in the country 'beyond the north wind,' where it was guarded by the dragon Ladon. Some confusion seems to have been occasioned as to the position of Mount Atlas, which was later understood to be in the west; the complication came about, possibly, in consequence of the generally received opinion that the land of the departed was westward with the sunset, and yet on the world mountain. In other accounts the mountain paradise is north-east, or even east, a consequence probably of the westward migration of the peoples after the polar significance had been forgotten. In the Talmud, for instance, the sun is said to be red in the east because of the roses of Eden, and to glow at eve because of the fires of hell.

Like Atlas the Indian Mount Meru bore a tree, Parajita, which perfumes the whole world with its blossoms; and India is called *Jambu-dwipa*, the land of myrtle blooms, from this tree, which grows at its centre. Its earthly position was hidden among the Himalayas, 'mountains of heaven.' In the Veda it is the heavenly Soma tree, dropping nectar for the gods. In the Avesta of the Persians the details are amplified, but the scene—the world, mountain of paradise—and the tree are the same. 'Haoma, golden flowered, that grows on the heights, Haoma that restores us, that drives death afar.' There is also a companion tree, and two birds roost on their branches. These mythical birds—'the two eagles of the sky, Amru and Chamru—are invoked as helpful powers. They nestle on the tree of life in the heavens.' On the highest peak grows the Haoma; from the sea of heavenly waters grows the other tree, which bears all seeds. 'When Amru sits on this tree the seeds fall down, and Chamru carries them away,' and they are rained down on the earth with the showers.

So all earthly trees as well as all the waters come to us from the central heaven, where all life originated (Duncker's Hist. Ant.). The more modern Persian Simurgh in Firdausi is the counterpart of the bird of the tree of life.

The northern world-ash, the high seat of the gods and prop of the sky, had the stars for fruit; around its stem was coiled Nidhogg the serpent, and on the topmost branch the eagle sang of creation and destruction. A tree like this is the fit habitation for such a bird as is well known in old fables under different names: and so in Eastern story the Garuda perches on a wonderful tree, from which it flies to seize the rhinoceros or elephant in its grip and bear them away.

In old Japanese lore there is a vast metal pine tree which grows in the north at the world centre. Our Saxon forefathers told of Irminsul the column of the sky—the 'Pole' in the double significance. The golden apple tree appears frequently in Folk Stories, usually in connection with a visit to the other world. In a Bohemian story an immense tree grows past the clouds. A princess desires to have of its fruit. Hans, the youngest son of a peasant—the male parallel of Cinderella, scorned but success-

ful—after all have failed, makes the essay. He starts, taking a
number of wooden shoes to drop one daily. After climbing some
days, he sees a light glimmering; it is the dwelling of a very old
woman; he asks how far it is to the top, and she answers: 'Thou
hast yet far to go, I am only Monday. Thou must come to Tuesday, Wednesday, and so on to Saturday.' In his long journey
upwards all this comes to pass. After leaving Saturday, he comes
to a stone wall, into which the stem of the tree had grown. He
goes through a little door, and in a golden meadow there is a
golden city, with splendours unendurable to human eyes,
golden creatures leaped in the pasture, and the fruit of the tree
was all of gold. ' Hans believed he was in heaven, and he
stopped there; others say he came down again to earth and related this story.' Monday, Tuesday, and the rest occupy the planetary spheres; the wall is the firmament.

There is a remarkable agreement in these legends of the
Greek, Babylonian, Hindu, Norse, and Finnish world mountain.
It stood at the North Pole, 'in the country of the Hyperboreans;'
it was of gold and precious stones, or of crystal, like the dome-
shaped mountains of glass in Folk Tales. At its apex grows the
great Tree of the Heavens, whose stem and branches of gold
carry stars of precious stones for fruit, and on whose highest
point perches the solar Phoenix. Here is the Earthly Paradise, the
Garden of the Sun, as is perfectly understood in the following,
extracts from the 'Romance of Alexander,' from Sir John
Maundeville, and from Dante.
    In India, Alexander and his army came to two paths, east-
ward and north; they try eastward, but it is impassable, and they
go back and attempt the other to the north, by which at last they
reach a cliff covered with diamonds, with hanging chains of red
gold. Two thousand five hundred steps there were, which they
ascend, and reach the clouds and 'wait for wonders.' They see
'a palais, one of the precioussest and proudest in earth, and built,
as the book says, with two broad gates and seventy windows,
of gold, carven, and clustered with gems.'
    There was a temple surrounded by a garden of golden vines
full of great fruit of carbuncle stones; it was the 'house of the sun'
and paradise. Alexander enters, and on a gorgeous bed he finds
a god, who asks him if he would have his future known by in-

quiry of the trees of the sun and moon; on his consenting, they approach two enormous trees, that of the moon was silver; the tree of the sun was gold, and on its crest sat 'a proud bird.' 'All gilded was her gorge with golden feathers.' 'Yon is a fearless fowl, a Fenix we call.' It is predicted that Alexander will never return.

'Of Paradise,' says Sir John Maundeville, 'I cannot speak properly, for I was not there. It is far beyond; and that forthinketh me, and also I was not worthy. But as I have heard say of wise men beyond, I shall tell you with goodwill. Paradyse terrestre, as wise men say, is the highest place of earth that is in all the world, and it is so high that it toucheth nigh to the circle of the moon there as the moon maketh her turn.' There, also, is the Well of Paradise, many precious stones, much lignum aloes, and much gravel of gold.

In Dante's system the point under the zenith of our northern heavens is occupied by Jerusalem; the antipodes of this is Mount Purgatory, which rises from the seas of the southern hemisphere, the land being drawn up to the mountain, leaving the sea all round. It is in the form of the Babylonian terraced pyramid of seven stages; the top is the earthly paradise, and he passes thence to the circle of the moon.

> 'Those who in ancient times have feigned in song
> The Age of Gold and its felicity,
> Dreamed of this place perhaps upon Parnassus
> Here vas the human race in innocence
> Here evermore was spring, and every fruit,
> This is the nectar of which each one speaks.'

Such was Beatrice's welcome, and then he sees—

> 'A little further on seven trees of gold.
>
> *   *   *   *   *   *
>
> But when I had approached so near to them,
>
> *   *   *   *   *   *
>
> The faculty that lends discourse to reason
> Did apprehend that they were candlesticks.'

It is thus as a light-bearer, a candelabrum, that the artificial tree would best fulfil a symbolic function in the representation of the great mysterious tree whose canopy forms the firmament

and bears the light-giving stars as its fruit—a symbolism which we appear to perpetuate, as year by year at the winter solstice we light the candles on the Christmas tree. In the East, where tradition 'lingers last, as loath to die,' the lighting is properly by means of a lamp-tree. 'There is in the Prince of Wales' collection a remarkable *candelabrum in silver gilt from Shringar, shaped like a conventional tree*, and ornamented all over with the crescent and flame device and hanging fishes, its design being evidently derived through Persia from a Turkoman original. The candelabra

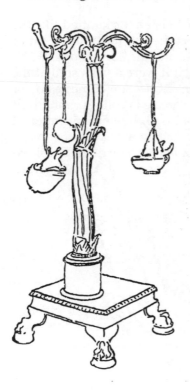

seen in Hindu temples constantly takes this tree form without the addition of the symbols of the sky and ether.' And not only in temples; 'the high brass tree, like candelabra, with a number of branches bearing little lamps filled with oil, and having a wick in each, are a marked feature in great houses in Lahore' (Birdwood, ' Indian Arts'). In the Indian Museum at South Kensington are several of these lamp-trees, one of which, figured on next page, is a very fine design; it has not very many leaves, but monkeys climb on the boughs. In another example the lamp bowls are shaped like birds.

The classic bronze candelabra that fill our museums almost universally follow the same thought through many modifications of design. Sometimes where there is but one stem it has vestiges of lopped branches, or leafy appendages at intervals; or the top bowl rests on the fork of three branches which have been cut off. Others again, perfectly plain, have an animal chasing a bird up the stem; still others, with or without an otherwise clearly defined tree form, have a snake coiled round the stem. There are examples of all of these

in the British Museum, two or three of each show that they are
types, not accidents. Close to these candelabra is a bronze
Hercules standing by the tree of the Hesperides; the guardian
serpent being coiled around its trunk, exactly like the serpent on
the candlesticks. We may hardly doubt that this bronze tree is a
candlestick, the branches of which bore suspended lamps. A tree
candelabrum found at Pompeii has hanging lamps in the form
of snails. These classic candlesticks wherever found, in Etruria,
Greece or South Italy, have this tree-like form. Of the Etruscan
ones Mr Dennis says:—

'The shafts are often fluted, or twisted, or knotted like the
stem of a tree. It was a favourite conceit to introduce a cat or
squirrel chasing a bird up the shaft, and the bowl above has often little birds around it, as though it were a nest, so that the
whole is then intended to represent a tree. Sometimes a boy or
monkey is climbing the shaft, or a snake is coiling round it. It
often terminates above, not in a bowl, but in a number of
branches, from which lamps were suspended.'

Dr Smith's Dictionary gives a similar account of the Greek examples. Even the later Roman marble candelabra carry forward
the tradition.

A parallel custom was for the lamp to have seven nozzles, the number of the planets, like an example of Roman work in the British Museum, and this became a very general form, and still seven lamps burn before the altars of many churches. We may also while speaking of the symbolism of lighting, remark that the hanging crowns of light in Christian Churches, of which that at Hildeshiem is such a fine example, were understood to symbolise the New Jerusalem with its twelve towered gates. Mr Morris, with fine insight, makes the solitary lamp in the 'House of the Wolfings' 'The Hall Sun.' That these should all be undying flames is, of course, of the essence of the symbolism.

Nor can we forget the seven-branched candlestick in the Temple, of gold, ornamented with 'knops and flowers;' the seven lamps symbolising to Josephus the seven planets. It seems to have been understood in the Middle Ages that this was a tree, for a fourteenth century poem on Bible history makes the birds flutter among the leaves when the golden treasure from Jerusalem is exhibited at the feast in Babylon. Mr Robertson Smith sees in the candlestick such a symbolic tree, the motive being taken from the almond.

Following the Jewish was the Christian candle tree. The description of Durham tells of a great paschal candlestick that rose even to the high vault, nearly as broad as the choir below, with seven flower-shaped branches for tapers. Great seven-branched candlesticks are frequent; those of Hildesheim and Vienna are the best known from the casts at South Kensington; the latter is called the 'Virgin's tree.' It appears from Mr Walcott's 'Dictionary of Archæology' that all important churches had a sevenbranched candlestick, and 'in some churches there was a magnificent series of branches grouped together called the Tree.' In Sta. Sophia, as finished by Justinian, were placed many candelabra in the likeness of trees; the whole effect was 'like a wood.'

At Delphi there was a bronze palm tree surmounted by a gilt statue of Athene, on it there were owls and imitations of fruit. Plutarch also describes in the same temple, a sacred palm-tree of bronze with frogs in relief around the base. Almost certainly these would be lamp bearing trees. Gerald Massey cites a description of a temple in Cambodia where a bronze tree, about which coiled a serpent, rose from a pool of water.

Athenæus says, 'Euphorion in his historical commentaries says that the young Dionysius, the tyrant of Sicily, dedicated in the prytaneum at Tarentum a candlestick capable of containing as great a number of candles as there are days in the year.' Like a many branched tree, it overhung the sacred hearth in the sky-like tholos.

Pausanias describes the light before the statue of Athene in the Erechtheum: 'And Callemachus made a golden lamp for the goddess. And when they fill this lamp with oil, it lasts for a whole year, although it burns continuously night and day, and the wick is of a particular kind of cotton flax, the only sort imperishable by fire; and above the lamp is a palm tree of brass, reaching to the roof, and carrying off the smoke; and Callemachus, the maker of this lamp, although he comes behind the first artificers, yet was remarkable for ingenuity, and got the name of Art Critic, whether his own appellation, or given him by others.' From Pliny it is apparent that this is no isolated artistic whim, but that it was well understood that the temples should be lighted with trees bearing lamps, like the golden fruit of the heavens. Candelabra (*lychnuchi pensiles*), he says, were placed in the temples, *or gave their light in the form of trees loaded with fruit*; such is the one, for instance, in the temple of the Palatine Apollo, which Alexander the Great, at the sacking of Thebes, brought to Cyme, and dedicated to that god. An instance this of Greek workmanship of considerable, perhaps of remote, antiquity.

A slab recently discovered in Rome, showing the Mithraic sanctuary, has on each side trees; one carries the sun as a demi-figure with a halo, and the other the moon with a crescent. Curiously enough, in St. Mark's at Venice there is such a representation in the mosaics; two lofty pillars are figured supporting each a chariot and horses; in the one is Phoebus, in the other Diana with the crescent, and against them is written, 'Stata Solis,' 'Stata Lunae,' a conception entirely the same as is found thousands of years before on Babylonian seals.

Dr Isaac Taylor says that the primitive Chinese symbol for light was the sun on a tree. In Japanese religious processions, sun and moon are carried about in trees. The sacred trees of Greece, Apollo's laurel at Delos, the olive of Athene in the Erectheium, and the oak of Dodona, may have belonged to crude tree worship, a subject treated at length by Mr Frazer in the 'Golden Bough.' Duncker, however, saw in Dodona another localisation of paradise with its mount, tree, and the water of heaven.

The slabs and gems of Assyria repeatedly and variously show us the sacred celestial tree, the complete composition having the tree in the middle, above it the winged sun disc of Asshur, and on either side guardian genii. It bears fruit, and is called 'The Shining Tree,' or 'Tree of Great Light.' There is no doubt that its image was set up in the temples; for a slab in the Louvre, figured by Perrot, shows the king standing before a tree of artificial construction; and such, too, was 'the graven image of the grove' that the apostate King of Israel placed in the Temple (2 Kings xxi. 7). It is also shown among the Temple furniture carried in processions. It was an ingeniously designed tree of metal, of great splendour; the fruit of that shown so clearly in the beautiful slab figured by Perrot (fig. 45, Vol. II.) was doubtless of jewels. It has been pointed out, by Layard and others, how the number seven enters into their composition.

In Assyria, at an age unknown, the copy in the Temple of the golden gem-bearing tree of the sky was probably first set up. In Egypt, however, we also meet the legend of the heavenly prototype, and farther we cannot strain our gaze into the past. Nut, the goddess of the heavenly ocean, whose body is decked with stars, has her abode in such a tree; the pilgrim to the lower world eats of its fruit, and the goddess, leaning from the tree, pours out the water of life. This was in the west, on the way travelled by the dead. To the east there was another tree, with wide radiating branches bearing jewels; up it the strong morning sun, Horus, the first giant killer, climbs to the zenith of heaven—

'The beautiful green tints on the horizon at daybreak and at the sunset are mythologically represented by the " Sycamore of Emerald," through the midst of which the sun god advances into the firmament ' (Renouf, 'Hibbert Lectures').

CHAPTER VI

THE PLANETARY SPHERES

'And after shewed hym the nine spheris
And after that the melodye herd he
That cometh of thilke speris thries thre,
That welleys of musyke ben and melodye
In this world here and cause of armonye.'
                                    —*CHAUCER.*

THE number seven is written on the sky. What time the seven planets were counted and individualised is beyond all history; probably not two in a hundred even now guess at any other planet than Venus; probably not two in a thousand have ever seen Mercury, certainly not without a telescope; yet all of them we find distinguished by names and grouped together as errant bodies among the fixed stars in the earliest traditions:—(1) The Sun, (2) the Moon, (3) Mars, (4) Mercury, (5) Jupiter, (6) Venus, (7) Saturn.

The first known and named probably of all constellations, the Great Bear, always visible above the horizon, 'never bathing in ocean,' as Homer has it, is a group of seven. The lesser Bear has the same form, which is repeated a third time by the great square of Pegasus, and the three bright stars in Andromeda and Perseus. Seven also are the symmetrical and splendid stars of Orion. In France, the Pleiades are still called the ' seven stars,' and the north is named the Septentrion, from the stars of the Great Bear.

The planets gave their names to the days of the week, and still distinguish them all over the world from France to China, and they are but slightly obscured for us by their northern names.

The seven days of the week are the nearest whole number to one-fourth of a month, a moon's quarter. The two days completing the month of thirty days were in Assyria intercalary.

Immense has been the influence of this magic number in philosophy, material and metaphysical. The life of man has been divided into seven ages. The first seven are the years of infancy. At three times seven—twenty-one—we become 'of age.' Three times twenty-one is the 'grand climacteric;' and seventy years is put as the time to die.

So the life of the world was in Middle Age histories divided into seven eras, of which we are in the last. There were seven material heavens; this middle world was divided into a like number of zones or 'climates,' and the under world into as many depths. In the philosophy of the schools every factor of the universe had a sevenfold division.

In the *Cursor Mundi* it is remarked that there are seven holes in the head, 'for maister sterres are there seven.'

So absorbing has been the nature of this number, that where groups occur, of anything from four to a dozen, let us say, they are almost sure to be 'seven sisters,' or 'seven brethren.' Sevenoaks, the seven hills of Rome, or of Constantinople, the seven holy cities of India, the seven architectural wonders of the world. Mr. Ruskin tells us he found great difficulty in limiting his 'seven lamps' so that they should not become eight or nine.

The seven planets have had a potent influence over architecture and the arts. The sun, the moon, and the five other planets were not only observed to move independent;y of the 'sphere' of the fixed stars, but independently of each other, in varying periods. As the whole moving heaven of the 'fixed stars' was a solid 'firmament' studded with stars revolving around a pivot, the earth mountain; so, as the system was perfected, other transparent spheres had to be imagined, one for each planet, carrying it around in its due time. The heavenly mountain of the gods is thus either entirely celestial, the exterior of our firmament, and the whole seven successive domed heavens; or it is the central mountain of this lower world. the prop and pole of the heavens, divided into seven stages, one to each planetary sphere. Practically it is impossible to keep these two notions separate, and to say which is the Olympus—the stepped mountain supporting the heavens, or the seven-fold heavens itself. Dr. Rink, speaking of the Esquimaux, says: 'The upper world, it would seem, may be considered identical with the mountain, round the top of which the vaulted sky is for ever circling.' Olympus, to the Greeks, was many peaked, or of many layers, like the stratum without stratum of the Iranian mountain of the stars. By the addition of a sphere for the fixed stars, and an outer and immovable envelope, the seven became nine heavens.

In the Vedas there are seven heavens. 'In the Hindu cosmogony,' writes Sir G. Birdwood, 'the world is likened to a lotus flower floating in the centre of a shallow circular vessel, which has for its stalk an elephant, and for its pedestal a tortoise. The seven petals of the lotus flower represent the seven divisions of the world, as known to the ancient Hindus, and the tabular torus, which rises from their centre, represents Mount Meru, the ideal Himalayas (Himmel), the Hindu Olympus. It ascends by seven spurs, on which the seven separate cities and palaces of the gods are built, amid green woods and murmuring streams, in seven circles placed one above another.' Here is a tree which perfumes the whole world with its blossoms, a car of lapis lazuli, a throne of fervent gold; 'and over all, on the summit of Meru, is Brahmapura, the entranced city of Brahma, encompassed by the sources of the sacred Ganges, and the orbits in which for ever shine the sun and silver moon and seven planetary spheres.' The old Japanese poems translated by Mr Chamberlain speak of a mountain at the 'earth's acme or omphalos, which extended even to the skies; on its summit was a beautiful house.'

The modern view in Siam is similar. Mr. Carl Bock writes: 'According to Laosian idea, the centre of the world is Mount Zinnalo, which is half under water and half above. The subaqueous part of the mount is a solid rock, which has three root-like rocks protruding from the water into the air below. Round this mountain is coiled a large fish of such leviathan proportions that it can embrace and move the mountain; when it sleeps the earth is quiet, but when it moves it produces earthquakes.' 'Above the earth and around this great mountain is the firmament, with the sun, the moon, and the stars. These are looked upon as the ornaments of the heavenly temples. Above the water is the inhabited earth, and on each of the four sides of Mount Zinnalo are seven hills, rising in equal gradations one above the other, which are the first ascents the departed has to make.'

The planets themselves, which were affixed to their several spheres, were apparently thought of as having the nature of self-lustrous metals or gems, as they were perceived to be diversified in colour—the golden sun, the silver moon, the red Mars of war. Thus the names of the several precious stones were given to the spheres.

In the Mohammedan scheme, as we have seen, the seven spheres have these distinctive colours. The first is described as formed of emerald; the second, of white silver; the third, of large white pearls; the fourth, of ruby; the fifth, of red gold; the sixth, of yellow jacinth; and the seventh, of shining light.'

Such being the conception of a holy mountain whose top reached to heaven; we need not wonder, we may expect to find many local identifications of it in the inaccessible snow-capped mountains of Pamir or the Himalayas; in Ararat, Parnassus, and the Thessalian Olympus. Inferior sites would also be artificially improved, thus Lenormant, in his article on Ararat and Eden (Contemp. Rev., Sept. 1881), thinks it clearly proved that Solomon and Hezekiah had this idea in the distribution of the waters which flowed from under the Temple in four streams, one of .. which was named Gihon. He quotes Obry: 'The Buddhists of Ceylon have endeavoured to transform their central mountain, Peak of the Gods, into Meru, and to find four streams descending from its sides to correspond with the rivers of their paradise.' And Wilford, in vol. viii. of 'Asiatic Researches,' says the early kings of India were fond of raising mounds of earth called 'Peaks of Meru,' which they reverenced like the holy mount. One of these near Benares bore an inscription which makes this clear. A country was divided into seven, nine, or twelve nomes or provinces, and the people into as many castes or tribes.

The Chaldeans had early perfected this universe of seven spherical strata, and with them we have stupendous architectural structures, known as *Ziggurats*, erected, 'as an imitation or artificial reproduction of the mythical mountain of the assembly of the stars' (Ararat and Eden).

'Now, the pyramidical temple is the tangible expression, the material and architectural manifestation, of the Chaldaio-Babylonian religion. Serving both as a sanctuary and as an observatory for the stars, it agreed admirably with the genius of the essentially siderial religion to which it was united by an indissoluble bond' ('Chaldean Magic').

These structures belong to a class not properly temples. They are rather Mounts of Paradise-terraced altars. 'God Thrones' might best explain their purpose. They represent the world from without as a seat rather than a shrine for the Deity. If the word temple is here used, it is only in deference to custom.

Herodotus describes the Ziggurat of Babylon thus: 'The sacred precinct of Jupiter Belus, a square enclosure two furlongs each way, with gates of solid brass, was also remaining in my time. In the middle of the precinct there was a tower of solid masonry, a furlong in length and breadth, upon which was raised a second tower, and on that a third, and so on up to eight. The ascent up to the top is on the outside by a path which winds round all the towers. When one is about halfway up, one finds a resting-place and seats, where persons are wont to sit sometime on their way to the summit. On the topmost tower there is a spacious temple.'

This great metropolitan 'God Throne,' Perrot gives as the type of the Chaldean temple; and from the mounds and the temples depicted on the slabs, he has, together with the architect M. Chipiez, made a series of restorations in the volumes on the Art of Babylon and Assyria. He says: 'In spite of the words of Herodotus, M. Chipiez has only given his tower seven stages, because that number seems to have been sacred and traditional, and Herodotus may well have counted the plinth or the terminal chapel in the eight mentioned in his description.'

Mr George Smith, indeed, deciphered a tablet which actually gave the dimensions of this Ziggurat for all the seven stages. The bottom stage was 300 feet square and 110 feet high; the second, 260 feet sloping upwards, and 60 feet high; the third, 200 feet, and 20 feet high; fourth, fifth, and sixth, 170, 140, 110 feet respectively, each 20 feet high. And the top stage, the seventh (evidently the sanctuary, from its change of form), was oblong, 80 by 70 feet, and 50 feet high; the whole height being thus 300 feet, exactly the same as the base. These dimensions are set out in the drawing that forms the frontispiece, which is believed to be the first published drawing founded on these measurements; that of Perrot and Chipiez being entirely conjectural. However doubtful the translation into English measure may be, the form and proportion remain, and the result is a majestic and mysterious suggestion of volume and stability.

Herodotus also gives an account of the city and palace of Ecbatana of the Medes: 'This fortification is so contrived that each circle was raised above the other by the height of the battlements only. The situation of the ground, rising by an easy ascent, was very favourable to the design. But that which was particularly attended to is that, there being seven circles altogether, the king's palace and the treasury are situated within the innermost of them. The largest of these walls is about equal in circumference to the city of Athens. The battlements of the first circle are white; of the second, black; of the third, purple; of the fourth, blue; of the fifth, bright red. Thus the battlements of all the circles are painted with different colours; but the two last have their battlements plated, the one with silver, the other with gold.'

Erech, the old sacred city of the Chaldeans, is called on a tablet 'The City of the Seven Zones or Stones' (Sayce).

At Borsippa, close to Baylon, there was a very ancient terraced temple or *Ziggurat*; it was restored by Nebuchadnezzar, and an inscription of his is preserved, which says: 'I have repaired and perfected the marvel of Borsippa, the temple of the seven spheres of the world. I have erected it in bricks which I have covered with copper. I have covered with zones, alternately of marble and other precious stones, the sanctuary of God.' Rawlinson writes: 'The ornamentation of the edifice was chiefly by means of colour. The seven stages represented the seven spheres, in which moved, according to ancient Chaldean astronomy, the seven planets. To each planet fancy, partly grounding itself upon fact, had from of old assigned a peculiar tint or hue. The sun was golden; the moon, silver; the distant Saturn, almost beyond the region of light, was black; Jupiter was orange (the foundation for this colour, as for that of Mars and Venus, was probably the actual hue of the planet); the fiery Mars was red; Venus was a pale Naples yellow; Mercury, a deep blue. The seven stages of the to-wer-like walls of Ecbatana gave a visible

embodiment to these fancies. The basement stage, assigned to
Saturn, was blackened by means of a coating of bitumen spread
over the face of the masonry; the second stage, assigned to Jupiter, obtained the appropriate orange colour by means of a facing of burned bricks of that hue; the third stage, that of Mars,
was made blood-red by the use of halfburned bricks formed of
a red clay; the fourth stage, assigned to the Sun, appears to have
been actually covered with thin plates of gold; the fifth, the stage
of Venus, received a pale yellow tint from the employment of
bricks of that colour; the sixth, the sphere of Mercury, was given
an azure tint by vitrifaction, the whole stage having been sub-
jected to an intense heat after it was erected, whereby the bricks
composing it were converted into a mass of blue slag; the seventh stage, that of the Moon, was probably, like the fourth,
coated with actual plates of metal. Thus the building rose up in
stripes of varied colour, arranged almost as Nature's cunning ar-
ranges the hues of the rainbow—tones of red coming first, succeeded by a broad stripe of yellow, the yellow being followed
by blue. Above this the glowing silvery summit melted into the
bright sheen of the sky' (Ancient Monarchies).

The order in which the stages encircled one another spreading outwards to the base, represented in correct sequence the
orbits of the planets, as was supposed, around the earth. The
small orbit of the moon at the top; the sun taking the place of the
earth, as it appears to journey through the twelve signs of the
year; and Saturn last of all. Generally, however, as in the walls
of Ecbatana, the sun and moon lead the planets in the order of
the days of the week. The order in which the days of the week
are named after the planets, Mr Proctor says, is obtained in the
following manner. If all the hours throughout the week are dedicated to the planets in the sequence of their observed distances—
Saturn, Jupiter, Mars, Sun, Venus, Mercury, Moon—then beginning with Saturday the planet which rules the first hour of the
next day will be the Sun, and of the next the Moon, and so on
for all the days of the week. This explanation takes for granted
that the days were divided into twenty-four parts before the
seven days were named after the planets.

Another of these Ziggurats, an adjunct to Sargon's palace, was
discovered by M. Place at Korsabad, and by him named the
Observatory; this was 143 feet at the base, and is supposed to

have been the same height. Three whole stages and part of a fourth, were still in existence. 'Coloured stucco, varying in hue from one stage to another, was still visible, and confirmed the statement of Herodotus as to the traditional sequence of the tints.' The stages of this building were each about 20 feet high. The first was white; the second, black; the third, red; the fourth, white; and fragments of other colours were found in the *debris*.

The plan of one of these temples, with the path making seven complete circuits before it reaches the centre and the top, is very much the same as the traditional form of the labyrinth of Crete, and intimately connected with it in origin; or rather, they are complementary ideas, the one representing the seven spheres of the overheavens, the other the seven circles of the under-world. But we will try to follow this clue of the labyrinth in the next chapter.

According to the poet Nonnos, Thebes was built by Cadmus circular in form; the main streets from the centre went north, south, east, and west, and every one of the seven gates was consecrated to a planet. It was thus quite a celestial city, and the seven gates retained their planetary designations in historical times.

In an article in the 'Journal of the Geographical Society' (vol. x.), Sir H. Rawlinson quotes, from an historian of Armenia of the fifth century of our era, a description of Atropatene, 'the second Ecbatana, or the seven-walled city.' He adds: 'The story of the seven walls is one of Sabæan origin, and the seven colours are precisely those which are used by the Orientals to denote the seven great heavenly bodies or the seven climates in which they revolve. Thus Nizami describes a seven-bodied palace, built by Bahram Gur (the Sassanian monarch), nearly in the same terms as Herodotus. The palace dedicated to Saturn, he says, was black; that of Jupiter, orange, or, more strictly, of sandal wood colour; of Mars, scarlet; of the Sun, golden; and Venus, white; of Mercury, azure; and of the Moon, green—a hue which is applied by the Orientals to silver.' Sir H. Rawlinson doubts the actual existence of seven concentric walls at Ecbatana with their several metals and colours, but thinks it likely that the city was dedicated to the heavenly bodies. In another account of Persian monumental symbolism, we find the whole series, not as before the Sun and Moon alone, represented by metals—The seven planetary metals. Origen quotes Celsus as to the mysteries of Mithras—' For in the latter there is a representation of the two heavenly revolutions, of the movement, to wit, of the fixed stars, and of that which takes place among the planets, and of the passage of the soul through these. The representation is of the following nature. There is a ladder with lofty gates, and, on the top of it, an eighth gate. The first gate consists of lead, the second of tin, the third of copper, the fourth of iron, the fifth of a mixture of metals, the sixth of silver, and the seventh of gold. The first gate they assign to Saturn, indicating by the lead the slowness of this star; the second to Venus, comparing her to the splendour and softness of tin; the third to Jupiter, being firm and solid; the fourth to Mercury, for both mercury and iron are fit to endure all things, and are money-making and laborious; the fifth to Mars, because, being composed of a mixture of metals, it is varied and unequal; the sixth, of silver, to the Moon; the seventh, of gold, to the Sun, imitating the colours of the two latter.'

The Buddhists held an exactly similar view as to the transmigration through several heavens before the heaven of heavens of Buddha was reached—the ascent, in other words, of the stages of the holy Mount Meru. We have shown before that the tope was the microcosm of the material sky as imagined by the Buddhists. These, too, would seem to have had their zones of planetary colours; for Fa-Hian, the Chinese pilgrim to the Buddhist shrines of India and Ceylon, at the end of the fourth century, describes nearly every tope he sees as ' covered with layers of all the precious substances,''the *seven* precious substances' (Legge). These precious substances are given by Mr Rhys Davids as gold, silver, lapis-lazuli, rock crystal, rubies, diamonds or emeralds, and agate. Major Cunningham gives a similar list, substituting amethyst for the diamond. In the tope at Sanchi, with the relics, he found seven beads of the 'precious things.' Indeed, we are told that after Buddha's enlightenment, a Raja built a hall for him of the seven precious substances, where he sat on a seven-gemmed throne.

Seven or nine-staged buildings were common all over India, Ceylon, Burmah, and Java, as Mr Fergusson's third volume sufficiently shows. All these, according to Col. Yule (Jour. R. Asiatic Soc. I 870), symbolised the mundane system. He quotes with approval from Koeppen: 'In Tibet, we are told every orthodoxly-constructed Buddhist temple either is, or contains, a symbolical representation of the divine regions of Meru, and the heaven of the gods, saints, and Buddhas rising above it.' He then describes the 'Pagoda' at Mengoon, in Burmah, as being 'intended as a complete symbolical representation or model of Mount Meru,' as it rises in seven-terraced stages, surrounded by jagged parapets of 'mountainous outline,' which figure the several zones of the heavenly mount. The Pagoda of Rangoon stands on a terrace 900 by 700 feet, and 166 feet high; there are four flights of steps, the eastern being the most holy. On this terrace stands the central shrine, 1355 feet round, and 370 high; this was surmounted by tiers of 'Umbrellas,' to which were hung multitudes of gold and silver bells of fabulous worth, and the whole mass was gilt.' The central edifice represents Mount Meru, and the circle of smaller buildings represents the mountains outside the world-girdling sea' ('The Burman,' Shway Yeo).

A remarkable temple at Jehol, in Mongolia, is described as 'a series of square buildings, each series higher than the other, till the last, which is eleven storeys high, and 200 feet at least square; the storeys are painted red, yellow, and green alternately... the tiles of the roof also are blue' (Williamson's Journeys).

The Heavens are nine in the Edda: 'I mind me of nine homes of nine supports. The great mid-pillar in the earth below.' Also in the Kalevala. 'The nine starry vaults of ether.' In China, long before Buddhist influence, the same symbolism obtained. Professor Legge gives a prayer addressed to *Shang Ti* (Heaven), dwelling in the sovereign heavens, looking up to the lofty *nine-storied azure vault*.' The 'Altar to Heaven' in Pekin, where this worship was celebrated, was in existence twelve centuries before our era. It consists of a triple circular terrace 210 feet wide at the base, 150 in the middle, and 90 at the top. 'The platform is laid with marble slabs, forming nine concentric circles; the inner circle consists of nine stones round the central stone, which is a perfect circle.' On this slab, 'flawless as a piece of the cerulean heavens,' the Emperor kneels. 'Round him on the pavement are the nine circles of as many heavens, consisting of nine stones, then eighteen, then twenty-seven, and so on in successive multiples of nine, till the square of nine, the favourite number of Chinese philosophy, is reached in the outermost circle of eighty-one stones. Four flights of steps of nine each lead down to the middle terrace, where are placed tablets to the spirits of the Sun, Moon, and Stars, and the Year God.' The order followed in worship is that of court ceremonial. First come the nine orders of nobility, and then the nine ranks of ofticers—the distinctions being indicated by different coloured balls on their caps: the Emperor being at the vertex (Edkins in Williamson's Journeys). Not only have we here the temple of heaven, but the celestial hierarchy and ritual.

Mr Squier, an American archæologist, points out a similar meaning in the structures of Mexico. 'The Mexicans believed in nine heavens, their conception differing only in this respect from that of the Hindus. The first or superior heaven was called "The Residence of the Supreme God;" the second, or next inferior, the *Azure Heaven*; the next, or seventh, the *Green Heaven*,' etc. And quoting from Lord Kingsborough: 'The Mexicans believed in nine heavens, which they supposed were distinguished from each other by the planets which they contained, from the colour of which they received their several denominations' (a native drawing is given as illustration, showing the nine heavens as so many ceilings studded with stars). 'It is not an assumption supported only by analogy that the Mexican *teocalli* were symbolical structures.' (He then cites Boturini's account of the reformer king of Tezcuco.) "This celebrated Emperor built a tower of nine stages, symbolising the nine heavens, and upon its summit erected a dark chapel, painted within of the fairest blue, with cornices of gold, dedicated to God the Creatorr who has His seat above the heavens" '(The Serpent Symbol in America). Prescott says the tower was 'nine stories high, to represent the nine heavens; a tenth was surmounted by a roof painted black, and profusely gilded with stars on the outside, and incrusted with metals and precious stones within. He dedicated this to the unknown God, the Cause of causes.' The finds at Warka, and some inscriptions, would go to show that the shrines in Chaldea surmounting the Ziggurat were also of the fairest blue, lapis-lazuli. Maspero and Perrot are disposed to accept the account of a Greek writer that the great Pyramid was decorated in zones of colour, with the apex gilt; and it would seem more than a coincidence that the earliest pyramids, attributed to the first four dynasties, should be in stages. That of Sakkarah still has six steps, decreasing from thirty-eight feet high at the bottom to twenty-nine feet for the top, in remarkable resemblance to the Ziggurat of Babel. And Mr Petrie has found that the pyramid of Medum was built in seven degrees before the outer and continuous casing was applied, 'producing a pyramid which served as a model to future sovereigns.'

In the outer circle of his underworld Dante sees the fields of peace of the great pagan dead. From his description and Botticelli's drawing, in the 1481 edition, with its seven circular walls, a high tower gateway in each, an Assyrian would know at once it was the city of the dead:-

> 'We came unto a noble castle's foot,
> Seven times encompassed with lofty walls,
> Defended round by a fair rivulet;
> This we passed over, even as firm ground;
> Through portals seven I entered with these sages;
> We came into a meadow of fresh verdure;
> People were there with solemn eyes and slow,
> Of great authority in their countenance;
> They spake but seldom, and with gentle voices.'
> —Canto iv.

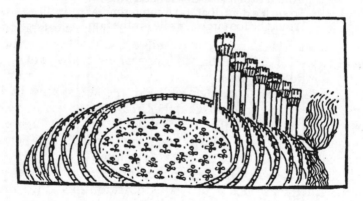

According to Sir George Birdwood, the regents of the planets that govern the days of the week in India are distinguished by the following colours: (1) The regent of the Sun and the first day of the week, bright yellow; (2) of the Moon, white; (3) of Mars, red; (4) of Mercury, yellow; (5) of Jupiter, also yellow; (6) of Venus, white; (7) of Saturn, black.

In making thrones, the same author says, 'The colour of any stone used should be that of the planets presiding over the destiny of the person for whom the throne is made.' We have already seen Buddha's throne, made of all the seven planetary substances, and that the vast pyramid structures of Babylon were thrones for the god to which the coloured terraces formed so many steps.

The tradition of the throne on the seven heavenly steps lasts on into the Middle Ages. A thirteenth century MS. at Heidelberg, which figures the universe, shows the Throne of the Majesty standing on seven decreasing circular steps forming to the earth the vaults of heaven. An inscription, 'seven steps in fashion of a hollow vault,' makes the meaning clear, and is especially valuable as giving us the scheme of Dante's Paradise, which has so puzzled the commentators. Dante, standing at the apex on the outer material heaven, looks up and sees over and around, another and another expanse. As he stands centrally under them, the steps of the throne form an inverted amphitheatre, 'the white rose'—

> 'And it expands itself in circular form
> To such extent, that its circumference
> Would be too large a girdle for the Sun.'

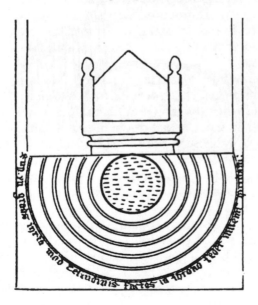

The throne high over all becomes a type; and all thrones must have seven steps. Compare the description of Solomon's throne in the Book of Chronicles and Josephus: 'Moreover the king made a great throne of ivory, and overlaid it with pure gold. And there were six steps to the throne, with a footstool of gold, which were fastened to the throne, and stays on each side of the sitting place, and two lions standing by the stays; and twelve lions stood there on the one side, and on the other side upon the six steps. There was not the like made in any kingdom' (2 Chron. ix. I7). Josephus varies slightly, but in both are the seven pairs of lions standing at seven degrees of height: "A throne of prodigious bigness, of ivory, and having six steps to it, on every one of which stood on each end of the steps two lions; two other lions standing above also; but at the sitting place of the throne hands came out to receive the king; and when he sat backward, he rested on half a bullock that looked towards his back; and all was fastened together with gold.' In the Talmud are also the seven pairs of animals, but, to add some ingenuity, the animals and birds are such as prey on one another 'symbolical of enemies dwelling together in peace.' 'And the wolf shall then dwell with the sheep.' Over the throne was hung a chandelier of gold, with seven branches, ornamented with roses, knops, bowls, and tongs; and on the seven branches were the seven names of the patriarchs engraven—Adam, Noah, Shem, Abraham, Isaac, Jacob, and Job.

The Arab writers add to the wonders. Two lions were made for the throne by genii and set at the foot; two eagles were placed above it; and when the king mounted it, the lions stretched out their paws, and when he sat down the eagles shaded him with their wings. All this seems to have been achieved in the throne in the imperial palace at Constantinople—constructed in imitation of and called Solomon's throne-where the beasts of goid rose to their feet and roared, and close by was the golden tree and singing birds.

But the steps should be adorned with the planetary colours, like the throne of Prester John, as vouched for by Sir John Maundeville. 'Of the steps approaching his throne where he sits at meat, one is of onyx, another of crystal, another green jasper, another amethyst, another sardonyx, another cornelian, and the seventh on which he sets his feet is of chrysolite. All these steps are bordered with fine gold, with other precious stones, set with great orient pearls. The sides of the seat of his throne are of emeralds and bordered full nobly with gold, and dubbed with other precious stones and great pearls. All the pillars in his chamber are of fine gold, with precious stones, and with many carbuncles, which give great light by night to all people, And althoughthe carbuncle gives light enough, nevertheless at all times a vessel of crystal, full of balm, is burning to give good smell and odour to the emperor, and to expel all wicked airs and corruptions.'

In the 'Romance of Alexander' the throne of the conquered Darius has seven such steps. They were of amethyst, smaragdine, topaz, garnet, adamant, gold and earth. The first keeps one from drunkenness, the second protects the sight, the topaz reflects an inverted image, the garnet is the brightest, the adamant, which is the hardest, attracts ships, gold is the chief of metals, and the earth reminded the King that he too was but dust.

Fa-Hian, in India, in the fourth century, sees a relic of Buddha exposed on 'a pedestal of the seven precious substances, and covered with a bell of lapis lazuli both adorned with pearls.'

In Egypt the covering of the throne and its footstool, figured the blue star set expanse of heaven. In Mexico also it was of azure. The King has everywhere been a god seated on the heavenly throne. There is still reason behind the most imaginative design.

The septfold planetary system holds in Heraldry. To quote from Baron Portal on the symbolism of colour:—' All coats of arms, says Anselm in the *Palais de l'Honneur*, are differenced by two metals, five colours, and two furs. The two metals are, or and argent; the five colours are azure, gules, sable, sinople (green), porpure; and the two furs ermine and vair. Aristotle in his time gave names to the metals and colours according to the seven planets. Or, was called the Sun; argent, the Moon; azure, Jupiter; gules, Mars; sable, Saturn; sinople, Venus; and porpure, Mercury, and each god was painted with his appropriate metal and colour.' In the Middle Ages, when the heavenly spheres had been increased to nine, with nine orders of spirits to govern them, the sevenfold arrangement of the metals and tinctures was increased to nine by two other tinctures—tenne (tawny), orange, and sanguine, blood colour. The 'Boke of St. Albans,' compiled in the fifteenth century by Dame Juliana Berners, gives us the Mediæval lore as to heraldry and the ninefold colours:-

'The lawe of Armes the wiche was effigured andbegunne before any lawe in the worlde, both the lawe of nature and before the commandementis of God.

'And this lawe of armys was grounded upon the IX dyveris orderys of angels in heven encrowned with IX dyveris precious stonys of colouris and of vertuys dyveris also of them are figured the IX colouris in armys.

' The first stone is calde Topazion, signyfiyng gold in armys ' (its virtue is truth), etc., etc.

The seven or nine perfect heraldic tinctures are thus the precious stones and metals of the seven planets or nine heavens. Well may Lydgate say of these stones ideally used in blazoning arms:-

'The which stones come from Paradise
Therefore they are so precious singular.'

In old-fashioned heraldry this tradition is preserved, and the tinctures called either by their ordinary heraldic names, by the names of gems, or of the planets, the first being used to blazon the coats of commoners, the gems for nobles, and the planets for sovereign princes.

Or	Topaz	Sol
Argent	Pearl	Luna
Sable	Diamond	Saturn
Gules	Ruby	Mars
Azure	Sapphire	Jupiter
Vert	Emerald	Venus
Porpure	Amethyst	Mercury

The natural colours of the planets as they appear to the eye, or under a low power, are said to be:

Saturn	Deep bluish.
Jupiter	White.
Venus	Yellow.
Mars	Red.
Mercury	Pale blue.

In comparing the lists, the Sun and Moon are the two metals, Mars is always red, Saturn always black, Venus is yellow or
green, Mercury blue or purple, and Jupiter is the least certain.
The heraldic correspondences given in the *Palais de l'Honneur*
may perhaps be accepted as authoritative. The significance of
colour is thus given by a modern magician (Eliphas Levi): 'Those
who love blue are idealists and dreamers; those who like red are
materialistic and passionate; yellow, fantastic and capricious;
green, mercantile and crafty; those who give their preference to
black are ruled by Saturn.' This accords with the rule of the planets over the several temperaments, as we preserve it in ordinary
speech—Jovial, Mercurial, and Saturnine or Melancholy.

We have seen above the association of the metals with the
seven stars; their correspondence is sufficiently obvious, and
they share in modern science the same signs, and in one case the
same name. There is a great deal of astrology in the sciences yet.

Sun	Gold.	Jupiter	Tin.
Moon	Silver.	Venus	Copper.
Mars	Iron.	Saturn	Lead.
Mercury	Mercury.		

Chaucer gives a list identical with this except that the quicksilver of Mercury is contracted to silver. Gower in the 'Confes-
sio Amantis' gives similar correspondences, except that 'Jupiter
the brass bestoweth.'

In the East the perfect metal was naturally an alloy of all
these.

Once grasp the colours and qualities of the seven planets, and
you possess the master key of Astrology. As these powers might
be present in the twelve houses of the heavens devoted to Birth,
Riches, Marriage, etc.; so would the fortune of the subject be
influenced. Two Capitals of the Ducal Palace at Venice show us
how they rule Man and the Sciences; one depicting the seven
ages, the other the seven liberal arts.

The Moon governs Infancy.
Mercury „   Boyhood.
Venus „   Adolescence.
Sun „   Young Manhood.
Mars „   Manhood.
Jupiter „   Age.
Saturn „   Decrepitude.

The seven arts were Grammar, Logic, Rhetoric, Arithmetic, Geometry, Music, and Astronomy.

The traditional association of colours and stones with the planets is barely yet extinct in the West, where old brooches may be seen of six coloured stones, and lavas set round a seventh central one, all with carved heads of the planets, and at the centre the rayed head of Apollo. In the East it is well understood. The gorgeous gold treasure from Burmah in the Indian Museum which has the splendour that only half barbaric work ever attains to, the bloom of red gold, and the profuse setting of uncut stones mesmerising the imagination into exaltation, has on most of the pieces eight precious stones set round an enormous ruby as large as a nut. This symbolic group is called *Nauratan* (nine gems). Throughout India 'they are the only stones esteemed precious.'

To come back again to the Chaldean world mountain, home of the gods, birthplace of the nations, and, like Meru, a mountain of precious stones. In the tablets it is called Nizar, and its summit by a name familiar to us as that of its architectural representation—Ziggurat. Madame Ragazoin puts this symbolic purpose clearly before us. 'So vivid was the conception in the popular mind, and so great the reverence entertained for it, that it was attempted to reproduce the type of the holy mountain in the palaces of their kings and the temples of their gods.'

'As the gods dwelt on the summit of the Mountain of the World, so their shrines should occupy a position as much like their residence as the feeble means of man would permit. That this is no idle fancy is proved by the very name of "Ziggurat," which means "mountain peak," and also by the names of some of these temples; one of the oldest, and most famous, indeed, in the City of Assur was named "The House of the Mountain of Countries." '

And Professor Sayce, in his Hibbert Lectures, is equally definite. 'As the peak of the Mount of the Deluge (Nizar) was called Ziggurat or temple tower, so, conversely, the Mountain of the World was the name given to a temple Ziggurat at Calah.' 'A fragmentary tablet which gives, as I believe, the Babylonian version of the building of the tower of Babel, especially identifies it with "the illustrious mound." The name given to the tower of the chief temple at Kis was 'The Illustrious Mountain of Mankind.'

Our last picture of the earthly paradise and world mountain shall be that of the Kingdom of Atlas, for which Plato gathers up just what he requires of tradition, and uses it with the realism of Swift. The successive zones of water and land, and the many-coloured walls, show it to be as real a legend of the heavenly Mount Meru as is the picture of a Buddhist paradise given here for comparison.

We will take first the story told by the Buddha to Ananda of 'The Great King of Glory :'—

'Kasavati was the royal city . . . and on the east and on the west it was twelve leagues in length, and on the north and on the south it was seven leagues in breadth.

'The royal city Kasavati, Ananda, was surrounded by seven ramparts. Of these, one rampart was of gold, and one of silver, and one of beryl, and one of crystal, and one of agate, and one of coral, and one of all kinds of gems.

'To the royal city Kasavati, Ananda, there were four gates; one was of gold, and one of silver, and one of jade, and one of crystal.

'At each gate seven pillars were fixed of the seven precious substances and four times the height of a man. The city was surrounded by seven rows of palm trees; of gold, of silver, and of gems; their fruits were jewels, from which, shaken by the wind, there arose delightful music. In this city was a palace of righteousness, a league east and west by a half-league north and south, with 84,000 chambers, each of gold, silver, beryl, and crystal; at each door stood a palm tree. The palace was all hung about with a network of bells of gold and silver, the music of which was sweet and intoxicating. There was a lotus lake lined with tiles of gold, silver, beryl, and crystal.

'I was that king, and all these things were mine! See, Ananda, how all these things are past, are ended, have vanished away!' (Rhys Davids, S.B. of East, vol. xi.)

Plato's island of Atlantis had in the centre a plain, in the midst of which was a mountain. Poseidon enclosed the hill all round, making alternate zones of sea and land, larger and smaller, encircling one another; there were two of land and three of water, which he turned as with a lathe out of the centre of the island, equidistant every way.

'His eldest son he named Atlas, and from him the whole island and the ocean received the name of Atlantic. In the first place they dug out of the earth whatever was to be found there, mineral as well as metal; and that which is now only a name, and was then something more than a name, orichalcum, was dug out of the earth in many parts of the island ... also whatever fragrant things there are in the earth, whether roots or herbage, or woods or essences which distil from fruit and flower, grew and thrived in that land.. .. All these that sacred island, which then beheld the light of the sun, brought forth fair and wondrous and in infinite abundance.

'They bridged across the zones and opened waterways from one zone to the other. . . . All this, including the zones and the bridge, they surrounded by a stone wall, on all sides placing towers and gates where the sea passed in.

'One kind of stone was white, another black, and a third red; some of their buildings were simple, but in others they put together different stones, varying the pattern to please the eye, and to be a natural source of delight. The entire circuit of the wall that went round the outermost zone they covered with a coating of brass; and the circuit of the next wall they coated with tin; and the third, which encompassed the citadel, flashed with the red light of orichalcum. The palaces in the interior were constructed on this wise:—In the centre was a holy temple dedicated to Cleito and Poseidon, which remained inaccessible, and was surrounded by an enclosure of gold. Here too was Poseidon's own temple, which was a stadium in length and half a stadium in width, and of a proportionate height, having a strange Asiatic look. All the outside of the temple, with the exception of the pinnacles, they covered with silver, and the pinnacles with gold. In the interior of the temple the roof was of ivory, adorned everywhere with gold, and silver, and orichalcum; and all the other parts of the walls, and pillars, and floor, they lined with orichalcum.

'In the temple they placed statues of gold: there was the god himself standing in a chariot—the charioteer of six winged horses—and of such a size that he touched the roof of the building with his head. . . . Enough of the plan of the royal palace. Leaving the palace and crossing the three harbours outside you come to a wall which began at the sea and went all round; this was everywhere distant fifty stadia from the largest zone or harbour, and enclosed the whole.

'Such was the vast power which the god settled in the lost island of Atlantis. They despised everything but virtue, caring little for their present state of life, and thinking lightly of the possession of gold and other property, which seemed only a burden to them: neither were they intoxicated by luxury; nor did wealth deprive them of their self-control, but they were sober, and saw clearly that all these goods are increased by virtue and friendship with one another' (Critias Jowett).

'Thou hast been in Eden, the garden of God; every precious stone was thy covering. Thou wast upon the holy mountain of God; thou hast walked up and down in the midst of the stones of fire.'

CHAPTER VII

THE LABYRINTH

*'Hast thou left thy blue course in heaven,
golden-haired son of the sky! The west
opened its gates, the bed of thy repose is
there. The waves come to behold thy beauty.
They lift their trembling heads. They see
thee lovley in thy sleep. They shrink away
with fear. Rest in thy shadowy cave, O
Sun! Let thy return be in joy.'*
— *OSSIAN.*

IN 'The Bible of Amiens' Mr Ruskin describes the labyrinth once inlaid on the floor of the nave of the cathedral, and in 1825 'removed to make the old pavement more polite.' In that outburst of fervour, from the middle of the twelfth to the end of the thirteenth century, wrought into the stones of the great cathedrals—speaking particularly of France—when the scheme of imagery and symbolism had been consummated, so that no part of the building should be without its teaching, one of these labyrinths belonged by right to the floor: 'a recognised emblem of many things to the people.'

This one of Amiens was octagonal, and forty-two feet across; the effigy of the architect was at the centre, and a legend containing the date 1288. There was another, similar, at St Quentin; and one at Rheims, square, and thirty-five feet across, was laid down in 1240 and destroyed in 1779. Another, about the same time, was broken up in the Cathedral at Arras. At St Omer, in the Abbey of St Bertin, mountains, animals, and towns were depicted on the pathway, and the Temple of Jerusalem in the centre. It has been suggested that the maze was a symbol of life and of the coil of sin. 'The whole device was deemed to be indicative of the complicated folds of sin by which man is surrounded, and how .impossible it would be to extricate himself from them except through the assisting hand of Providence' (Didron's *Annales*).

At Bayeux there is a maze formed by patterned tiles in the chapter-house. At Sens there was a fine example; and another still exists in St Stephen's Abbey at Caen. One, especially beautiful, at Chartres, inlaid with dark stone on light, has a pathway of some six hundred and sixty feet round and round to the centre. In the thirteenth century sketch book of the architect Viliars de Honecourt, there is a drawing of a maze like this of Chartres, indeed, it is identical in planning. These French labyrinths appear to have been called '*la lieue*' or '*Chemin de Jerusalem*;' they were placed at the west end of the nave, and people made a pilgrimage on their knees, following the windings of the pathway to the centre, which is said to have been called *Sancta Ecclesia* or *Ciel*.

There is a German example in the Church of St Severius, Cologne. In England there was one at Canterbury, but none now remain in our churches. There are, however, a great number cut in turf. One of these, at Saffron Walden, is a hundred and ten feet across: wholly overgrown with grass, its form is made out by alternate ridge and furrow. Others are at Wing, in Rutlandshire; Alkborough, in Lincolnshire; Boughton Green, Northants; St Catharine's Hill, Winchester; Sneiton, Nottinghamshire; and Pimpern, near Blandford. They were given the names of Miz-Maze, Julian's Bower, Troy Town, or Shepherd's Race.

Their age is not known, but, according to the country historian, some sort of spring festival seems to have been held at that of Saffron Walden. Those formed by clipped hedges, 'green mazes,' are an ordinary part of ornamental gardening, and designs for them may be found in Serlio and other writers. There was a fine regular one at Theobald's old palace, and the maze at Hampton Court is known to everybody. One, of water, in the *Hypnerotomachia*, on which tiny shallops floated and seven gate-towers divided the stream, is evidently symbolical of life.

In Italy some beautiful examples are found—one at Ravenna, in St Vitale, is here represented; another is in St Michele, Pavia; and two others are in Rome, at S.M. in Trastevere, and S.M. in Aquiro.

Through Roman examples on pavements and gems we are led back to the Greek coins of Crete, where, in the fifth or sixth century B.C. the device first appears. (For illustrations see Didron's *Annales*, De Caumont, 'Archæological Journal,' and 'The Architectural Dictionary.')

Of course the varieties in the mere design of mazes would be infinite; their resemblance is the striking fact, so that, considered merely as a device or pattern, the tradition is one for the two thousand years from the Greek coin of Gnossus to Botticelli's print in thc Renaissance, and we wonder how it passed from place to place. There are no false paths, not a single *cul-de-sac* but simply the longest involved path, from the entrance to the eye, you follow far enough, and necessarily reach the centre. When the root of tradition was broken away from at the Renaissance, all this was altered, and mazes became inventions, every one different from the others—spiders' webs of enticing false paths.

The windings and doublings of the inlaid one at St Quentin are identical beyond all possibility of merely fortuitous coincidence with the one on the green at Alkborough, as is also that of Sens with that at Boughton Green. The Chartres labyrinth is absolutely the same in design as one on the door jamb at Lucca, with this difference, that the former, thirty feet across, is ornamented at the centre, and the latter is but a scratched line. This one in turn is exactly like that on the Hereford Map of the World, and that one also in the sketch book of Viliars de Honecourt, with the only exception that this last is reversed. These four, then, severally in Italy, France, and England, are absolutely related-in form and proportion, number of walls and planning of their revolutions, they are transcripts of one another or a common original. Those at Ravenna, on Botticelli's engraving, and on a picture at Cambridge, are but slight variations

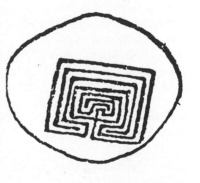

frorn this typical form, or from a Roman one scratched on a wall at Pompeii, and the original Cretan examples here given from the coins.

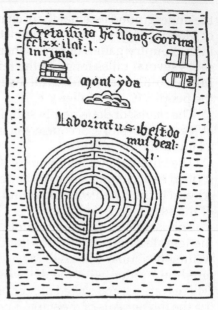

All the time it was understood to be the labyrinth of Dædalus, in Crete, into which, aided by Ariadne's thread, Theseus penetrated and safely returned. This is the subject of Botticelli's engraving. On the Hereford Map the plan of the labyrinth nearly fills the whole map of Crete: it is inscribed *Labarintus id est domus Dealli* (see next page). The great floor labyrinth at Amiens was inscribed Maison de Dalus. In the Lucca example there is also an inscription—' This is the labyrinth which Cretan Dædalus built, out of which nobody could get who was inside, except Theseus; nor could he have done it unless he had been helped with a thread by Ariadne, all for love' ('Fors Clavigera').

At Pavia the Minotaur is represented at the vortex in the form of a centaur. That at Pompeii had written against it, '*Labyrinthus hic habitat Minotaurus.*' Those on the Greek coins belong to the town founded by Minos himself, where the labyrinth was said to have been built; and the reverses of the coins have the head of Theseus, who thus accompanies the symbol of his 'life's problem.' So, from the earliest Greek to the Renaissance there is an unbroken sequence of examples giving this form to the house of the Minotaur. We can well understand that, once existing and associated with rites of pi}grimage or penance, they would easily acquire different local names—'The way to Jerusalem,' and the rest—but the form and the rite existed before any such titles.

That in Roman times they were marked out on turf pavements, and that there was a popular custom of following the windings of the pathway, is shown by Pliny,who, speaking of the underground assemblage of chambers, the socalled labyrinth of Moeris in Egypt, says,—'Nor is it as we sometimes see drawn in the country games of boys, where a small strip contains passages several miles long.' In the reign of Commodus, Q. Julius Miletus built a labyrinth as an institution for the amusement of the people. (C. O. Muller.)

The *choros*, or dancing-place, built by Dædalus for Ariadne— as it existed in story, of course, not in stone —was probably such a labyrinth.

The Hindu dance in honour of Krishna, as the sungod, is described as a 'circular sunwise dance, in which the dancers twisted, and turned, and wheeled round about in supposed imitation of the sun, moon, and planets.'

This is repeated in the sevenfold star-wise procession around the temple of Jagannatha, or the Caaba of Mecca. M. Reville, writing of similar dances in Mexico, says, that worshippers entered into union with the deity by imitating his movements. 'There were several sacred dances having the character of imitating the movements of the stars.' Knowing the right form of these involutions was of the greatest importance. Mr A. Lang tells us that to savages 'those who don't dance our dance are foreigners.' And the plot of one of our folk stories-'Child Rowland'— is the awful consequences of running round a church 'widershins' or contra sunwise.

Here in England 'the boys to this day divert themselves with running in it one after another, the first leading them by many windings quite through and back again. Stukeley supposes that it is called Julian from Iulus and the Trojan games in Virgil' (Fosbroke 'Encyc. Antiq.' 1840). Mr Gerald Massey tells us mazes are 'still figured in the children's games in Cornwall and Wales, and consist of seven circles round a centre cut in the grassy sod.' In the Western Counties anything untidy and confused is said to be 'like Troy Town.'

Herodotus opens with a fourfold legend of the origin of the war of Troy—the stories of Io, Europa, Medea, and Helen, all seemingly varients of one 'far told tale' of a princess enticed away over sea. A hero in a foreign land is set to do a great deed and to endure a great peril; the king of the country sets the task in malice; but his daughter sees, loves, and helps the hero; he overcomes, and they fly away over the sea together; but fate suffers it not so for long, and then comes a sorrowful parting. 'Everywhere there is the search for the bright maiden who has been stolen away, everywhere the long struggle to recover her: the war of Ilion has been fought out in every Aryan land ' (Sir G. Cox).

Europa's son, Minos, becomes the great king and lawgiver of Crete, and the whole story is repeated. A vast prison-house has been built by Dædalus to confine the Minotaur, and a tribute is imposed on Athens of seven youths and seven maidens yearly sacrificed to the hidden monster. On a year one of these is Theseus, the hero who is to end 'the infamy of Crete.' 'When Theseus arrived in Crete, according to most historians and authors, Ariadne, falling in love with him, gave him a clue of thread, and instructed him how to pass with it through the intricacies of the labyrinth. Thus assisted, he set sail, carrying off Ariadne.' (Plutarch.)

Minos, the king, has three characteristics in classic lore; he is, above all, the great administrator of law; he is the judge of the under world of the dead; he is the lord of the labyrinth. Already, when we first meet his name in the Homeric poems, he is the earthly king of Crete and the ruler of the dead in Hades. Odysseus describes his descent to the house of Hades,—'There, then, I saw Minos, glorious son of Zeus, wielding a golden sceptre, giving sentence from his throne to the dead, while they sat and stood around the prince, asking his dooms through the wide-gated house of Hades.... And Ariadne, the daughter of Wizard Minos, whom Theseus on a time was bearing from Crete to the hill of sacred Athens' (Odyss. XI.)

The story is closely parallel to that of Osiris, in Egypt. Osiris, overcome by the powers of evil and darkness, goes to be the judge of the under world, in the hall of justice, which is surrounded by walls, wherein are twelve or fifteen successive gates to be passed. This is reached by tortuous ways past finding out, were it not for the guide book of the departed, 'The Book of the Dead.' Isis goes in quest of her lover, and the powers of darkness are at last overcome by Horus, the rising sun of a new day. The Egyptian myth has been universally regarded as solar, the

House of Osiris with its seven halls being the under world, 'the nocturnal abode' through which the sun nightly finds his way back to the east.

'Osiris is the setting sun. Plutarch identifies him with Hades. Both, he says, originally meant the dwellings, and came to mean the god of the dead ' (Lefebure).

'Osiris is the sun of yesterday, who was overcome by Night in the person of Set, who, in his turn, was vanquished by Horus, the son of Osiris.... Horus is the sun in full strength ' (Renouf).

The power of darkness is represented as the giant serpent Apap, 'with which,' says Lenormant, 'the sun, under the form of Ra or Horus, contends during his nocturnal passage round the lower hemisphere, and over which he is destined to triumph before reappearing in the east. The conflict of Horus with Apap is ever renewed at the seventh hour of the night, a little before sun rising.'

In his recent book, the 'Golden Bough,' Mr Frazer regards Osiris as a god of vegetation. Should this be accepted, it will not conflict with the conclusion reached in this chapter. Whether Sun or Vegetable Life, it is still the dark under world to which he withdraws—house of darkness, winter, and death.

Theseus, it is generally allowed, is a duplication of Hercules, the solar hero. Melkarth, the sun-god of the Phoenicians, Horus, of the Egyptians, and the other parallels make it clear that his achievement of the labyrinth was one of many descents into the nightland to fight the serpent, dragon, or minotaur of death and darkness.

The story of Herodotus of the founding of the city of Ecbatana by the great lawgiver of the Medes is closely allied to the foundation of Gnossus and the building of the labyrinth by Minos, who instituted law in Crete. Without necessarily questioning the existence of an actual Ecbatana with seven walls, each dedicated to a planet, or a real Dioces, we may see the close connection of this history with other stories of the Just Judge in the underground, seven-walled, world of the dead. The labyrinth of Minos, as found on the coins, is such a seven-walled citadel.

Dioces, the first king of the Medes, says the Father of History (or of Folk Lore), 'applied himself with great zeal to the exercise of justice, and the people chose him for their king. And, as the Medes obeyed him in this also, he built lofty and strong walls, which now go under the name of Ecbatana, one placed in a circle within the other.' . . . ' He established the following regulations:—That no man should be admitted to the king's presence, but every one consult him by means of messengers, and that none should be permitted to see him . . . that he might appear to be of a different nature to those who did not see him. He was very severe in the distribution of justice; and the parties contending were obliged to send him their cases in writing . . . and all other things were regulated by him; so that, if he received information that any man had injured another, he would presently send for him and punish him in proportion to his offence; and for this purpose he had spies and eavesdroppers in every part of his dominions.' Is not this a Minos apportioning justice to all men in the lower world rather than a human king in an earthly city? We must not, however, forget that kings and tyrants have secluded themselves; Mokanna, the veiled prophet, for instance, and divine monarchs generally.

Strabo, speaking of Avernus, near Cumae, where the Italian peoples supposed the descent to be, says:—' There is here a spring of water, near to the sea, fit for drinking, from which, however, every one abstained, as they thought it water from Styx. They thought, likewise, that the oracle of the dead was situated somewhere here. Ephorus, peopling the place with Kimmerii, tells us that they dwell in underground habitations, and that these communicate with one another by means of certain subterranean passages; and that they conduct strangers through them to the oracle, which is built far below the surface of the earth. They lived in the mines together, with the profits accruing from the oracle and grants made to them by the king. It was a traditional custom for the servants of the oracle never to behold the sun, and only to quit their caverns at night. At last, however, these men were exterminated by one of the kings, the oracle having deceived him; but the oracle is still in existence, though remoyed to another place. Such were the myths related by our ancestors.'

Duncker cites a Greek author of the second century, who, in describing the Sabæans, gives an echo of a similar tradition. 'Their chief city, Mariaba, lies on a mountain. Here lives the king, who pronounces justice for the people; but he is never allowed to leave his palace. If he acts otherwise, he is stoned by the people, in obedience to an ancient oracle.'

Peoples now living in a low phase of development account for the judgment of the dead in exactly the same way. 'It is a belief of the Australians, as, according to Bosman, it was with the people of the Gold Coast, that a very powerful wizard lives far inland; and the negroes held that to this warlock the spirits of the dead went to be judged according to the merit of their actions. Here we have a doctrine (quoting Mr Andrew Lang in "Myth and Ritual") answering to the Greek belief in the wizard Minos, Æacus, and Rhadamanthus, and to the Egyptian idea of Osiris as judge of the departed.'

In Herodotus a story is related of Rhamsinitus, in whose reign, he tells us, 'there was a perfect administration of justice.' 'He descended alive into the place the Greeks call Hades, and there played at dice with Ceres, and sometimes won and at other times lost.' A ceremony was instituted imitating this descent, and in another story, this same king possesses a wonderful treasury-house, which is ingeniously robbed by a master of theft—a plot, as Mr Clouston has shown, which is found in the folk tales of many peoples, even to this day, and which may, after all, be what Sir G. Cox, approaching from another point of view, sees in it—the sun breaking through the prison-house of the under world, always with all people the treasury of riches.

The Greek story of Theseus and Ariadne had its Phoenician co-relative in Adonis and Astarte, the Tammuz and Istar of the Assyrians. 'One of the most popular of old Babylonian myths,' says Professor Sayce, 'told how Istar had wedded the young and beautiful sun-god Tammuz, and had descended into Hades in search of him when he had been slain by the boar's tusk of winter.' Istar 'was the goddess of the evening star.' In the narrative of her adventures in the lower world, 'the house out of which there is no exit,' we seem to get a clear idea of the point of departure of these stories, in thought if not in geography. The following is taken from Lenormant's 'Chaldean Magic':—

'The country whence none return is divided into seven zones, like those of Dante's Inferno, upon the model of the seven planetary spheres.... Seven gates gave admission, each guarded by a porter.... This idea of the circles of the under world is also found in the Egyptian mythology of the ritual of the dead—the deceased had to pass through fifteen pylons in his descent.' In the centre of this grave-land was the palace of the ruler and a temple of justice. As Istar passes through each of the seven gates the porter requires her jewels and apparel. At the first, her crown; at the second, the rings from her ears; at the third, her necklace of precious stones; at the fourth, the pectoral from her bosom; at the fifth, her girdle of gems; at the sixth, bracelets; at the seventh, her robe.

In the version given by Perrot it is not merely a country divided into zones, but a *city of seven walls*—a structure like the labyrinth of Dædalus. 'We know from the narrative of Istar that they looked upon it as an immense building situated in the centre of the earth, and bounded on every side by the great river whose waters bathe the foundations of the world. This country of the dead is called 'the land where one sees nothing,' or 'the land from whence is no return.' The house is surrounded by seven strong walls. In each there is a single door, which is fastened by a bolt as soon as a new comer has entered.'

The descriptive epithets show it as very clearly imagined. ' The house in which the evening has no morning, whence there is no return. There, too, stand the foundations of the earth, the meeting of the mighty waters.' The earth being convex and hollow, like an inverted bowl, the palace of the ruler of the dead was in the void beneath, around flows the earthly ocean, and on that rests the foundations of the over sea.

The seven spherical envelopes passing under the earth, as above in the heavens, divide it into as many regions. Tammuz, Theseus, Horus—the strong sun—penetrate this prison-house, and rise out of the eastern gate, but the path is so involved that none of the dead find their way back. This is the origin of the labyrinth, nor can we wonder that mediæval mystics made use of its symbolism at the non-sacred end of their churches.

This under world of seven walls is quite universal. In Origen there is an account of the Ophites, with their invocations to seven demons, who guarded as many gates in the passage of the soul. The Zoroastrian fragments in Cory preserve the same plan for the under world. Over the earth there were seven successive firmaments for the planets, and below us: 'Stoop not down, for a precipice lies below the earth, drawing under in a descent of seven steps, beneath which is the throne of dire necessity.'

In the later Persian, *Shah-Nameh* of Firdausi, Rustem, the Hercules of Iran, undertakes seven great labours in seven days, when he reaches a place called the seven mountains, he fights a demon 'within a deep and horrible recess.'

In India the same scheme of a labyrinthine under world would seem to have existed from the Vedic time, for such appears to be the cave to which the cloud cattle of the sun are driven off by a trackless path. In the Hindu system, under the Olympian Mount Meru, with its seven zones, 'there are seven lower worlds, which are all beautiful paradises, though inhabited by demons and nagas; the latter are half men and half serpents, and are governed by three great snakes, which reign over all the snakes on earth.'

The Mohammedan cosmogony is very similar. According to Lane there are seven material heavens, and seven earths, one below the other; Jahennem is also divided into seven stages; to which, according to D'Herbelot, there are seven great portals. In the Jewish traditions of the Cabbalah there are seven infernal halls. The lowest Buddhist hell, called in the Chinese 'earth prison,' is surrounded by a sevenfold iron wall. This verse from the poetic Edda shows the thought of the Northmen, which was also that of our old English ancestors:—

'Without and within
I seemed to go through all
The seven lower worlds.'

Professor Rhys (Hibbert Lect.) quotes a story of the descent of the Celtic hero to the land of Shades. The words might as well be uttered by Istar herself, so typical they are:—

'When I went to the land of Scath,
There was the fort of Scath, with its lock of iron;
I laid hands upon it.
Seven walls there were around this city;
Hateful was its stronghold.'

Dante, confessedly in the *Convito*, founds on the planetary spheres (following Ptolemy, and to the seven adding two others, for the spheres of the fixed stars and the primum mobile) his nine-fold arrangement of the circles of Paradise and the Inferno. It is most remarkable how he relates his descent, to that of Theseus in the Labyrinth of Dædalus. Minos is the guardian and judge who assigns to each his proper circle, and, guarding the way to the seventh circle, he encounters the Minotaur:—

'And on the border of the 'broken chasm
The infamy of Crete was stretched along.
My sage towards him shouted: "Peradventure
Thou think'st that here may be the Dulke of Athens,
Who in the world above brought death to thee ?
Get thee gone, beast, for this one cometh not
Instructed by thy sister, but he comes
In order to behold your punishments."'

Does not the description of the Malebolge seem as if it was founded directly on such a labyrinth as that on the floor at Ravenna, which must have been familiar to him ?

'Right in the middle of the field malign
There yawns a well exceeding wide and deep,
Of which its place the structure will recount.
Round then is that enclosure which remains
Between the well and foot of the high, hard bank,
And has distinct in valleys ten its bottom.
As where, for the protection of the walls,
Many and many moats surround the castles,
The part in which they are a figure forms
Just such an image those presented there;
And as about such strongholds, from their gates
Unto the outer bank are little bridges,
So from the precipice's base did little crags
Project, which intersected dykes and moats,
Unto the well that truncates and collect them.'
—Canto xviii.

It has been too much the custom to see mere arbitrary inventions in Dante's system but he wrote in quite another temper than did Miiton. Dante embodies no fancies of his own; but follows the universe system of his age. In the words of Dean Milman, 'Dante is the one authorised topographer of the mediæval hell ;' topographer is the word.

In some instances we have the sun in the lower world, not obscured by any impersonation, as in the 'Rest in thy shadowy cave, O sun,' of Ossian, quoted under the heading of this chapter, which agrees remarkab}y with what Pytheas, the traveller of Marseilles, was told in the north regarding the sun: 'The barbarians used to point out to us the lair or sleeping-place of the sun; for the nights at one place were only three hours long, at another place only two hours.' (Compare Dr. Tylor's Anthropology, pp. 332, 349).

Mr A. Lang quotes, in his 'Myth and Ritual,' an account given by the Piute Indians: 'Down, deep under the ground, deep, deep, under all the ground, is a great hole. At night, when he has passed over the world, looking down on everything, and finished his work, he, the sun, goes into his hole, and he crawls and creeps along it till he comes to his bed in the middle part of the earth. So then he the sun, stops there in his bed all night. This hole is so little, and he, the sun, is so big, that he cannot turn round in it; and so he must, when he has had all his sleep, pass on through, and in the morning we see him come out in the east. When he, the sun, has so come out, he begins to hunt up through the sky to catch and eat any he can of the stars, his children, for if he does not so catch and eat he cannot live. He, the sun is not all seen. The shape of him is like a snake or lizard. It is not his head that we can see, but his belly, filled up with the stars that times and times he has swallowed.'

The moon, it goes on to say, is his wife, and sleeps in the same hole, but when he returns and is cross, she comes away. As in Hesiod, one home cannot contain them both; and so sun and moon do not appear at the same time in the upper world.

Such, then, have been the thoughts of men regarding, the land peopled by their dead, the cavernous deep whose dark windings the sun has nightly to thread, to reappear in the morning victor over the powers of darkness. Well may the Dawn, Moon, or planet Venus furnish the clue by which the new day is won, and greet him on his issuing from the gates; but not for long can they be together—Ariadne must be left behind at Naxos, as the sun hastens westward. This is the subject of the 'gest' of Theseus. Hesiod, indeed, wrote a 'Descent of Theseus,' now lost, and such an adventure seems interwoven in the 'Odyssey,' where Circe, the enchantress, counterpart of Istar, furnishes Ulysses with directions for his visit to the land of the shades.

The root of the story thus being the going down of Tammuz into the seven-walled city of the dead, it would naturally be asked, Where is the gate of this city? And, as it was always 'in the west,' alike to Egyptian, Babylonian, Phoenician, and Greek, the place depended on the country where the question was asked. The story of Europa, and of Theseus and Ariadne, is acknowledged to be Phoenician; and we can well understand how, looking out from the Syrian sea-board, Crete, the island in the west, became one of the first of many such points, which, as civilisation came westward, removed farther and farther to the setting sun. Sicily, in the story of Persephone; and again, beyond the Pillars of Hercules. Procopius has a story how the dead assembled on the coast of Gaul and were ferried over to Britain; they were, indeed, invisible, but the bark sank deep into the waters with the burden, and its speed answered to an unknown force.

Teneriffe was another such site, so that in a Spanish map of 1346 it bears the name of the Island of Hades; Ireland had 'St Patrick's purgatory;' beyond, again, it is the New Atlantis of the western ocean; and in the time of Columbus the people still had a tradition of a country to which they gave the name of 'Seven Cities.' Stories also would naturally enough arise of persons who by accident or by enticements strayed over that threshold. Pausanias tells us of a man of Gnossus who strayed into a cave and was overcome by a sleep that lasted forty years; Pliny has a similar tale; and such are the mediæval stories of Tannhauser, Thomas the Rhymer, and Ogier the Dane, for which see Wright's 'Patrick's Purgatory,' Baring Gould's 'Curious Myths,' and Hartland's 'Science of Fairy Tales.'

In another set of stories entirely parallel, it is the maiden who is carried off to the dark under world. Persephone gathering the crocuses and the white lilies of the fields in Enna is borne off like

Europa, not to Crete, but to the dark labyrinth of the under world by its lord Pluto, to spend a portion of her time away from the bright summer world, 'she herself the spring,' as Dante says. Such a story finds its explanation in this other from the Romance of Alexander.

In farther India, Alexander,having seen most of the wonders of that land of wonders, comes 'to a district where he beheld women, who being interred during the winter sprung up to life on the approach of summer, with renovated grace and beauty, or, as it is prettily expressed in the metrical romance of 'Lambert li Cors,' as given by Dunlop:—

'Quant l'este revient, et le beau temps s' espure
En guise de fleur blanche revienient a nature.'

And so it comes in all the pretty stories that this imprisoned heroine has to be awakened by the kiss of the hero, of the Theseus or Sigurd type; and so, too, their palace is set round with ring fences, seven. In Hindu story, Rama dreams of a peerless beauty, and is told that she lives afar off in (1) a glass palace, (2) round the palace runs a river, (3) round the river is a garden of flowers, (4—7) and round the garden are four thick groves of trees. Thousands of princes have failed to overcome these difficulties; all, until the chosen hero comes. In another, *Panch-Phul Ranee*, 'The Queen of the five flowers,' dwelt in a small house round which were seven wide ditches and seven great hedges of spears (Old Deccan Days).

In the Russian stories the hero goes to the other world through a hole in the ground, he slays a vast snake or composite creature, Koshchei the deathless, and frees the captive maiden. In the Servian version he regains earth by the flight of an eagle. The best known of all these tales is ' The Sleeping Beauty,' 'La Belle au Bois Dormant' of Perrault. Grimm's 'Briar Rose,' who sleeps within a maze of briars that none may penetrate until the hero and the time—the spring—are come.

In the Ramayana Sita, called 'daughter of the furrow,' is carried off by Ravana the king of the under world and lord of riches; she is won back by Rama, but the earth ever claims her again;

as Professor Max Muller, speaking of Brynhild says, thus we see
that the awaking and budding spring is gone, carried away by
Gunnar; like Proserpina by Pluto; like Sita by Ravana.'
A story similar to this, told of 'the Queen of the flowers,'
'Rosebriar,' or Rosa-Mundi, gets attached to a real Rosamond
Clifford, 'the fairest flower in all the worlde.' The maze of
Woodstock thus appears in Stow:—'Rosamond, the fayre
daughter of Walter, Lord Clifford, concubine to Henry Il. (poi-
soned by Queen Eleanor, as some thought), dyed at Woodstock
(A.D. 1177), where king Henry had made for her a house of
wonderful working; so that no man or woman might come to
her, but he that was instructed by the king, or such as were right
secret with him touching the matter. This house after some was
named Labyrinthus or Dedalus worke, which was wrought like
a knot in a garden called a maze; but it was commonly said that
lastly the Queen came to her by a clue of thridde, or silke, and
so dealt with her that she lived not long after; but when she was
dead she was buried at Godstow in an house of nunnes, beside
Oxford, with these verses upon her tomb

'Hic jacit in tumba, Rosa mundi, non Rosa munda:
Non redolet, sed olet, quae redolere solet.'

We will leave the myth with the beautiful story in
Maundeville of the daughter of 'Ypocras' changed into a serpent,
'and they say that she shall remain in that form until the time
that a knight come who shall be so bold that he dare come to her
and kiss her on the mouth, and she lies in an old castle in a cave,
and appears twice or thrice in the year.' The castle in the cave,
not the maiden, is all that properly belongs to our subject.

This imagery of the under world, as the labyrinth of the dead,
had a further influence on architecture than the figured mazes
of the floors. It formed the ideal plan of the tomb.
Maspero is clear as to this. 'During the day the pure soul was
in no serious danger, but in the evening, when the eternal waters which flow along the vaulted heavens fall in vast cascades
adown the west and are engulphed in the bowels of the earth
the soul follows the escort of the sun and the other luminary
gods into the lower world bristling with ambuscades and per-

ils. For twelve hours the divine squadron defiles through long
and gloomy corridors, where numerous genii, some hostile,
some friendly, now struggle to bar the way, and now to aid it
in surmounting the difficulties of the journey. Great doors, each
guarded by a gigantic serpent, were stationed at intervals, and
led to an immense hall full of flame and fire, peopled by hide-
ous monsters and executioners, whose office it was to torture the
damned. Then came more dark and narrow passages, more
blind gropings in the gloom, more strife with malevolent genii,
and again the welcoming of the propitious gods. At midnight
began the upward journey towards the eastern region of the
world; and in the morning, having reached the confines of the
Land of Darkness, the sun emerged from the east to light another
day.' The tombs of the kings were constructed upon the model
of the world of night. They had their passages, their doors, their
vaulted halls, which plunged down into the depths of the mountain.' The wall-paintings carry farther this same intention; if the
planning gives the geography these give the very scenery of the
lower world. 'At Thebes as at Memphis the intention was to se-
cure to the double the enjoyment of his new abode, and to usher
the soul into the company of the gods of the Solar Osirian cycle
as well as to guide it through the labyrinth of the infernal regions. Taken as a series, these tableaux form an illustrated narrative of the travels of the sun and the soul through the twenty-
four hours of the day and night. Each hour is represented, as also
the domain of each hour, with its circumscribing boundary, the
door of which is guarded by a huge serpent. These serpents have
their various names, as "Fire Face," "Flaming Eye," "Evil Eye."
He was assailed like Dante and Virgil at the gates of Hell, by
frightful sounds and clamourings. Each circle had its voice not
to be confounded with the voices of other circles. Here the sound
was as an immense humming of wasps; yonder it was as the
lamentation of women for their husbands, and the howling of
she beasts for their mates; elsewhere it was as the rolling of the
thunder. The sarcophagus as well as the walls were covered with
these scenes of joyous or sinister import.'

This interpretation is fully borne out by Perrot. 'The soul had
to appear before the tribunal of Osiris, the sun of night.... The
tomb had its snares and narrow passages, its gaping depths, and
the mazes of its intersecting corridors. Thus the tombs of the

Theban period embody the Egyptian solution of the problem which has always exercised mankind. Their subterranean corridors were a reproduction upon a smaller scale of the leading characteristics of the under world.' ... 'A reproduction in small of the regions of the other world.'

Miss Edwards writes of the Tombs of the Kings: 'To go down into one of these great sepulchres is to descend one's self into the lower world, and to tread the path of the shades; crossing the threshold we look up, half expecting to read those terrible words in which all who enter are warned to leave hope behind them. The passage slopes before our feet; the daylight fades behind us. At the end of the passage comes a flight of steps, and from the bottom of that flight of steps we see another corridor slanting down into depths of utter darkness.'

The tomb of Seti I. penetrates 470 feet and is 180 feet deep in the earth; another has some 24,000 square feet taken up by the passages, halls, staircases, pits, and chambers of the tomb. The inside of the magnificent alabaster sarcophagus of Seti I. in the Soane Museum is entirely covered with engravings giving the course of the sun and the passage of the gateways to reach the Hall of Justice. This is an Egyptian atlas, nor were they without a handbook to the land from which no tourist returns, for the guide-book for the dead was laid in the coffin, telling them of all the turnings, and of all the ruses of the wicked spirits who would entice them away from the one true path. Just as Mr Carl Bock tells us that, when a chief dies in Borneo, directions are chanted so that the dead shall not mistake the way and may avoid tempting but false allurements.

On a wide comparison, important tombs are generally labyrinthine; and it may be suggested that the carved maze-like patterns—those incised on the Mycenæ slabs, for instance, as shown by Schliemann—had sometimes the intention of figuring the grave land. The Etruscan tomb chambers are particularly involved, as may be seen in the plans given by Dennis. The tomb of Lars Porsenna is thus described by Pliny:—' He was buried under the city of Clusium, in a spot where he has left a monument of rectangular masonry, each side whereof is three hundred feet wide and fifty high, and within the square of the basement is an inextricable labyrinth; out of which, no one who ventures in without a clue of thread, can ever find an exit.'

In the initiations and mysteries, imitations of the labyrinth of the dark world seem to have been built. Professor Sayce quotes from an Assyrian tablet which describes the initiation of a priest of the Sun-god Samas, who is 'made to descend into an artificial imitation of the lower wor]d.' And the Elusinian Mysteries embodied the same thought. In Buddhist story we are told that Asoka in his evil days actually built 'a hell' and tortured people there.

Another widely distributed myth in connection with old buildings, that of the underground passage would seem a parallel thought, perhaps best explained by this underway of the sun, which everyone felt assured must go under his own particular temple. Be this as it may, we are likely to be told in many old church and abbey in England, especially if ruined, that 'there is a passage underground which runs from here for miles and miles; it crosses under the river, and the other end is at the castle.' The story is told in France, in one instance, of all the way from Arles to the amphitheatre at Nimes. Sir H. Layard heard the same tale in the wildest part of Persia; just as it was told Herodotus in Egypt that there was a subterranean gallery from the Great Pyramid to the Nile; or to the French traveller Theveniot, that it passed from the Pyramid to come out of the head of the great Sphynx. The Euphrates Expedition spent some time in searching for a passage which was reported to have existed under the river (Ainsworth). A story like this, once having obtained a hold on the imagination, seems to have an undying vitality.

CHAPTER VIII

THE GOLDEN GATE OF THE SUN

> *...The eastern, gate*
> *Where the great sun begins his state.*
> —MILTON.

> *'The doors of Heaven seem slowly to open,*
> *and what are called the bright flocks of the*
> *Dawn step out of the dark stable, returning*
> *to their wonted pastures. . . . Not only the*
> *east, but the west and the south and the*
> *north, the whole temple of Heaven, is*
> *illuminated.*
> —MAX MÜLLLER (Comp. Myth.).

WHEN the earth, or rather the wall of mountains surrounding the utmost bounds of ocean, was the foundation of the solid sky, some contrivance was necessary to account for the disappearance and return of the sun. A new sun, it was thought, was created in the morning to die at night, the creature of a day. Others believed that when it reached the ocean it was floated round by the north to the place of rising in the east; or that, as the earth rose in the north like a great mountain, the sun was periodically hidden behind it. The general early view, however, was that there were two openings —the Gates of the East, and the Gates of the West. Through the one the sun enters in the morning the mundane temple, to pass out at the other in the evening, and thence pursue its way back by the dark path of the under world.

Thus Hesiod:—

'There night and day, near passing, mutual greeting still
Exchange, alternate as they glide athwart
The brazen threshold vast. This enters, that
Forth issues, nor the two can one abode
At once contain. This passes forth and roams
The round of earth. That in the mansion waits
Till the due season of her travel come.'

In the Veda:—' The dawn shone with brilliance and opened for us the doors that open high and wide with their frames.'

In Babylonia the same scheme is shown, in such texts as the invocations to the rising sun, given in 'Records of the Past,' and by Lenormant, of which the first is curiously like Hesiod. 'He opened great gates on every side; he made strong the portals on the left hand and on the right; in the centre he placed luminaries. The moon he appointed to rule the night and to wander through the night until the dawn of day.'

'Sun, thou shinest in the lowest heavens: Thou openest the bolts which close the high heavens: Thou openest the gate of Heaven.' Or:—' In the great door of the high heavens in the opening which belongs to thee.' Steps led up the sky from the east gate and descended to the west (Lenormant). Dr Hayes Ward in the American Journal of Archæology (Vol. 3), shows some dozen Babylonian seals, with intaglios of the Sun-god passing through the double-valved gate of the East and beginning to climb the mountain of the sky. The gate has two guardian figures.

To the Egyptians, the sun was The Opener. The gates to the grave land are often mentloned in the Book of the Dead, and are figured on the tombs.

In Virgil, it is the slamming of these great portals of the firmament that makes the thunder resound from the whole vault of heaven; probably a primitive thought, as it is such a good explanation, 'quem super origens porta tonat caeli' (Georg. iii. 260).

To the Phoenicians, Hercules (Melkarth) the sungod, established in the distant west the Pillars of Hercules, identified afterwards with the mountains on either hand at the Straits of Gibraltar; but even as late as Tacitus it was not decided where they were, nor what.

Such being the gates of the world structure, we may expect temple doors to have a definite relation to their great prototypes; and accordingly in chapter iii. we saw that not only did the building offer its four walls to the four heavenly aspects, but it was the universal early practice for the great door to be 'the Gate of Sunrise.' This door of enormous size was properly the sole opening to the temple, serving as much for light as to enter by; it was thrown open at dawn, and the sun thus entered the world temple and its microcosm at one bound. His symbol signs as we shall see the temple gates, and by a natural reaction, what belongs to one idea is reflected in the other.

In Egypt the gates of the under world through which the sun passes are shown in the illustrations to the Book of the Dead as great pylons like the entrances to the temples. Every temple pylon becomes a sun gate, and sculptured and painted on the centre of its lintel is the red disc of the sun. 'The winged globe,' says Wilkinson, 'always having its place over the doorways.' And Perrot and Chipiez, 'It was generally ornamented with the winged globe, an emblem which was afterwards appropriated by the nations which became connected with Egypt. This emblem in its full development was formed by the solar disc, supported on each side by the uraeus, the serpent which meant royalty. The disc and its supporters are flanked by two wide-stretching wings with rounded fan-shaped extremities, which symbolized the untiring activity of the sun in making its daily journey from one end of the firmament to the other. Egyptologists tell us that the group as a whole signifies the triumph of right over wrong, the victory of Horus over Set (light over dark). An inscription at Edfou tells us that after this victory Thoth ordered that the emblem should be carved over every door in Egypt, and in fact there are very few lintels without it.' That is, there was a sacred legend saying that the God of Wisdom ordered the sun to be represented on every portal, to symbolise the victory of the sun over darkness, in the struggle at daybreak at the gates of the east.

These colossal gates are the all-important features to which the shrines are but secondary; so much so that an Egyptian temple might be defined as a series of gates. They were most impres-

sive in themselves and their ritual significance must have awed into thought and silence whoever entered. Miss Edwards thus describes Karnak, Denderah, and the rock-cut temple at Aboo Simbel. 'Crossing this court in the glowing sunlight we came to a mighty doorway. Only a jutting fragment of the lintel stone remains. That stone when perfect measured forty feet and ten inches across. The doorway must have been full a hundred feet in height' (Karnak).

'The winged globe depicted upon a gigantic scale on the curve of the cornice seems to hover above the central doorway' (Denderah).

'On certain mornings in the year, in the very heart of the mountain, as the sun comes up above the eastern hill-tops, one long level beam strikes through the doorway, pierces the inner darkness like an arrow, penetrates to the sanctuary, and falls like fire from Heaven upon the altar at the feet of the gods. No one who has watched for the coming of that shaft of sunlight can doubt that it was a calculated effect, and that the excavation was directed at one especial angle in order to produce it. In this way Ra, to whom the temple was dedicated, may be said to have

entered in daily, and by a direct manifestation of his presence
to have approved the sacrifices of his worshippers' (Aboo
Simbel). Sculptured over the door is a figure of Horus bearing
the sun disc.

An inscription of Rameses II. on the temple of Ptah, at Memphis, might well boast.—

'Its gates are like the heavenly horizon of light.'

The Phoenicians likewise signed with the sun the centre of
their doorways, borrowing the Egyptian orb at Byblos. At Ebba
the sun rises between two moons (see above from Perrot). The
great ceremonial propylae to the temples, as shown on the coins,
have the sun and moon depicted immediately above them. And
in the ruins at Medeba, in Moab, Dr Tristram found upon a lintel over an ancient doorway the sculptured emblems of the sun
and moon. The acroterion of the portico of the Heraum at Olympia, the oldest known temple in Greece,was a solar disc; and
another instance of the same kind is given by Lebas and
Waddington.

In the classic period of Syrian art most of the great temple doors had sculptured on the under side of the epistyle an enormous eagle with expanded wings. The great eastern door of the sun temple at Baalbek, 'city of the sun,' is the finest of these; it is 21 feet wide, and therefore, some 40 feet high, as the approved proportion was twice as high as broad. 'Here on the lower surface (lintel of the door) is the celebrated figure of the crested eagle, beautifully wrought, holding in his talons a caduceus, and in his beak strings of long garlands extending on each side where the other ends are borne up by flying genii. The crest shows that it was not the Roman eagle; but as the same figure is found in the great Temple of the Sun at Palmyra, Volney and others regarded it as the Oriental eagle consecrated to the sun' (Robinson 'Palestine Researches').

The lintel of Palmyra is figured by Wood and Dawkins. The door faces due east, and the great eagle appears to fly into the temple, the wings expanded ten or twelve feet; the rest of the space is occupied by stars, and two genii of the dawn. In front, on the eastern side of the vast court, 700 feet square, is a magnificent propylon.

The Memoirs of the Palestine Exploration Society describe remains of a temple of similar style at Kades, fronting full east, with three doorways, the centre one being very large. 'The lintel, which lies broken in front of the doorway, bears on the under side a representation of the winged deity, the Sun; it resembles the lintel of the small temple at Baalbek.'

Another remarkable instance is the great eastern portal of the temple of Baalzamin, figured and described by De Vogue. Here is, first, a 'solar head with rays' on the lintel; the lower side of the architrave of the pillared portico has the solar bird, and on its front face is a large sculptured disc.

The cornice or arch of the door was at times only charged with a circular sun-disc, as that of the tomb at Shefa Amr, in Galilee, here figured. It was this tradition that was afterwards followed in the universal Syrian Christian custom of placing a disc with the sacred monogram or cross on the lintel, usually with ribbon-like appendages, right and left, which are direct survivals of the Egyptian uraeus, that in a similar position accompanied the sun's orb. This becomes a decorative commonplace in Byzantine art, either at Constantinople or Venice.

In Persia also the gates were dedicated to the sun. At Hatra,
a temple, supposed to have been erected under the Parthian
dynasty, has the sun rising between two moons displayed on the
eastern door; this, and many others, have birds right and left,
emblems of dawn. Later, under the Sassanian kings, the tradition was preserved on the great arch of Chosroes II., at Tak-i-

Bostan. Flandin shows at its crown a crescent moon, and on either hand flying genii. There was also, Rawlinson thinks, a ball,
'thus presenting to the spectator, at the culminating point of the
whole sculpture, the familiar emblems of two of the national
divinities.'

A symbol of the sun is placed in the same way centrally over the great ceremonial gates of the enclosure of the Buddhist topes, which face the cardinal points, the ritual providing that the procession should enter by the gate at the east, circle round the dome—representing the firmament—and go out at the west. These wheel symbols of the sun remain at Sanchi; and the custom would seem to have been followed generally, for an ancient native authority says that the Raja of Ceylon inserted gems in the centres of *the four suns* in the great tope. 'This, perhaps,' adds General Cunningham, 'points to the absorption of the ancient sun-worship into Buddhism; for the wheel was one of the common and obvious emblems of the sun.' (In the Talmud the sun was the great whirling wheel. 'But for the noise of the solar wheel, the hubbub of The City (Rome) might be heard; but for the noise of the city, the sound of the revolving wheel.')

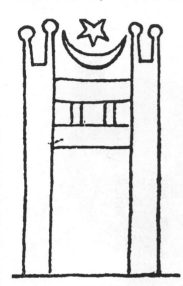

In Orissa, we find not only the sun, or sun and moon, but the whole of the planets ' The *Nava Graha*, or nine planets, adorn the lintels of all the temples of the Kessari line' (Fergusson). Sometimes they are sculptured figures, at others merely nine bosses.

It is impossible not to compare the great Buddhist gateways, with their triple lintels and sun-discs, to the propylons of Phoenician temples preserved in semblance on coins (see that of Paphos, figured below). These have double lintels binding the otherwise isolated sideposts, and over the centre of the lintel are the sun and moon. Probably the doorposts of the sun-gates in the East and West are the origin of the two pillars that served for symbol of Melkarth in Phoenician temples, for this symbol was not a single stone, a shapeless ærolith, but a pair of pillars of metal or emerald glass, almost certainly connected by a lintel. They are bethels and 'Gates of Heaven' dedicated to the Opener. Perrot remarks that, ' in speaking of the Phoenician and Syrian temples, classic authors often mentioned the tall pillars which rose in couples before the sanctuary. In the temples of Melkarth, at Gades, they were of bronze, eight cubits high, and bore a long inscription. In the shrine of the same deity at Tyre the admiration of Herodotus was stirred by the sight of two shafts, one of pure gold and the other of emerald, that is, of lapis lazuli or coloured glass. These shafts or stelae probably stood in similar places to those occupied at Jerusalem by Jachin and Boaz, the two famous bronze columns, which rose at the threshold of a building also erected by a Phoenician architect.'

Such pillars have been found engraved as a symbol of Melkarth on a votive stele (see Perrot's Phoenicia), and they really form a gateway, a trilithon, for, standing apart, they are connected by a lintel; over them are the sun and moon—a counterpart of the gateway to the temple on the coin of Paphos.

Professor Robertson Smith, in the recent volume of the 'Encyclopædia Britannica ' (art. Temple), says definitely: 'Such twin pillars or twin stelae in stone are of constant occurrence in Phoenician sacred art, and are still familiar to us as the Pillars of Hercules.'

The Egyptian obelisks that flank the great portals of the temples, at once occur to us as having a corresponding intention. In both ancient and modern times the symbolism of these is understood to be solar. 'Dedicated to the sun,' says that at Rome set up by Augustus. According to Pliny, they 'represent rays of the sun.' 'The obelisks,' says Ebers, 'were sacred to Ra, the sun.' It has been remarked that sometimes they were entirely gilt, that the apex was at other times covered with gilded bronze, and some at least appear to have carried spheres or discs, also of gilded metal.

An inscription describes two obelisks erected by Queen Hashop, the sister of the great Thothmes: 'Their tops are covered with copper of the best war tributes of all countries; they are seen a great many miles off. *It is a flood of shining splendour when the sun rises between them*' (Brugsch). The Assyrian slabs and bronzes seem to make it clear that 'sun pillars' flanked the entrances, or were set up right and left of an altar.

In India, pillars supporting sun-wheels are found at the entrance gates to sacred buildings. Fergusson says: ' My impression is that all the pillars surmounted by lions in front of the caves, as at Karla, supported originally a wheel in metal.' Such 'chakra pillars' are frequent on the Buddhist sculptures, and the wheels appear to have been turned on an axle. In Orissa, Dr Hunter tells us, 'sun pillars' are surmounted by the charioteer of the god, or by an eagle.

In Peru and Mexico we get exactly the same interpretation of the universal thought. At the gold-plated temple of Cuzco 'the doors opened to the east, and at the far end was the golden disc of the sun, placed so as to reflect the first rays of the morning on its brilliant surface, and, as it were, reproduce the golden luminary.' 'Columns of the sun' were erected in Peru. 'They were regarded as "seats of the sun," who loved to rest upon them. At the equinoxes and solstices they placed golden thrones upon them for him to sit upon.' Quadrants were traced at the base as dials (Reville, Hibbert Lectures).

The monolithic doorway at Tiahuanco has on the centre of the lintel 'a figure, probably representing the sun' (Clements Markham).

In China it is the same. A tomb doorway at Canton, figured by Dresser, has the entire lintel sculptured with the sun rising from the clouds; but the most usual form is to charge the beam or the ridge of the great roofed gates (*Pailoos*) with a flaming sun rising between two guardian dragons.

The custom of erecting such a fore-gate is still maintained at the Shinto temples of Japan. Dr Dickson says the temple enclosure 'is marked by a stone *torii* or sacred portal. The torii is characteristic of all Shinto shrines; it consists of two upright posts, on the tops of which rests a horizontal beam, projecting slightly on each side; beneath this is a smaller cross beam, whose ends do not project. The material used is generally wood, but may be stone or bronze. The original purpose of the torii was to serve as a perch for the sacred fowls, *kept to give warning of the daybreak*; but after the introduction of Buddhism it came to be regarded as a gateway.' We may remark here, that the weathercocks on every church are gilded birds that greet the sun.

In M. Bing's recent book on Japanese art it is remarked that everything is symbolical in the architecture of Japan. 'The torii is a "roost," as the word indicates, and its two bent beams are made in order that the sun, the King of Nature, may come, like a bird, and perch there.' Hokusai, the great Japanese artist, has devoted a book to this very subject, and he accounts for the curves of the massive roofs of the temple porches thus: 'The sun, represented by a large circle on a horizontal line, is supported on its right and left by four smaller circles, representing the four seasons.' Though a diagram which he gives really seems far fetched, it is interesting that he associates the sun thus definitely with the gate; and our wide comparison sufficiently answers the question of the writer who quotes this from Hokusai in the firstnamed work, and asks, 'Has this explanation any historical value, or is it only ingenious and poetical? At any rate, it is enough that it should come from a Japanese artist, who does not limit to that extent his indications of a like nature in order to prove how strong is the conviction in Japan that architectural forms come, more or less, from hazy recollections of some ancient symbolism.'

The suggestion that the torii were primarily roosts either in purpose or by etomology is certainly not well founded, although it was made by Mr Satow. They were doubtless derived with Buddhism from the gates to the Indian topes there called torana, 'Celestial gates.'

In Japan, the palace of the god-king at Kioto is entered by 'The Gate of the Sun' (Reid); and Dr Dresser saw pilgrims worshipping the rising sun as seen between two rocks connected by a straw-band, from which Shinto symbols were pendant.

These Shinto symbols are the torii itself, the mirror, slips of paper attached to a wand, and the rope. This last is of rice-straw, 'varying in thickness from the heavy cable which often hangs across a torii or temple entrance to that no thicker than a finger, which is suspended across house doors.' In Peru a chain was suspended from two rocks across a valley to catch the sun (Frazer, 'Golden Bough'). The two pillars in front of the temple of Paphos, C. O. Muller says, were joined by a chain. In Hindu temples a chain is sometimes found festooned across the top of the portal. The thought of localising the sun by catching him at the eastern door would thus seem general. The actual sun, we may remember, was often thought to be chained in the performance of his daily toil.

In Arcadia, Pausanias visited a grove of Zeus:—' And on the highest crest of the whole mountain there is a mound of heaped-up earth, the altar of Zeus Lycaeus; and the most part of Peloponnesus can be seen from that place; and before the altar stand *two pillars facing the rising sun, and thereon golden eagles* of yet more ancient workmanship ' (viii. 2).

At the most ancient of the sacred sites in Greece —the pre-Homeric oracle of Zeus of Dodona —were two columns; on one was a brazen bowl, on the other a brazen statue. Against the bowl it was arranged that balls attached to chains should strike, swayed by the wind. It cannot be doubted that the chain-work and pomegranates around the bowls on the pillars of Solomon were intended, in the same way, to form æolian bells, shivering out music to every breath of wind, like the golden bells suspended about the exterior of Burmese temples, which are definitely intended to recall the sweet sounds of paradise. For these gates of Solomon and Herod see the chapter 'Toran' in Ferguson's 'Temple of the Jews.'

The gate, according to Josephus, had no doors, 'for it symbolised the heavens, everywhere open and everywhere visible.' In the Talmud it is said that it was 40 cubits high and 20 broad. Above the pillars were five beams of wood, each of which projected at the ends a cubit more than the one below. 'A golden vine was spread over this gateway of the temple, and it was carried on the supporting beams.' (Other Syrian gateways were ornamented with sculptured vine; and this gives us another Byzantine origin.) The whole porch and inner doorway were entirely covered with gold. This was opened at the moment of sunrise; when the noise, it was said, of loosing the bolts was heard even to Jericho. Across the porch hung a veil embroidered with stars.

The Greek *Propylaea* of the Acropolis follows the same thought; and it is of some interest to note that the early Greek and Etruscan doorways were of forms suitable and common to these isolated structures —the jambs inclined, and the lintel widely over-lapping them.

The Japanese say that 'unless you passed under the toran on entering the temple your prayers would not be listened to' (Fergusson); and some Christians who were obliged to give up their faith had to pass under one of these torii, as a sign; for this, too, is none other than the gate of heaven. Probably the custom of squeezing between pillars has been at times associated with this thought. St Willibald, in the eighth century, says of the Ascension Church: 'the man who can creep between the wall and the columns is free from his sins.'

Pairs of pillars are associated together also as memorials of the dead, or used to record the past. The two brazen columns in the temple of Hercules at Gades bore a long legend. And Procopius, in 'Wars of the Vandals,' says that in his time two huge stone stelae existed in the Numidian town of Tirgisis, inscribed by the inhabitants, in Phoenician, with the legend, 'We are they who fled from before Joshua, the robber, the son of Nun.' A yet older record was said to preserve, in this way, the learning of those before the flood. 'The sons of Seth wrote the knowledge of things celestial upon two columns.' 'And that their inventions might not be lost before they were sufficiently known, upon Adam's prediction that the world was to be destroyed at one time by the force of fire, and at another time by the violence of water, they made two pillars, the one of brick, the other of stone; they inscribed their discoveries on them both, that, in case the pillar of brick should be destroyed by the flood, the pillar of stone might remain, and exhibit these discoveries to mankind, and also inform them that there nas another pillar of brick erected by them. Now this remains in the land of Siriad to this day.' (Josephus, I.-II.)

The pair of immense pillars before the temple at Hieropolis were said to have been in some way connected with the flood.

The most characteristic and persistent type of tomb was the dolmen, or trilithon; ranging from the rudest balancing of rough stones to perfectly finished work —a pair of columns with an entablature. In this form they are especially found in Syria and places connected with Phoenicia; but the custom is of wider distribution than can be attributed to contact with any one country. Fergusson, in 'Rude Stone Monuments,' has already pointed out the affinity with the toran gateway, giving an illustration of a Buddhist tomb of the toran form as corresponding to the Western sepulchral trilithons. As in Egypt, and generally to the peoples of antiquity, the soul was expected to pass through the gate of the west; and as in most early tombs —those of Persia and Lycia, for example— there is a false door, a mere representation of a doorway, with two guardian watchers; as, furthermore, we have seen that the grave was the under world in double: shall we not be justified in regarding these sepulchral trilithons as at once the door of the tomb and portal of the under world? It was so certainly in Egypt. Maspero tells us how in the tombs of early or later dynasties the chief object is a false door, the entrance to the 'eternal home' of the dead. It is often found in the west, but that position was not prescribed by rule (?). In the earliest times it was indicated like a real door, low and narrow, framed and decorated like the door of an ordinary house, but not pierced through. An inscription graven upon the lintel, in large readable characters, commemorated the name and rank of the owner.' In the pyrarnid of Unas (sixth dynasty), the chamber was lined with alabaster, and engraved to represent great monumental doors; and carrying the duplication even farther, 'small obelisks, about three feet in height, are found in tombs as early as the fourth dynasty. They are placed on either side of the door which leads to the dwelling of the dead.'

In the 'Encyclopædia of India' (Balfour, art. 'Toran') this same suggestion is made: 'The dolmen or trilithic altar in the centre of all those monuments called Druidic, is most probably a toran, sacred to the sun-god, ... to whom (in India), as soon as the temple is raised the toran is erected.'

The Egyptian obelisks were pre-eminently used for important inscriptions, and their symbolic suitability as everlasting records will be reinforced by what Perrot says of the hieroglyphic significance of the obelisk:—' It was used to write the syllable men, which signified *firmness or stability.*' From the Bible Dictionary we learn that *Boaz* and *Jachin*, the names of the pillars of Solomon, had an equivalent value. Jachin, 'he established;' Boaz, 'in him is strength.' Renan reads: 'May the double column firmly stand.' We can hardly doubt longer that twin columns represent the eternal and immovable pillars of the sky-Heaven's gate—through which the worshipper must pass to the temple; or the soul to the other world.

Portals must have guardians. The gateways of the Assyrians were in this respect like the sun gates of the east and the west, where the solid firmament rested on two winged genii in the form of bulls. 'The "path of the Sun" to the "great twin gates" was guarded by the pair of scorpion kerubim ' (Boscawen, Bab. Record).

'We read invocations to the two bulls who flanked the gate of the infernal abode, which were no longer simulacra of stone, but living beings, like the bulls at the gates of the celestial palaces of the gods.'

'The invocation which follows is addressed to the ears of the bull "placed on the right of the bronze enclosure," because they imagined the gate of hell to be flanked by human-headed bulls *like those which guarded the gates of the Assyrian palaces*; only these bulls were living genii: "O great bull, very great bull, which stampest high, which openest access to the interior ! "The bull on the left of the bronze enclosure is invoked in his turn ' (Lenormant).

It is clear at this point that these are not the characteristics of the temple and palace gate read into the solar gateway to the under world, but the exact reverse; for these guardians were known to story ages before it was possible to realise such 'simulacra' in stone as are to be seen in the British Museum. In the inscription on the bull of the gateway at Khorsabad, its great builder says: 'I opened eight gates in the direction of the four cardinal points. I have named the large *gates of the east the gates of Samas* (the sun) and of Bin.' Another king ornaments with silver 'the gate of the sunrise.'

The huge human-headed bulls were reproductions for the gate of the palace, of the creatures that guarded the sun gates of the east and west, to which they were dedicated. 'Such,' says Lenormant, 'are the readings furnished us, from the cuneiform inscriptions, upon the nature and significance of the genii in the form of winged bulls with human countenances whose images were stationed as guardians at the portals of the edifices of Babylonia and Assyria.' These representations of the guardians of the sun gate had a magical and beneficent influence, as is shown in an inscription of Esarhaddon: 'Bulls and lions carved in stone, which with their majestic mien deter wicked enemies from approaching: the guardians of the footsteps, the saviours of the path of the king, who constructed them at the gates.... May the bull of good fortune, the genius of good fortune, the guardian of the footsteps of my majesty, the giver of joy to my heart, for ever watch over it! Never more may its care cease.'

In Egypt the gates of the under world were guarded by creatures in the form of animals which are often mentioned in the Ritual. We saw also that the sun disc was placed over the gateway in memory of the battle between Horus, the rising sun, and the Power of darkness: to wage this war Horus took the shape of a human-headed lion, the sphinx; and this creature is called the 'sun on the horizon.' Are not the sphinxes which guard the entrances of the temples—a single pair, or an avenue of hundreds—evidently derived from these?

It is the same in the East and in Greece. 'The Vedic poets,' says Professor Max Muller, 'have imagined two dogs belonging to Yama, the lord of the departed spirits. They are called the messengers of Yama, bloodthirsty and broad-snouted, brown, foureyed, and pale—the "dawn children." The departed is told to pass by them on his way to the fathers, who are rejoicing with Yama. Yama is asked to protect the departed from these dogs; and finally the dogs themselves are implored to grant life to the living, and to let them see the sun again. These two dogs represent one of the lowest of the many conceptions of morning and evening.... Greece, though she recognised Hermes as guide to the souls of the departed did not degrade him to the rank of the watch-dog of Hades. These watch-dogs, Kerberos and Orthros, represent, however, the two dogs of Yama—the gloom of morning and evening, here conceived as hostile and demoniacal powers.'One of them was black, and the other was spotted.

Now let us compare all this with Homer's conception of a palace as it ought to be, the palace of Alcinous: 'Brazen were the walls, which ran this way and that, from the threshold to the inmost chamber; and round them was a frieze of blue; and golden were the doors that closed in the good house. Silver were the door-posts that were set on the brazen threshold, and silver the lintel thereupon; and the hook of the door was of gold; *and on either side stood golden hounds and silver*, which Hephæstos wrought by his cunning to guard the palace of great-hearted Alcinous, *being free from death and age all their days.*'

This view has already been suggested by Mr Keary in his 'Outlines of Primitive Belief': 'The two gods (of the palace door) have, I fancy, a special meaning. I see in them the descendants of the Sarameys, or whatever in early Aryan belief preceded these guardians of the house of death, who are own brothers to the two dogs of the Wild Huntsman, Hackelburg. The garden which surrounds the palace of Alcinous distinctly presents the picture of a home of the blessed. It is just like the gardens of the Hesperides, and like all pictures which before or after have been drawn of the earthly paradise.'

It is interesting to find these two guardian dogs of the entrance to the death land exist still in Irish observance. Lady Wild tells us that mourners are enjoined not to wail for some time after the passing of the spirit, for fear of waking the two dogs who guard the way, so that they tear the pilgrim when he comes to the gates.

The two great beasts, rampant supports of a central pillar above the Lion gate at Mycenae, are but the guardians of the 'jaws of death, the gate of hell.' An exactly parallel treatment may be found in the British Museum in the gables of the Lycian tombs, where sphinxes guard the false door. Or at times there is a central pillar, like the Mycenae composition, where, unfortunately, the chapiter is broken away. Two such sphinxes, with the pillar, are placed over the central epistyle of the early temple of Assos; and the arrangement afterwards becomes one of the common-places of design, but for long rightly associated with the door of the temple or the tomb. The Chaldean prototype is shown in George Smith's 'Chaldea' Two composite creatures, scorpion-men, 'warders of the sun,' stand on either side of a pillar-like object, and above hovers the symbol of the sun.

This practice of putting horrible human or composite monsters in effigy at the doorway of entrance is universal. The custom probably has a root in the simple nature of things, the at-once-felt appropriateness of it; but there can be no doubt that the guardians of the sun gate were put there in answer to the question, 'Why do the dead return not ?' These beasts 'fawn on all who enter,' but rend all who would pass thence again. 'Easy is the descent to Avernus.'

All over the East, in India, China, Siam, Japan, the gates are so protected. Before the temples of the latter two statues are placed, called 'the Avengers' (Dixon); and Miss Bird tells us that house doors and even cupboards have prints of these warders. Some of the Indian temples have enormous rearing horses, with their riders spearing enemies.

In the early Buddhist structures in Ceylon the gates are guarded by giant creatures, who fulfil the same purpose of magical protection as the genii of Assyria. They are named *dvarpal*, 'guardians of the approaches.' 'These grotesque demon figures were supposed to be endowed with a mysterious power, vested in their intense hideousness, of scaring away enemies.' The groups of flesh-tearing lions at the gates of Lombard churches are identical in their intention. The early Christian use, as shown by De Vogue of Syria, was to put Michael and Gabriel on either side of the door; sometimes also instead of the figures, the disc on the centre of the arch had the letters X. M. G. for Christ, Michael, and Gabriel. The Byzantine 'Manual of Iconography' says these archangels should be painted right and left, inside the door; and Mrs Jameson tells us they were also painted on the jambs of the triumphal arch to the chancel.

If the gate is the doorway of death, it would interpret that curious primitive custom by which to touch the threshold was ominous of evil. Early travellers in the East tell us how carefully this had to be avoided; and we know how brides had to be lifted over the threshold.

It has often been said that we see a system, and read our modern methods of thought into old observances that were followed without an intelligent motive. This is no doubt perfectly true, but it should be urged in reply that a method may explain even the *unconscious* developments of thought. It is no answer to Mr Ruskin to say that Turner allowed that the critic saw more than the painter did in his pictures: that is the critic's justification.

The gateway of one of the Peruvian temples is pierced through a single enormous stone, perfectly squared, and entirely covered with sculptures. So fascinating has been the idea of 'monolithism,' that probably only the supreme difficulty made it infrequent. Tavernier mentions seeing a doorway to a mosque at Taurus 'cut out of a great transparent white stone, four-and-twenty feet high and twelve broad.' The three stones of jambs and lintel were the nearest practicable approximation.

Pausanias tells us of many temples, that their doors were only thrown open once a year. He says the door of the tomb of Helen of Adiabene, at Jerusalem, 'cannot be opened except on one particular day of the year. And then it opens by the machinery alone, keeping open for some time, and then shuts again.'

It was usual to cover the east door itself with shining metal. Nebuchadnezzar says of the temple of Babylon:—The gate of glory I made as brilliant as the sun.' So well known was this practice in Greece, that Aristophanes makes a passing allusion to gilded temple doors. In Syria it was the same; at the temple of Mabog (Hierapolis) the doors were gilded, as also was the entire sanctuary, walls and ceiling. Two immense columns, one hundred and eighty feet high, flanked the door, inside which, on the left, was placed the throne of the sun. The great eastern gate of Herod's temple was entirely gilt, and also a region of the wall surrounding it. So it is that we get the 'Golden Gate' of the Protevangelion; and in Jerusalem to-day the gateway entering the sacred area has the same name. Constantinople and Ravenna had such gates, and so had Rome, for the 'Mirabilia' speaks of the Porta Aurea. In Egypt, as we have seen, the obelisks were gilt, so probably were the doors; and the custom holds good in modern India and Burmah. At the Palace of Spalato, the four gates at the cardinal points were called gold, brass, iron, and the sea gate. Some of the Greek temple doors were overlaid with ivory. The earliest Christian buildings naturally looked to the temple as a type, and it would appear from Eusebius, that even the toran found a place in the new structures. Describing the Church of Tyre, he says that a magnificent propylon was built, far off toward the sun-rising, to attract the passer-by; passing through the court and other gates, the entrance to the temple itself was reached, which also fronted the rising sun, and was covered with brass.

Later, when the churches were entered opposite the setting sun, the power of the old symbolism was lost, but it survived long, if largely unconsciously. Right into the Middle Ages shining metal was the only fit material for the doors of entrance. Those of the basilica of St John, at Damascus, were of silver; those of Constantinople and Rome of gilt bronze.

It was also customary throughout the Middle Ages to sculpture the signs of the zodiac on the arch of the great west door. The doorways of Venice, especially, have very generally the sun and moon sculptured at the crown of the arch; and there is a fine instance at Piacenza, with the signs of the zodiac up the arch, and the sun and moon at its zenith. In the 'Stones of Venice,' Mr Ruskin says: 'The sun and moon on each side of the cross are constantly employed on the keystones of Byzantine arches.'

Of the archivolts of the central doorway of St Mark's, he says: 'The sculptures of the months are on the under surface, beginning at the bottom, on the left hand of the spectator as he enters, and following in succession round the archivolt; separated, however, into two groups at the centre by a beautiful figure of the youthful Christ, sitting in the midst of a slightly hollowed sphere, covered with stars, to represent the firmament, and with the attendant sun and moon set one on each side, to rule over the day and over the night.'

But to return—when Josiah cleared the Temple of Jerusalem of the idolatrous objects and symbols that had been set up there by his apostate predecessor, it was from the eastern gate that the symbolic chariot of the sun was removed. 'And he took away the horses that the kings of Judah had given to the sun at the *entering in* of the house of the LORD ... and burned the chariots of the sun with fire.' It was, doubtless, a throne for the sun like that at Mabog.

The beautiful Greek metope of Phoebus rising in his quadriga, found at Ilium, represented as it is coming directly outwards, was evidently intended for a position over the eastern entrance portico; either alone in the centre, or balanced by the declining car of night. As Dr Schliemann says: 'Helios here, so to speak, bursts forth from the gates of day, and sheds the light of his glory over the universe.' This, the actual moment of sunrise, is a fine and fitting subject for the eastern entrance of a temple; it is found yet more dramatically in the eastern pediment of the Parthenon. The scene of the sculpture is Olympus, and the central subject is the birth of Athene. In the left angle of the pediment—to quote Mr Murray—' Helios is represented emerging in his chariot from the waves. It has been noted by Michaelis that the angle in which this figure was placed is the darkest spot in the eastern pediment, and that it is only fully illuminated at the moment of sunrise. The right angle of the pediment belongs to the car of the goddess of the night ... the horse a marked contrast in motive to the pair in the opposite angle. The heads of the horses of Helios are thrown upwards with fiery impatience as they spring from the waves; the downward inclination of the head here described, and the distended nostril, indicate that the car of Selene is about to vanish below the horizon.' It is the precise moment of the double action at sunrise, as given by Homer and Hesiod, 'where herdsman hails herdsman as he drives in his flock, and the other who drives forth answers the call. There might a sleepless man have earned a double wage, the one as neat-herd, the other shepherding white flocks; so near are the outgoings of the night and the day.'

Next to Helios, the mountain god reclines, and next again the Hours. 'Self-moving ground, upon their hinges the gates of Heaven, *whereof the Horae are warders*' (Il. v. 749).

Bournouf, in his *L_gende Ath_nienne*, examines the orientation of this temple: a carefully engraved line of axis on the pavement points I4⁰ 11' north of east, where he thinks the first ray of dawn appears at the equinoxes. The pediment pictures the eternal drama of the dawn, 'the whole subject is a reflection of the sky as in a mirror.'

The great portico of the Parthenon is the very gate of the sun. Out of *it* the sun rises and the night withdraws, above *it* stand the gods on Olympus.

Finally the gate is one of the most essential symbols, religious or political. Holy places like Babel were 'God's gates,' and at the gate the king met the people in judgment. Eastern palaces had a porch like Solomon's, 'a porch for the throne where he might judge, even the porch of judgment' (I Kings vii. 7).

Having traced the tradition, we are in a position to sketch the ritual of the sunrise at the eastern portal with the aid of the fine description by Ezekiel of the 'abominations done in Israel.' 'And he brought me into the inner court of the LORD'S house, and, behold, at the door of the temple of the LORD, between the porch and the altar, were about five-and-twenty men, with their backs toward the temple of the LORD, and their faces toward the east, and they worshipped the sun toward the east.'

It is the moment of sunrise, chill and expectant; all the gates are thrown open to the east. The worshippers are waiting, and the golden tips of the obelisks are already burning. The sun shows its red rim through the open ceremonial gate of the outer court. They prostrate themselves.

There is a sudden awaking sense of heat and life and light, a passing vibration in the air. The little bells festooned from pillar to pillar shiver out silver notes; a deep strain vibrates from the sanctuary. They stand on their feet. The great gates of the temple close with a clangour that reverberates like thunder.

Baal has entered into his temple.

CHAPTIER IX

PAVEMENTS LIKE THE SEA

'...The sea, flat like a pavement of lapis-lazuli, ascended imperceptibly to the sky on the horizon.'
—FLAUBERT.

IN the 'Stones of Venice' Mr Ruskin wrote of the floors of the basilicas of Murano and St Mark: 'We feel giddy at the first step we make on the pavement, for it is of Greek mosaic, waved like the sea, and dyed like a dove's neck.' 'Round the domes of its roof the light enters only through narrow apertures, like large stars; and here and there a ray or two from some far-away casement wanders into the darkness, and casts a narrow phosphoric stream upon the waves of the marble that heave and fall in a thousand colours along the floor.'

Mr Street, in 1854, described 'the wild beauty of the pavement' in St Mark's as swelling up and down like a petrified sea; and he went on to suggest that this *undulation of surface* was an intentional making of the floor in the semblance of the sea. This, magnificent as it would be as imagination, has not generally been approved, and the balance of evidence from technical examinations of the construction and settlements is against the theory. As a parallel, Mr Street referred to the pavement of the 'Mother Church' at Constantinople as representing water in its design; but the floor is entirely covered with matting, and it has never been drawn, nor precisely described.

The story of its representing water which appears in many recent books on Constantinople, is borrowed from Von Hammer's description of the church. The original is given by Codinus, an officer of the Imperial palace at Constantinople, who wrote an account of Sta. Sophia in the fifteenth century, from which a friend has made the following extracts. In the church, as finished by Justinian, 'the varied hues of the pavement were like the ocean.' This was destroyed when the roof fell in; and in the repairs undertaken by Justin, the nephew of Justinian, 'as he could not otherwise obtain variegated stones, he sent Marses, the patrician, to Proconnesus to quarry marble as near like it as possible. Four rivers of leek-green marble were laid, like the four streams which flow from Paradise to the sea.' The marbles named are those known to us as pavonazzetto and verde antico: and some friends who examined the floor, as far as it might be seen through the chinks of 'that accursed matting,' say that it is laid in slabs of whitish marble with green bands; but it is impossible without more evidence to say that this is the original floor.

It is only in story that we can find *ideal* architecture—the pure thought unrelated to cost and utility. The romance writers delighted in decorating their dream edifices with marvellous pavements; bronze in the palace of Alcinous, in 'Cupid and Psyche' mosaic pictures of jewels, in mediæval story jasper, onyx, paste of coral, or alternate squares of gold and silver for living chess. But actual pavements have been hardly less remarkable. Some were areas of black marble or wholly of white slabs, 'like snow,' says Procopius of a floor in a church built by Justinian. Another, in the palace at Constantinople, 'imitated the flowers of the field.' In mediæval pavements, the subjects usually are chapters from Nature's story, and in this they follow Roman and Eastern tradition. The four Seasons, for instance, was a favourite subject for classic pavements, whether in Carthage or in Cirencester. A mosaic from a Christian church at Tyre was brought from Syria by Renan, which represented the *Seasons, Months, and Winds*. In Italy, the Year is often enthroned in the centre, holding Sun and Moon, and surrounded by the Months with the several appropriate *Labours of the Fields*. The four Rivers of Eden are poured out of great vases, and the angles are filled up with the beasts of the earth. At Brindisi and Otranto are floors of fine design, whatever may be their meaning:—' The principal divisions are formed by gigantic trees resting upon elephants and extending far into the nave; the branches are alive with animals of all kinds.' These motives, Woltmann says, are borrowed from the designs of Oriental carpets. We find, again and again, that to follow up any thought in decorative design leads to the East, apparently to Persia; and as the farther East was influenced as much by Persian art, we may see here the centre of at least true Aryan design.

When Ahasuerus made his feast at Shushan the floor was 'of porphyry, and marble, and alabaster, and stone of a blue colour' (lapis-lazuli). There is a beautiful Assyrian pavement in the British Museum, of alabaster, wrought like a tapestry; and Sadi tells us of a tomb floored with marble and turquoise. Philostratus describes a temple of the sun seen by Apollonius in India, the walls of which were of red marble, like fire with streaks of gold; on the pavement was an image of the sun, with its rays imitated in dazzling profusion of rubies and diamonds.

We might have expected to find floors with geographies; but—except the carpet of Chosroes, representing a garden with its paths, trees, and running water-courses, with parterres of spring flowers of the brightest hues: and a carpet belonging to one of the Fatimite caliphs, which represented the earth with its mountains, seas, rivers, highways, and cities, especially Mecca and Medinah, each marked with its proper name—none have been found described.

But far beyond all these realised or imagined designs the finest is the floor like the sea; the thought of which penetrates us like certain vibrations in music. It is the pavement in the heavenly temple of the Apocalypse:—

'And before the throne there was a sea of glass, like unto crystal.' 'Them that had gotten the victory ... stand on the sea of glass, having the harps of God' (chs. iv. and xv.) Compare the firmament, like 'the terrible crystal,' on which was placed the sapphire throne in Ezekiel, also 'the paved work' of clear sapphire in Exodus (xxiv. IO). The pseudo Enoch, in his vision of heaven, entered a spacious habitation of crystal, 'its walls, as well as its pavement, were formed with stones of crystal, and crystal likewise was the ground.'

This is the ultimate conception on which is founded the crystal floors of romance; but probably, as we shall see, it was not taken directly and consciously from the Revelation. In Lydgate's 'Warre of Troy,' the floor of the hall in Priam's palace is of jasper. In the 'Gest Hystoriale' of the Destruction of Troy, Hector, while suffering from his wounds, was laid in the proud ' Palace of Ylion':—

> 'Hit was pight up with pilirs all of pure stonys
> Palit full proudly; and a proud floor
> Wrought all with crystall, clere as the sonne.'

In each corner was a pillar, and on it an image of gold with 'gematry justly ajoynet.' The design is repeated again in the tomb of Hector 'trayturly slayn,' the same figures and floor of 'clere crystall.' 'As Dares tells in his treatise,' is the authority given for all these wonders; but Dares and Dictys say nothing half so nice in their bald and dreary narrative. The genealogy for the palace of romance probably ascends through the Alexander stories, and Apuleius in Cupid and Psyche, to the Eastern cities of gold, of which Homer's palace of Alcinous is a Greek version.

Justinian, at Constantinople, appears definitely to have set himself to rival Solomon as a builder. His throne was not only made in the fashion of Solomon's, but actually called 'Solomon's throne;' and when he had erected Sta. Sophia, the most splendid church Christendom has ever seen, he exclaimed: 'Glory be to God! who has esteemed me worthy to achieve a work so sublime; O Solomon, I have surpassed thee!' It is said that he intended at first to floor his church with gold, like the Temple; but, fearing man's supidity, he substituted the floor of marble, resembling water.

Now, there is an Eastern legend of Solomon laying a floor like the sea in his wonderful palace in Jerusalem:—' When the Queen of Sheba heard of the fame of Solomon, she came to prove Solomon with hard questions' (Book of Chronicles). These, according to Eastern tradition, were riddles, like those which passed between Solomon and Hiram of Tyre. But 'there was nothing hid from Solomon,' and, *en revanche*, he retorts by transporting the throne of Queen Balkis to his palace by the aid of the genii who ever served him, so that on her arrival she was con-

fronted by her own throne. 'It was said unto her: enter the palace. And when she saw it she imagined it to be a great water, and
she discovered her legs, by lifting up her robe, to pass through
it. Whereupon Solomon said unto her: Verily, this is a palace
evenly floored with glass (Koran xxvii.) Or, as some understand,
adds Sale, this was in 'the court before the palace, which Solomon had commanded to be built against the arrival of Balkis; the
floor or pavement being of transparent glass, laid over running
water in which fish were swimming. Fronting this pavement
was the royal throne, on which Solomon sat to receive the
Queen.'

A similar floor is given to the palace of *The City of Brass*, in
the 'Arabian Nights,' probably the most wonderful piece of
architectural imagination in literature. The Emeer Moosa and his
followers came to a high-walled city, from the midst of which
shines the tower of brass. They entered and pressed on to the
palace, and found a saloon constructed of polished marble,
adorned with jewels. 'The beholder imagined upon its floor was
running water, and if any one walked upon it he would slip. The
Emeer Moosa therefore ordered the Sheykh Abd-Es-Samad to
throw upon it something that they might be enabled to walk
upon it; and he did this, and so contrived that they passed on.'

The story, incorporated in the Koran soon after the year 622,
is probably from the Talmud, which contains this version:—All
the kingdoms congratulated Solomon as the worthy successor
of his father David, whose fame was great among all nations,
save one, the Kingdom of Sheba, the capital of which was called
Kitore.

To this kingdom, Solomon sent a letter.

'From me, King Solomon, peace to thee and to thy government. Let it be known to thee, that the Almighty God has made
me to reign over the whole world, the kingdoms of the north,
the south, the east, and the west. Lo, they have come to me with
their congratulations, all save thee alone. Come thou also, I pray
thee, and submit to my authority, and much honour shall be
done thee; but if thou refusest, behold I shall by force compel
thy acknowledgment.

'To thee, Queen Sheba, is addressed this letter in peace, from
me, King Solomon, the Son of David.'

When Solomon heard that the Queen was coming he sent Benayahu, the son of Yehoyadah, the general of his army, to meet her. When the queen saw him she thought he was the king, and she alighted from her carriage.

Then Benayahu asked, 'Why alightest thou from thy carriage?' and she answered, 'Art thou not his majesty the king?'

'No,' replied Benayahu, ' I am but one of his officers' Then the queen turned back and said to her ladies in attendance, 'If this is but one of the officers, and he is so noble and imposing in appearance, how great must be his superior the king.'

And Benayahu, the son of Yehoyadah, conducted Queen Sheba to the palace of the king.

Solomon prepared to receive his visitor in an apartment laid and lined with glass, and the queen at first was so deceived by the appearance that she imagined the king to be sitting in water.

And when the queen had tested Solomon's wisdom and witnessed his magnificence, she said, 'I believed not what I heard, but now I have come and my eyes have seen it all; behold, the

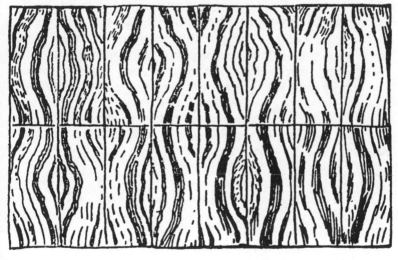

half has not been told to me. Happy are thy servants who stand before thee continually, to listen to the wisdom of thy words. Blessed be the Lord thy God, who hath placed thee on a throne to rule righteously and in justice.'

There is a practically identical story in another of the quarry books of the world, the Sanscrit epic of the *Mahabharata*, which sings the long strife of rival royal houses. One of the Rajas celebrates a royal sacrifice. 'When the sacrifice had been fully accomplished, Duryodhana entered the place where it had been performed, and saw very many beautiful things that he had never beheld in his own Raj at Hastinapur. Amongst other wonders was a square, made of black crystal, which appeared to the eye of Duryodhana to be clear water, and as he stood on the margin he began to draw up his garments lest they should be wetted, and then throwing them off he plunged in to bathe and was struck violently on the head against the crystal. Then he was much ashamed and left that place.'

Mr Talboys Wheeler suggests that this may be borrowed from the Koran, but allows that it may have had an independent origin. There can, however, be little doubt that these transcendental palaces, which are handed on through milleniums of Indian story, find their origin in the structures of the land which is not subject to winter's wind, nor any decay—The City of Gold founded in the waters above the firmament.

In the fifteenth century Italian romance, called the *Hypnerotomachia*, the author seems to have collected all the architectural wonders of history and romance; but how should he come by this same story? Poliphilus, after penetrating zone after zone of gardens, which occupy an island, comes at last to a circular temple, open to the sky, and on entering it was astonished to find 'a marvel more grand and stupefying than anything he had ever seen;' the whole area of the amphitheatre was apparently paved with one sole stone of obsidian, entirely black and of invincible hardness, so polished and shining that at the first moment he feared destruction by walking into an abyss. It reflected the light of day so perfectly that he contemplated the profound and limpid sky as in a quiet sea: everything was reflected as in a polished mirror.

According to the story in the Koran, Solomon's throne seems to stand on the waters, just as was imagined of God's throne. 'It is He who hath created the heavens and the earth in six days, but His throne was above the waters, before the creation thereof' (Koran xi.). 'For the Mohammedans supposed this throne, and the waters whereon it stands—which waters they imagine were supported by a spirit or wind—were with some other things, created before the heavens and the earth. This fancy they borrowed from the Jews, who also say that the throne of glory then stood and was borne on the face of the waters by the breath of God's mouth' (Sale). An account of this pavement of waters above the firmament is given in Smith's 'Dictionary of the Bible'—'Further, the office of the *rakia* (firmament or solid expansion) in the economy of the world demanded strength and substance. It was to serve as a division between the waters above and the waters below.... and accordingly the rakia was created to support the upper reservoir (Psalms cxlviii. 4 and civ. 3), where Jehovah is represented as "building His chambers of water," not simply in water, that being the material of which the beams and joists were made.'

In Ezekiel's vision of a perfect temple, after he has seen every court and chamber, and measured them with his reed, he is brought again to the door:—'And, behold, waters issued out from under the threshold of the house eastward: for the forefront of the house stood toward the east.' The waters came from the south of the altar, and after passing through the court and the outer gate became a mighty river flowing to the sea. It is the river of the water of life, 'and everything shall live whither the river cometh.'

To return to Constantinople once more: an account of the emperor's bed-chamber, in the imperial palace, is given by Bayet (*L'Art Byzantin*.), quoting from Constantine Porphyrogenitus. A range of the palace called 'Cenourigion,' was built by Basil, the Macedonian; one of the rooms had sixteen columns, of green marble, and of onyx, sculptured with branches of the vine, and the vault was covered with golden mosaic. 'But nothing could equal the royal bed-chamber. The pavement was of mosaic, the centre was a peacock in a circle of Carian marble, surrounded by rays, and an outer circle. From this second circle issued, as it were, streams or rivers of green marble of Thessaly, which flowed, seemingly, to the four angles of the room (*comme des ruisseaux ou des fleuves de marble vert de Thessalie*); the four interspaces left between the marble streams had eagles wrought in mosaic, which seemed to live and to breathe. The lower part of the walls were encrusted with glass, in many pieces of varied colour, in the forms of flowers. Above a gold band, the walls were covered with mosaic, on the golden field of which were enthroned Basil and Eudoxia, and their children around them. In the centre of the ceiling glittered a cross of emerald glass on a star-lit sky.' In the same book (Bayet) is a story taken from

Codinus, of flooding Sta. Sophia with water, which, although not questioned by the author, seems ta be an expedient so impracticable and injurious as to be obviously a myth—just such a myth as would arise to account for a pavement representing water. 'When the dome fell in Anthemius and Isidore were dead, but the latter had left a nephew, who was charged with the works. He increased the elevation of the cupola, and at the same time gave greater solidity to the great arches. They this time left the centres longer in place, and all the scaffolding. *They also inundated with water the lower part of the church*, so that pieces of wood in falling should not cause any injury.'

In the great area of Sta. Sophia it is not possible to see the floor, but in one of the galleries a green marble pavement is still uncovered. It is formed of very large slabs of antique Cipollino (Browning's 'onion stone'), the slabs being laid in such a manner that what were the two faces of the division made by the saw in the original-block are opened out side by side, thus obtaining a symmetrical wave-like veining. Mr Brindley, the best English authority on marbles, says—' Cippolino produces, when sawn across the bed, sea-wave like effects, to which the Roman and Byzantine architects were very partial.'

In St Mark's at Venice where the floor is generally covered by the most varied and intricate mosaic in existence, there is, just in the most important place of the area, centrally in front of the choir screen, a similar 'sea' of marble. Twelve immense slabs of Cipollino, each thirteen feet long by five feet wide, are arranged in the same way as to matching one another, covering an area thirty feet by twenty-six feet with their rippled veining. The marble block from which these slabs were cut was brought from the east, and the slabs were laid down in quite evident imitation of the floor of Sta. Sophia.

If the ceiling belonged of right to the sky, the floor is yielded to the sea When Galla Placidia escaped from shipwreck, she dedicated a pavement in St John the Evangelist at Ravenna—a picture of the shipwreck recalling the peril of the queen by its likeness to the storm-tossed waves of the sea. Mr Baring Gould describes a pavement he discovered in a Gallo-Roman palace near Pau:—' In the principal room the pavement was very elaborate; the design was, however, rudely interrupted by a monstrous cross, nearly twenty feet by thirteen feet, with its head towards the south and its foot at the head of a flight of marble steps descending into what we were unable to decide whether it was a bath or a vestibule. The ground of the cross was white, the limbs were filled with cuttle, lobsters, eels, oysters, and fish *swimming as though in their natural element;* but the centre, where the arms intersected, was occupied by a gigantic bust of Neptune with his trident.

Sir Charles Newton says:—' On a mosaic found at Oudnah, in Algeria, we have a representation of the sea, remarkable for the fulness of details with which it is made out. The mosaic lines the floor and sides of a bath; and, as was commonly the case in the baths of the ancients, serves as a figurative representation of the water it contained. On the sides are hippocamps, figures riding on dolphins, and islands on which fishermen stand; on the floor are fish, crabs, and shrimps.'

The baths of Caracalla, in Rome, have such sea pavements treated pictorially, as well as patterns in a conventional rendering of sea waves. And the baths of Titus even had a floor of lapis lazuli—a great pool of ultramarine.

If we take any collection of Roman mosaic floors—as, for instance, those now exhibited on the staircase of the British Museum, or the drawings at South Kensington—it is most remarkable how often the floor is designed as a sea; there are subjects such as Neptune and Amphitrite; Ulysses in his ship; or a fisherman in a boat, the rest of the area being filled with fish: or, more frequently, only fish and marine monsters 'swimming as though in their natural element;' the sea being represented by the flowing lines of the plain white mosaic, with a darker broken line here and there in various directions. One of the most beautiful of these is an English example that was discovered at Cirencester, and figured by Lysons.

We can hardly suppose that all of these were in baths. At Lydney on the Severn, a mosaic was found forming the floor of a temple to the Celtic 'God of the Deeps,' to whom the pavement was dedicated; inscribed offerings proved that this was a temple. Great sea serpents and fish swim over the expanse of the floor (C. W. King).

The best authenticated specimen of Greek mosaic floor, that of the pronaos of the temple of Zeus, at Olympia, of which only a small fragment exists, represents a triton and fish swimming. Within the temple, directly in front of the great statue of Zeus enthroned, by Pheidias, and right across the sanctuary, was an area of black marble twenty-two feet square, and slightly sunk below the rest of the floor. Pausanias describes it, and the foundations yet show its place. Shining with the oil thrown over the ivory figure, and reflecting it and the lights, it must have resembled the deep still sea, the sea of heaven which bore the throne of Zeus, and in which the stars floated. There is an irresistible suggestion of water in these marble floors when highly polished. Miss Beaufort, for instance, saw in a Damascus mosque, what every worshipper of the throned Zeus must have seen and understood in the Temple of Olympia—' The polished marble floor shone darkly, like a lake of black water, reflecting back the few lamps like stars.'

A representation of the sea of heaven with its stars is especially appropriate to the floor of the holy place, which bears the figure of the god, or the altar.

It was quite general in the Middle Ages to figure the signs of the zodiac on the floor of the sanctuary, thus marking it like the 'paved work' of heaven.

'Look how the floor of heaven
Is thick inlaid with patines of bright gold.'
—*Merchant of Venice.*

Left behind in the west end of the church was the labyrinth of the lower world, but the holy place, raised seven steps, was heaven itself. In England we have a fine zodiac on the floor at Canterbury. The choir of St Remi, at Rheims, had a pavement of marble and enamel; on one side of which was figured the earthly paradise with the four rivers, the earth seated on ocean, and the seasons; on the other side were the four cardinal points, the zodiacal circle, and within the last the two bears of the North Pole studded with stars. Some British-Roman pavements display the sun in the middle surrounded by the planets.

In the Dome of the Rock at Jerusalem, a slab of dark stone inlaid in the floor is said to be a piece of the pavement of paradise.

Many of the churches of Italy have wave patterns on the floors, and in some instances we are able to identify them as set imitations of the waters. In the crypt of an early church at Piacenza the space before the altar has a mosaic pavement with undulating lines of waves in which fishes swim, and circular discs contain the zodiacal signs; these heavenly signs floating on the water appear to mark it as the oversea.

In the great basin of the Baptistry at Pisa the floor again definitely represents the water it contains.

At Florence, the floor of the Baptistry is laid in patterns suggesting running and rippled water, with the sun and zodiacal signs. (*See* figures.)

With all these examples, it cannot be doubted that the wave-like patterns of the central space at Grado, or portions in St Mark's, represent the sea by a traditional pattern.

To the Egyptians the realm of Osiris was watered by a network of smiling canals. Wilkinson writes of the happy dead admitted to these Elysian fields:—' Horus introduces him to the presence of Osiris, who, in his palace, attended by Isis and Nepthys, sits on his throne in the midst of the waters, from which rises the lotus, bearing upon its expanded flower the four genii of Amenti.' In the plate given by Wilkinson of the scene from which he takes his description, Osiris is shown under a pillar-borne canopy, seated on a throne placed on the waters, the water being shown by a parallelogram covered with zigzag lines.

In some of the Egyptian temples, the lower part of the side walls is painted with growing water plants, and next the floor is the zigzag line of water. The bases of the columns are wrapped round with water leaves; the shafts themselves being bundles of water reeds.

The gods are sometimes shown supported by the oversea, Ra floating in his bark, or enthroned (like that discovered by Miss Edwards' party at Aboo Simbel) on a platform of blue spangled with stars. As the Pharaoh had the effigies of his enemies painted on the soles of his shoes so that he might tread them in the dust, as his footstool was carved on its sides with prostrate captives: so, with symbolic intention, the thrones and footstools shown at the Ramessium, and in the tombs of the kings, were covered with tissue of blue sprinkled with stars. The king, godlike, crushes his enemies under his footstool, and treads underfoot the azure flood in which float the stars. No mere accident this, but an ordered symbolism; it occurs many times, the stars being treated exactly as they are on the star ceilings of the temples, an acknowledged symbol of the sky and heavens reserved for sacred places.

The most beautifully worked and preserved Babylonian tablet in the British Museum represents the king before the sun-god Samas. It is carefully engraved by Lenormant (*Histoire Ancienne de l'Orient*), and by Perrot. The image of the god sits on a throne, under a canopy; before him is a great sun disc, with flaming rays on it, which is revolved by means of ropes as the king is led forward. The floor of this composition, on which stands the throne, the sun altar, and the worshippers, is an area of water, and on it are a row of stars—without doubt stars, for above the god are engraved the forms of the sun, moon, and stars; and the stars on the pavement repeat the last with exactitude. The text says it represents the king before Samas in his temple at Sippara, and it seems possible that the floor there really represented the oversea. It is not without some relation, we might suppose, to these thoughts that an Assyrian pavement in the British Museum is entirely patterned over with the lotus.

There is abundance of evidence besides what has been given, that the celestial sea forms the floor of the over-world; our dome being the under side of the pavement, as in Blake:—

'Lo ! the vault of paved heaven.'

In the Brahmanical system, the paradise is well watered with broad, beautiful lakes. ' These lakes are covered with water-lilies, red, blue, and white, each blossom having a thousand petals; and on the most beautiful of all these calm lakes floats a throne, glorious as the sun, whereon Krishna the beautiful reposes ' (Miss Gordon Cumming). Indeed, the whole city of Krishna is built on the waters.

To the Buddhist, the 'lotus throne' of Buddha rests on the waters—Buddha being called 'the Jewel on the lotus.' Even in the Rig Veda, Yama, the lord of death, is 'the assembler of men who departed to the mighty waters,' 'the heavenly ocean;' and Varuna dwells in a golden palace, where he 'sits throned in unapproachable light, on the waters of heaven.' In the Avesta, the 'lofty mountain,' the exterior of the domed firmament is the seat of the gods, and the source of all the waters of earth. The paradise of the Burmese has 'gorgeous palaces, with crystal pavements, golden columns, and jewelled walls.'

Doubtless to a parallel phase of the thought belong the vast sacred lakes attached to the temples of India, on which, as the homes of the gods, they seem to float. It was the same in Greece, in Syria, Babylon, and Egypt; here the priests imitated the voyage of the sun, and here swam sacred fish. 'At Sais, in the sacred precinct... is a lake ornamented with a stone margin, formed in a circle, and in size it appeared to me much the same as that at Delos, which is called the circular. In this lake they perform by night the representation of that person's adventures, which they call mysteries' (Herodotus).

Nebuchadnezzar, in one of his inscriptions, speaks of surrounding the temple he had built with a lake. And in India the golden temple of Amritzur seems to float on an artificial sea, crossed by a single causeway, entering on which, as Lady Dufferin remarks, the pilgrim puts off his 'earthly shoes.' At Marttand the temple court was filled with water, in which stepping-stones were placed, leading from the gateway.

The fountain of ablution is common to the religions of the East. Although its use is obvious, both for practical and symbolic purity, yet the water was 'holy water,' and represented the fountain of life. Professor Sayce, in his Hibbert Lectures, says 'the temples of Babylonia were provided with large basins filled with water, and used for purificatory purposes, which resembled *the sea* made by Solomon in his temple at Jerusalem, and were called *deeps* or *abysses*.' Pausanias also mentions seas in Greek temples.

That there is something impressive to the imagination in thus making the floor to appear like a sea, is sufficiently borne out by the following instances from modern romance and poetry; from French, German, and English authors. To take them respectively:—

Flaubert thus describes the assembly at the temple in Carthage: 'The elders sat on the ebony benches, having thrown over their heads the ends of their long robes. They remained motionless, with their hands crossed in their wide sleeves; and the mother-of-pearl pavement resembled a luminous stream, that ran under their bare feet, from the altar to the door.'

In Eber's Egyptian romance, 'Uarda,' a temporary palace is built, in which to welcome back Rameses from the war in Syria. As the author leans so on his correct archæology, the floor of the banqueting-hall may be taken from a wall painting. 'This (the palace) was of unusual height, and had a vaulted wooden ceiling, which was painted blue, and sprinkled with stars, to represent the night heavens. Thick carpets, which seemed to have transported the sea shore on to the dry land—for their pale blue groundwas strewn with a variety of shells, fishes, and waterplants—covered the floor of the banqueting-hall.'

Mr William Morris makes use of the thought in the description of a new fourteenth century church, in 'A Dream of John Ball': 'The white shafts of the arches rose out of the shining pavement in the moonlight as though out of a sea, dark, but with gleams struck over it.' In the story of 'Cupid and Psyche,' in his 'Earthly Paradise,' it seems as if the floor is taken from the account of the reception of Queen Balkis by Solomon, for the idea is not found in the story by Apuleius.

> 'At last she came into a chamber cool,
> Paved cunningly in the manner of a pool,
> Where red fish seemed to swim through the floating weed;
> And at the first she thought it so indeed,
> And took the sandals quickly from her feet;
> But when the glassy floor these did but meet,
> The shadow of a long-forgotten smile
> Her anxious face a moment did beguile.'

The last instance is that in Southey's 'Thalaba,' which is not so much a continuation of the tradition as a reverting to the original idea which underlies the whole series—an imitation by human hands, in an artificial paradise, of the water or transparent crystal pavement above the firmament, where stands the throne. Shedad, who, according to Arab story, lived in the early ages of the world, built to himself such a lordly pleasure-house and garden of delights:—

> 'Here emerald columns o'er the marble courts
> Fling their green rays, as when, amid a shower,
> The sun shines loveliest on the vernal corn;
> Here Shedad bade the sapphire floor be laid
> As though with feet divine to trample azure light,
> Like the blue pavement of the firmament.'

CHAPTER X

CEILINGS LIKE THE SKY

> 'He first framed,
> For the children. of earth,
> The heaven as a roof—
> Holy Creator! '
>
> —CAEDMON.

> 'Look you, this brave, o'erhanging
> firmament,
> This majestical roof fretted with golden fire
>
> —HAMLET.

WE speak of the sky as a vault, a dome; but before domes or vaults were invented it evidently could have been likened to neither. It was then without doubt a ceiling, a flat extension.

Of course the sky was understood to be hollow, semi-spherical, at a very early time indeed; but it is evidently a more advanced and philosophical view than the other.

If we may take it as proved that the architectural dome was known and first reared in Chaldea (see Perrot) by a people who saw in the sky a solid hemisphere, and much given to nature symbolism in their buildings; may not the design and daring construction of the cupola be attributed to the form of the heavenly dome, and the desire that the 'ceiling' of the temple should still recall the ceiling of the great nature temple?

There is such a clear and constraining congruity between them that to describe a dome seems to call for the simile to the firmament: St Paul's, for instance—

'Whose sky-like dome
Hath typified, by reach of daring art,
Infinity's embrace' (Wordsworth).

It may be said that at great periods of architecture ceilings were always skies. Viollet-le-Duc tells us, in his *Dictionnaire de l'Architecture* (Art. *Peinture*), that the whole scheme of interior colour had to be readjusted in the thirteenth century to harmonise with the vaults, which were painted the most brilliant of blues, *parsemee*, with gold stars, against which nothing could hold its own but vermilion, black, and more gold. The *Sainte Chapelle* of Paris may be taken for example; and in England,'Conrad's glorious choir,' built in 1150. In Italy, at the same time,

the practice was universal. It will suffice to refer to Siena and Orvieto Cathedrals with their vaults, stars on azure; in Orvieto, still untouched, in wonderful harmony of changing and decaying colour, blue to emerald, like the evening sky while as yet the earliest star alone burns there.

In Giotto's Arena Chapel at Padua, the walls are covered with pictured panels, the background of all alike being of blue leading up to the sky of the vault. Again in Italy—but this time in pure Byzantine style direct from Constantinople—the dome of the Mausoleum of Galla Placidia, at Ravenna, is a magnificent instance in brilliant mosaic; blue, powdered with a profusion of stars to the zenith. (See figure.) In Sta. Sophia itself, the ciborium over the altar was supported on four silver pillars, the under side of the dome twinkling with stars. The manual obtained by Didron on Mount Athos describes how ceilings should be designed as heavens.

In 'Roman' Rome, the gorgeous taste of Nero seems to have affected these ceilings at the Golden Palace; and Tacitus gives an account of the scene at Pompey's theatre on the occasion of the reception of an Eastern prince:—' The stage and the whole inside of that noble structure were cased with gold: such a profusion of wealth and magnificence had never been displayed to view. To screen the spectators from the rays of the sun, a purple canopy, inlaid with golden stars,was spread over their heads.' A Roman example may be seen in Smith's ' Dictionary ' (Art. *Penates*).

As showing that it touched the imagination and was no mere decorative tradition, better than facts, we have fiction and legends, the twelfth century guidebook to the eternal city, the *Mirabilia Urbis Romae* (Nichols) contains the account of 'a temple that was called *Holovitreum*, being made of glass and gold by mathematical craft, where was an astronomy with all the signs of the heavens, the which was destroyed by St Sebastian.' A MS. of the fourteenth century, incorporated in the same book, tells of the wonders of the Flavian amphitheatre. 'The Colosseum was the temple of the sun, of marvellous greatness and beauty, disposed with many diverse vaulted chambers, and all covered with a heaven of gilded brass, where thunders and lightnings and glittering fires were made, and where rain was shed through slender tubes. Besides this, there were the signs super-celestial and the planets Sol and Luna, that were drawn along in their proper chariots. And in the midst abode Phoebus—that is, the god of the sun—which, having his feet on the earth, reached into heaven with his head, and did hold in his hand an orb, signifying that Rome ruled over the world.' Our own Higden, in the *Polychronicon*, adds to the might and marvel of the sun-god in this place:—'This brazen statue, gilded with imperial gold, continually shed rays through the darkness, and turned round in even movement with the sun, carrying his face always opposite to the solar body; and all the Romans when they came near worshipped, in token of subjection.' The story of a temple of glass is especially interesting. Benjamin of Tudela about the same time describes another as existing at Damascus.

In the Dietrich Romances, King Laurin of the Rose Garden has a subterranean palace to which he carries off his bride. In it 'the walls were of polished marble inlaid with gold and silver;

the floor was formed of a single agate, the ceiling of a sapphire, and from it there hung shining carbuncles like stars in the blue sky of night.'

In the 'Parsifal,' Titurel, the ancestor of the hero, builds on Mount Salvatch a temple worthy to enshrine the sangreal. It was discovered that the rock or core of the mountain was one entire onyx of enormous size, and this was flattened into a flooring and polished with great care. One morning the plan was found miraculously marked out and all the materials ready, and with supernatural aid the temple was soon completed. It was circular in form, and had seventy-two octagonal choirs and thirty-six belfries. In the midst was a tower with many windows, its topmost point a ruby, out of which rose a cross of clear crystal surmounted by a golden eagle with outstretched wings. 'Within the building, sculptured vines, roses, and lilies twined about the pillars, forming bowers, on whose branches birds seem to flutter as if alive. At every intersection of the arches was a glowing carbuncle that turned night into day; and *the vauted roof was blue, of saffire, in which a miracle of art was to be seen. The sun, moon, and stars, placed there by the builders, moved in the same order as the real lumineries in the heavens.* In the wide inner space of the great temple a second and smaller sanctuary was built, resembling the first, but far more beautiful. This was the place intended for the sangreal should it come down to earth' (Wagner and M'Dowall).

The alliterative Romance of Alexander (Early English Text) describes the palace of Candace as built all of gold, encrusted with precious stones, on pillars of polished porphyry. An inner chamber was by sorcery wonderfully founded, and ' made by marvel to move.' 'Twenty tamed oliphants turned it aDoUt,' and, as the Queen and Alexander entered, it began to revolve.

Similar imagery is used in the popular medieval history, 'The Ipvention of the Cross' in Caxton's ' Golden Legend,' and other earlier Cross poems. One of the thirteenth century, published by the Early English Text Society, says: There was a king named ' Cosdre ' (Chosroes). He conquered many lands. He came to Jerusalem and took possession of a part of the sweet Cross, which he removed to Persia.

> 'A swithe heig towr of gold and seluer he let him sone a-rere
> Of gimmes and of stones precious ther aboute he lette do;

Tourne of sonne and mon and of sterres also
Schinen, as hit themself were and tornen a-boute faste
And thunderinge he made eke that the folk ofte agaste
'Mid small holes throwh queyntyse that water ofte ther
He made hit ofte to grounde falle as they hit reyn were
As ferforth as couthe eny mon make mid queyntyse
The fourme as it an heYene were he made on alle wise.'

Here he rears a throne, and set himself up as a god. Heraclius,
the emperor, makes war on Chosroes, and finds him on the
throne in his false heaven where he slays him, and then restores
the sacred wood to Jerusalem.

Sir H. Rawlinson, writing of Ecbatana in the 'Journal of the
Geographical Society,' quotes Cedrenus, the Byzantine historian,
on the wars of Justinian and Heraclius against Chosroes.
Heraclius, when he took possession of Canzaca, 'found the
abominable image of Chosroes; a figure of the king enthroned
beneath the globular dome of the palace, as though he were
seated in the heavens; around him were emblems of the sun and
moon and stars, to which, in his superstition, he seemed to offer adoration, as if to the gods, while sceptre-bearing angels ministered on every side, and curiously-wrought machines distilled
drops of water, to represent the falling rain, and uttered roaring
sounds in imitation of the peals of thunder. All these things the
emperor consumed with fire, and, at the same time, he reduced
to ashes the temple and the entire city.'

Canzaca was taken by Heraclius in 628. Rawlinson (VII. Mon-
archy) tells us of the even greater splendours of Dastagherd:—
'The Orientals say that the palace was supported on forty thousand columns of silver, adorned by thirty thousand rich hangings upon the walls, and further ornamented by a *thousand globes
suspended from the roof* (p. 528). 'The royal crown—which could
not be worn, but was hung from the ceiling by a gold chain exactly over the head of the king when he took his seat in his
throne-room—is said to have been adorned with a thousand
pearls, each as large as an egg. The throne itself was of gold, and
was supported on four feet, each formed of a single enormous
ruby' (p. 640). The globes were 'probably of crystal or gold.' A
curtain shut off the king from ordinary gaze, and the courtiers
were organised in seven ranks. In the paradise attached were
beasts for the chase—lions and tigers, gazelles, peacocks and
pheasants. But the most splendid of these palaces was that of

Ctesiphon, taken by the Arabs not ten years later than the campaign of Heraclius, the façade of which stands to-day with its great arched portal, seventy-two feet wide and eighty-five feet high. 'In the centre was the Hall of Audience—a noble apartment one hundred and fifteen feet long and eighty-five feet high, with a *magnificent vaulted roof, bedecked with golden stars so arranged as to represent the motions of the planets along the twelve signs of the zodiac*—where the monarch was accustomed to sit on a golden throne.' The treasury was full of gold, gems, and arms; spices, gums, and perfumes. 'In one apartment was found a carpet of white brocade four hundred and fifty feet long and ninety broad, with a border worked in precious stones of various hues, to represent a garden of all kinds of beautiful flowers. The leaves were formed of emeralds, the blossoms and buds of pearls, rubies, and sapphires, and other gems of immense value.' There was a horse of gold with a jewelled saddle, and a camel of silver; suits of gold armour, scimitars, and 'cuirasses of Solomon' (Rawlinson (VII. Mon. 565).

There can be no doubt that these many notices show us the ceremony of the Persian court continued through centuries. The king was a god, 'brother of the sun and moon,' as he calls himself; and he sat in the middle of a universe of his own, ministered to by the seven orders of the heavenly hierarchy—as in China, there are nine who surround the throne.

It accords well with the theatrical genius of Nero that he should have copied this solemn and magical symbolism (which, we have also seen, formed part of the Mithraic ritual) in a mere supper-room of his palace.

Of this wonderful palace, called the Golden House, sober annalists give accounts marvellous in comparison even with the marvels of romance. 'In nothing,' says Suetonius, 'was he more prodigal than in his buildings. He completed his palace by continuing it from the Palatine to the Esquiline Hill, calling the building at first only "The Passage ;" but after it was burnt down and rebuilt, the "Golden House." Of its dimensions and furniture it may be sufficient to say thus much: the porch was so high that there stood in it a colossal statue of himself a hundred and twenty feet in height, and the space included in it was so ample that it had triple porticos a mile in length; and a lake like a sea, surrounded with buildings that had the appearance of a city;

within its area were cornfields, vineyards, pastures, and woods containing a vast number of animals of various kinds, both wild and tame. In other parts it was entirely overlaid with gold, and adorned with gold and mother-of-pearl. The supper-rooms were vaulted, and compartments of the ceilings, inlaid with ivory, were made to revolve, and scatter flowers; while they contained pipes which shed unguents upon the guests. The chief banqueting-room was circular, *and revolved perpetually, night and day, in imitation of the motion of thc celestial bodies*. The baths were supplied with water from the sea and the Albula. Upon the dedication of this magnificent house, after it was finished, all he said in approval of it was: 'That he had now "a building fit for a man."'

It is said, by Philostratus, that Appolonius of Tyana, when in Babylon, 'visited an apartment belonging to the men, the ceiling of which was domed in the form of the heavens, and covered with sapphire which is a stone of an azure colour resembling the sky. Under this canopy were suspended the images of their reputed deities, wrought in gold, and shedding a light as if from heaven. Here it is where the king sits in judgment. Four golden figures in form of birds are hung from the roof.' It was doubtless in such a place that Ahasuerus sat, god-like, when Esther feared to approach. In Persia, where modern ceilings still imitate the sky, it would seem to be an unbroken tradition from the earliest days. Not a ceiling remains to us from the buildings of Assyria, but it is significant that an inscription reads: 'I caused a ceiling of cedar wood to be made, beautiful as the stars of heaven, adorned with gold.' It is probable that the shrines were lined over the ceiling and walls with lapis lazuli, or blue tiles, as fragments have been found. In Mexico, the shrine represented a star-strewn sky; and in China, the roofs of the sacred buildings of Pekin are covered with azure porcelain.

In the temples of Syria, zodiacs are sculptured on the stone ceilings. The Hindus, in the temples of Orissa, followed the same custom.

In Athens, it is said in the third cent. B.C. concave ceilings were emblazoned with the heavenly signs. The many fragments we have of Greek ceilings found in excavation, and figured in books, show that they were usually divided into small square panels or coffers, the field of which was blue, each charged with a golden star. The British Museum, and other modern classics, follow this method; sometimes the coffers were slightly concave.

A modern ceiling designed with a real feeling for mystery, is that arranged by the Marquis of Bute at Mount Stuart House, where the aspect of the heavens at his birth is correctly set out on the library ceiling.

It is in Egypt that we shall find this dedication of the ceiling to the sky the most completely accepted, and that not only in the temple but in the tomb also; there, on the table of offerings, are food and wine for sustenance, and on its walls are figured all the works of the days of the earthly year and its pastimes; no mere decoration, but a 'double' of the things of earth, so that the dead may suffer no want in his long habitation. Over all is the sky in semblance; the deep blue of night with its stars, cloudless and still; never intended to be seen by other eyes than the eyes of the dead.

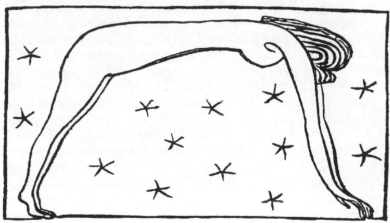

In sacred pictures the upper edge of the scene is occupied by the ideogram for sky or ceiling, a horizontal bar with a nib turned down vertically at each end, sometimes blue and the field for a line of stars. 'By the band of stars along the top of each scene, they represented the sky, or the ceiling of the temple, where the ceremony which is made the subject of the picture was supposed to have taken place. In fact, the ceilings of temples are very often decorated with white stars, with a red spot in the middle, scattered on a blue sky; these stars sometimes cover the whole ceiling, and form then the only decoration' (*Description de l'Egypt.*).

This hieroglyph is also the symbol of the impersonation of the sky, Tpe. Wilkinson says: 'She was a deification of the heaven itself, or that part of the firmament in which the stars are placed; she is sometimes represented under the hieroglyphic character signifying "the heavens" studded with stars, and sometimes as a human figure, whose body, as it bends forward with outspread arms, appears to overshadow the earth and encompass it, in imitation of the vault of heaven, reaching from one side of the horizon to the other. In this posture she encloses the zodiacs as at Esneh and Denderah.'

Champollion says: 'The Egyptians compared the sky to the ceilings of an edifice, and those of the greater part of the temples are painted blue, powdered with stars.... The goddess of the

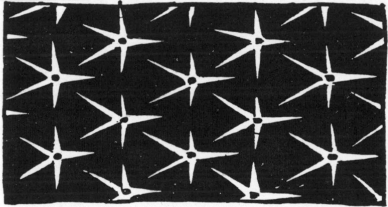

sky is figured under the form of a woman, whose body, placed horizontally, and out of all proportion long, embraces a large space, circumscribed by the legs and arms, which are vertical.... It is to be remarked that the body of the goddess Tpe, shown on the astronomical sculptures, is disposed in a manner to recall the form of the hieroglyph.'

Sometimes two goddesses are shown, who are thus described by Lenormant: 'Two female figures posed in such a manner that their bodies form, as it were, a flat ceiling, of which the legs and arms are of each end the supports; they are Tpe, the sky, and

Nut, the celestial ocean.' The ceiling of the portico at Phila, figured in the *Description* of the French Commission, has both these
figures extended on the ceiling; their bodies are laid down in
profile, with legs and arms bent at right angles to the torso, the
Egyptians never drawing the figure in full face until a late time.
At Denderah, this difficulty has been surmounted, and the goddess is full face, and particularly well rendered! The third figure, sometimes found, which the over-shadowing goddess
touches with finger tips and toes, is Seb, the earth.

In the first volume of the *Description* there are other examples
given. At Esneh, the ceiling of the portico has one of these figures at each end, perfectly rectangular in form, and the space is
filled with zodiacal signs as well as stars. At Erment, three sides
of the ceiling are surrounded by one of these figures, the body
being drawn out to immense length, and ruled perfectly straight,
filling the longitudinal side of the ceiling, which exceeds by
three times the ends occupied by the arms and legs.

The ceiling of the portico at Denderah furnishes the most
exaggerated example of all. The bodies of the goddesses, covered with the zigzag of water, stretch along the sides, like long
streams, on which float lines of stars, the mid-space being, occupied by the signs of the zodiac, and other astronomical figures
and stars.

Much earlier, and by far the most impressive, is that in the
tombs of the kings at Thebes, of the great period of the nineteenth
dynasty. This nude figure is beautifully proportioned, drawn
with the precision of a Greek vase painting, and fearlessly coloured the brightest lapis lazuli blue. The watchful goddess of the
sky, all-embracing, lost in the darkness in the farther part of the
chamber, peers down from the ceiling, her body bedecked with
the planets as bright discs, 'the stars on the body of the heavenly
goddess Nut'.

There is another variety of sky ceiling at Denderah. A square
apartment has a large circle touching its sides; around an outer
zone are the signs of the zodiac, and the central space is filled
with the northern constellations.

The simpler form, of stars only, thickly strewn as daisies in
a meadow, is the most beautiful representation of 'the intense,
clear, star-sown vault of heaven.' A good coloured plate of one
of these is given in Lepsius. On a bright blue sky large white

five-rayed stars (why do stars appear to have five rays?), are regularly spaced, almost touching one another. In the middle of every one is a spot of bright red, which, on the white with the surrounding blue, seems to make them dance and flicker before the eyes; others have white stars on an expanse of black, as in the pyramids of Dashour; or, again, the stars may be gold. 'The ceilings of the temples of Thebes had generally a blue ground, upon which vultures, with their great wings outspread, floated among golden stars' (Perrot). Not to give a catalogue of these, we will content ourselves by looking at an early one.

In 1881, Maspero opened a pyramid at Sakkarah, belonging to a king, the last Pharaoh of the fifth dynasty. Here, at a time to which no man can number back the years, 'the side walls are covered with fine hieroglyphs, painted green, and the roof sprinkled with stars of the same hue.'

Last of all, more pathetic than temple or tomb with their ceilings like the sky, the coffin itself was adorned in the same way. Coffins in the British Museum of a late period have their lids painted on the under side to resemble the sky, a greenish-blue studded with stars; along the margins are the signs of the zodiac in two rows; in the middle of these, longways, is the goddess of the heavens, in full face, white and serene, her eyes for ever looking down into his whom she watches and guards.

These men of Egypt loved the same sky that we also love.

CHAPTER XI

THE WINDOWS OF HEAVEN AND THREE HUNDRED AND SIXTY DAYS

> 'Stop! stop! O man stop! for the sake of
> three hundred and sixty-five, which are in
> the year.
> —*SERVIAN FOLK LORE.*

THE parallelism so often made out between the childhood of the individual and of the race is well sustained in the gradual apprehension of number by both. With them both, numeration begins by 'One, two,' and 'Ever so many;' both use the symbol of a determinate number for a great multitude; and by both, as the process is carried further, the numbers are instinctively connected with the 'digits' of the hand. Reckoning by fives seems to have preceded the decimal system of both hands, and is still in use, in taking in merchandise by tale—the man in charge chalking on some shutter, or other tally-board, four upright strokes, and then the fifth as a diagonal. As children help their addition or subtraction on their little fingers, so it was in the beginning. As they hold up their hands in dumb show for five, or ten, so did the infant man. His tally-board was always at hand, just as his measure of length, the palm, span, or foot, the cubit, or the fathom, was never mislaid. The Chaldean table books 'measures of length' began, 'five fingers one hand,' in a way still familiar in measuring horses.

Of the most primitive stage of number, Sir John Lubbock gives some account. The Bushman had not names beyond 'two;' three would be called 'two—one,' and four 'two—two,' and so on. They seldom lose oxen, for they discover a loss not by numbering the head, 'but by the absence of a face they know.'

'All over the world the fingers are used as counters; and although the numerals of most races are so worn down by use that we can no longer detect their original meaning, there are many savage tribes in which the words used are merely the verbal expressions of the signs used in counting with the fingers. Where names are given to the first four numerals, five is " one hand," and beyond it is one, two, three, four, on the second hand—ten being "two hands." Hence, no doubt, the decimal system in mathematics, ten, has been selected because we have ten fingers.'

Vitruvius points out all this: 'It is worthy of remark that measures universally used in all buildings, and other works, are derived from the members of the human body, as the digit, the palm, the foot, the cubit, and that these form a perfect number, called by the Greeks *teleios*. The ancients considered ten a perfect number, because the fingers are ten in number, and the palm is derived from them, and from the palm is derived the foot. Plato therefore called ten a perfect number; for nature having formed the hands with ten fingers, a number composed of units, called *monades* in Greek, that number advancing beyond ten as to eleven, twelve, etc., is not perfect until another ten is completed.'

It will be sufficiently obvious to affirm that the first recurring period noticed and counted would be that of the moon's phases, twenty-nine days, twelve hours, forty-four minutes; the nearest whole number in 'a moon' thus being thirty days—'six hands.' Then the year would be measured: twelve moons—three hundred and sixty days; the true primitive year. How the Egyptians and the Greeks set about correcting this is told by Herodotus: 'The Egyptians were the first to discover the year, which they divided into twelve parts, and they say they made this discovery from the stars; and, so far, I think they act more wisely than the Grecians, in that the Grecians insert an intercalary month every third year, on account of the seasons; whereas the Egyptians, reckoning twelve months of thirty days each, add five days each year above that number, and so with them the circle of the seasons comes round to the same point.' That three hundred and sixty days was the original year, improved by five additional days, is amply proved by the investigators of the monuments. The five days thrown in over were set apart as festivals, and a story that Osiris should not be born in the year, was fulfilled by his being born on one of the five days. That the original Greek year was also of three hundred and sixty days, is seen more clearly in another passage of Herodotus (1-32) and in Homer, as quoted later on.

Plutarch says of the Romans, that before Numa 'they had no idea of the difference between the annual course of the sun and that of the moon, and only laid down this position, that the year consisted of three hundred and sixty days.'

It was the same in Assyria, as astronomical tablets have made evident. 'Twelve months to each year, three hundred and sixty days in number, as recorded.' The course of the sun through the stars was partitioned according to the twelve months—the twelve signs of the zodiac—and these, sub-divided by their thirty days, gave the three hundred and sixty degrees, the basis since for all angular measure; the day was divided into six parts, each subdivided by sixty, and the same for the night, as is still the case in Japan.

In the Bible account of Noah and the Flood, exactly five consecutive months made one hundred and fifty days; therefore the year must have had three hundred and sixty. The Hindoo year of the Veda was the same, the sun-god having seven hundred and twenty twin children, three hundred and sixty days and nights. In the 'Mahabharata,' a young Brahmin descends through a cavern to the city of the serpents. He sees two women weaving a veil, the one with white, the other with black threads, of day and night. He sees a wheel with twelve spokes; three hundred and sixty rays issue from the nave—the days of the year. In Mexico, the number of days was evidently at first the same, for five days were intercalary.

Thus twelve, and three hundred and sixty, became important and easily recognised numbers—fixed points in a sea of abstractions. 'As many as the moons;' 'As many as the days in a year.' These important stepping-stones so far are ten, twelve, thirty, three hundred and sixty; not very even in their stride certainly, but sure and firm. If, however, we halve one, and double the other, of the two middle terms, the series will be much improved—six, ten, sixty (ten by six), three hundred and sixty (sixty by six) three thousand six hundred (sixty by sixty), etc. If this view of the growth of numeration is or is not right in every particular, it is sufficiently confirmed for Assyria by mathematical tablets, the scale having a sexagesimal base with ten: sixty, six hundred, three thousand six hundred (Boscawen). And Berosos even tells us the names of these: 'Now a *sarus* is esteemed to be three thousand six hundred, a *neros* six hundred, and a *sossus* sixty.'

Of the use of this system, the Chaldean account of the flood gives reiterated instances: 'And the God, the immutable lord, repeated the command in a dream, "Build a vessel and finish it. By a deluge I will destroy substance and life. Cause thou to go up into the vessel the substance of all that has life. The vessel thou shalt build, six hundred cubits shall be the measure of its length, and sixty cubits the amount of its breadth and of its height." I poured on its exterior three times three thousand six hundred measures of asphalte, and three times three thousand six hundred measures of asphalte within, three times three thousand six hundred men porters brought on their heads the chests of provisions. I kept three thousand six hundred chests for the nourishment of my family, and the mariners divided among themselves twice three thousand six hundred chests' (Lenormant).

This important number three hundred and sixty—as many as the days in the year—is largelv the basis of those long periods we find in early mythical chronology. In Babylonia, according to Berosos, the ten kings before the deluge reigned each in multiples of this period, making a total of four hundred and thirty-two thousand years (three hundred and sixty, by twelve, by one hundred), and from the deluge to the Persian Conquest three thousand six hundred years. In India the sacred chronology proceeds by the same method, as shown by the following from Sir G. Birdwood: 'The year of the gods consists of three hundred and sixty mortal years. The first age lasted four thousand eight hundred years of the gods, the second three thousand six hundred, the third two thousand four hundred, and the fourth, the present or black age, which began about B.C. 3101, is limited to one thousand two hundred years of the gods.'

The day of Brahma lasts four thousand three hundred and twenty millions of years (three hundred and sixty by twelve): this is the Brahmanical chronology, but there is another system 'based in the reigns of successive Manus, evidently handed down from Vedic times; each Manu was supposed to reign for four million three hundred and twenty thousand years (three hundred and sixty by twelve thousand).

In accounting for the coincidence of chronological numbers, Bunsen made out a cycle of sixty years, but the number of the days in the year is clearly the explanation for the Egyptian period, as given by Manetho at a late time, when a highly corrected solar year was known of 365.25 days. He tells us that the old Egyptian chronicle comprised thirty-six thousand five hundred and twenty-five years in as many volumes—a hundred times as many as the days of the year.

Pliny says that the labyrinth of Egypt had lasted three thousand six hundred years.

This number is the first of any considerable sum to meet us in Greek literature (Od. XIV., 20), as noticed by Mr Gladstone, 'Among all the numbers used in Homer the highest which he appears to use with a clearly determinate meaning is that of the three hundred and sixty fat hogs under the care of Eumæus in Ithica. The reason for considering this number as having a pretty definite sense in the poet's mind is that it stands in evident association with the number of days as it was probably then reckoned in the year.'

In China, says Huc, 'This number (three hundred and sixty-five), which corresponds with the days of the year, expresses, according to the geniius of the Chinese, a great multiple, an uninterrupted series.'

It is told of a certain builder that his method of estimating was to guess the quarter, and multiply by four; the ancients would appear to have multiplied by three hundred and sixty. Professor Max Müller tells us how as early as 600 B.C. 'every verse, every word, every syllable of the 'Veda' had been carefully counted;' the number of the syllables was given as four hundred and thirty-two thousand, a number we have already seen formed by a base of three hundred and sixty. Vitruvius says the circuit of the earth was ascertained by Eratosthenes of Cyrene to be two hundred and fifty-two thousand stadia; that is, a hundred fold the number of the degrees by the mystical number of the planets. And Dante, in the *Convito*, says the wise men of Egypt had counted the stars of heaven as twenty-two thousand, which is the nearest round number to three hundred and sixty by sixty (twenty-one thousand six hundred). In the Talmud there are said to be 'as many thousands of myriads of stars as the three hundred and sixty-five days in the solar year,' and in the Persian book, the *Bundahish*, there are six thousand four hundred and eighty stars (three hundred and sixty by eighteen).

In Plato's ideal Republic the inhabitants are five thousand and forty (three hundred and sixty by fourteen).

In the Orphic system there were three hundred and sixty gods, and the Gnostics acknowledged this number of genii.

But it was not alone for the calculation of the unknown quantity in mythical periods, the multitude of the stars, or circle of the earth, that this number was used: for the distance of places and size of countries it was of equal service to the ancient geographers as to the historians and astronomers. Herodotus, Strabo, and Diodorus use it frequently, but apparently without fear of inaccuracy: Strabo, for instance, gives the course of the Euphrates as thirty-six thousand stadia, the distance from Paphos to Alexandria three thousand six hundred, and the Appian way, Rome to Brundusium, three hundred and sixty.

As a measure of circumference, especially for the walls of cities, it was even more largely and more appropriately used; says Herodotus, 'the lake named from Moeris, near which the labyrinth is built, occasions greater wonder; its circumference measures three thousand six hundred stades, or sixty schoenes, equal to the sea coast of Egypt.'

Rawlinson extracted from the accounts given of Babylon, for the circuit of its walls :-

Ctesias	. .	360 stades
Clitarchus	. .	365 „
Q. Curtius	. .	368 „
Strabo	. .	385 „

And he is disposed to accept these as being sufficiently accurate estimates: but if we allow, with the editor of Strabo (Bohn's edition), as to the number three hundred and eighty-five, 'critics agree in this being a mistake for three hundred and sixty-five; the number of stadia in the wall, according to ancient authors, corresponded with the number of days in the year;' the whole series become but dimensions in mythland. Carthage, the same ancient writer says, 'is situated on a peninsula, comprising a circuit of three hundred and sixty stadia, with a wall of which sixty stadia are upon the neck of the peninsula, and reached from sea to sea;' also, he tells us, there was a space fortified on the isthmus of the Chersonesus—three hundred and sixty stadia. Diodorus Siculus says that one stadium of the walls of Babylon was erected every day by the two millions of men employed by Semiramis, so that the circumference was completed in a year. He says that three hundred and sixty thousand men were employed in building the great pyramid. Also, that it was the custom in an ancient Egyptian festival for three hundred and sixty priests to take water from the Nile in as many vessels, and pour them out in a cistern which would not retain the water, thus representing the lapse of the days. And at the Tomb of Osiris, at Philae, three hundred and sixty vases were daily filled with milk during the days of lamentation.

Herodotus, too, makes good use of the number. Darius, he says, divided his empire into twenty satrapies who paid tribute in gold or in kind; five of them paying three hundred and sixty talents, and the Cilicians, 'three hundred and sixty white horses—one for every day.' Also, in connection with Babylon, he tells us 'when Cyrus, in his march against that city, arrived at the river Gyndes, one of the sacred white horses, through wantonness, plunged into the stream, which carried him away and drowned him. Cyrus was much enraged with the river for this affront, and threatened to make the stream so weak that, henceforth, women should easily cross it without wetting their knees. After this menace, deferring his expedition against Babylon, he divided his army into two parts; and having so divided it, he marked out by lines one hundred and eighty channels on each side of the river, diverging every way; then having distributed his army, he commanded them to dig.

His design was indeed executed by the numbers he employed, but they spent the whole summer in the work. When Cyrus had avenged himself on the river Gyndes by distributing it into three hundred and sixty channels, and the second spring began to shine, he then advanced against Babylon.' Pliny says that the Mesopotamian valley was three hundred and sixty miles in breadth, and Herodotus, that when the Persians built two bridges of boats across the Hellespont for the invasion of Greece, one had three hundred and sixty, the other three hundred and fourteen boats. From Egypt, according to the last author, the King Amasis sent a corselet as a present to the Lacedaemonians. 'This corselet was made of linen, with many figures of animals inwrought, and adorned with gold and cotton wool: and on this account each thread of the corselet makes it worthy of admiration, for though it is fine it contains three hundred and sixty threads all distinct.' Pliny gives the number as three hundred and sixty-five.

'It is said that there is a Persian song in which is reckoned up three hundred and sixty useful properties of the Palm' (Strabo). More modern Persian makes much the same use of the number, for Sadi says of the veins, that the body is a meadow through which are flowing three hundred and sixty rivulets. The crocodile, it was said by the ancient writers on Natural History, had three hundred and sixty teeth, and laid eggs sixty at a time. Gibbon tells us the Arabs found in Spain a table of emerald supported on three hundred and sixty-five legs. In Cashmere there was a village with three hundred and sixty fountains dedicated to the moon. *Ayeni Akberi*, quoted by Maurice.)

Tavernier, in the court of the chateau of Augustbourg, in Denmark, was shown a tree so extraordinarily large that it sheltered a number of tables ranged underneath. 'Je ne les ay pas contées mais le Concierge nous dit qu'il y en a autant que des Jours en l'an.'

A Chinese book of birds, which in 'Mythical Monsters' is said to be of the third or fourth century, describes their Phoenix the 'Fung Hwang' as the principal of three hundred and sixty different species of birds. A monument of the seventh century quoted by Huc says that after the primitive and pure religion was forsaken, three hundred and sixty-five sects arose and upset all ideas. In a Japanese work of the beginning of this century, translating a Chinese original some two thousand years old, the mystical relation between the world and man as a microcosm ('Little Heaven and Earth') is drawn out with a detail amazingly like that of mediæval mystagogues. 'Man receives his human form from heaven and earth, and therefore he resembles heaven as to his head, which is round, and earth to his feet, which are square. If in heaven there are five elements, fire, water, wood, metal, and earth, in man there are also the corresponding viscera: lung, heart, liver, stomach, and kidneys; if in heaven there are the five planets or stars, the fire star, the water star, the wood star, the metal star, and the earth star, in man also we find the five fingers and nails; if in heaven there are the four seasons, the twelve months, and the three hundred and sixty days, man displays also the four limbs, twelve great joints, and three hundred and sixty minor articulations' (Fauld's Nipon). Many things seem to have been arranged on a correct numerical plan at Constantinople: in the royal college burnt, it is said, in the reign of Leo the Isaurian (but Gibbon appears to doubt if it ever existed) the president was named the Sun of Science, his twelve associates were Signs of the Zodiac, and the number of books in the library was three hundred and sixty-five thousand. Justinian is said by Codinus to have allotted three hundred and sixty properties to Sta. Sophia, and to have devoted a year's tribute from Egypt, three hundred and sixty-five hundred thousand sesterces, to the construction of the ambo and solia. Sir John Maundeville makes Prester John to be served by three hundred and sixty knights: and tells us that King David had a like number of wives and concubines. They were as many in the story of Hasan in the Arabian Nights, 'three hundred and sixty, according to the number of days in the year.

It is to cities and buildings that the number 'as many as the days in the year ' has the most frequent application; from the earliest descriptions of Babylon and Carthage, as we have seen, to the present day in England, the number and phrase are universally current. It is told of Blenheim; Heriot's Hospital, Edinburgh; Castletown, near Dublin; Syon House, and of many besides, that they have as many windows as the days of the year; but the story is more striking when applied to an ordinary 'Squire's House' in the country. It was told of a house of this sort, to the writer when quite a little child, and the memory of this, as something mysterious, is the origin of this chapter. In some instances, Salisbury Cathedral for example, the comparison is extended through days of the year, weeks, months, and even hours and minutes.

At Calais, landing under the great revolving flashes of the new lighthouse, you are told that it has as many steps as the days in the year.

In the Edda, Thor's palace has five hundred and forty halls: and—

> 'Five hundred doors
> And forty more,
> Methinks are in Valhalla.'

That is, one might suppose, sixty to each storey in the nine-fold heavens.

Lucian describes the city of the Isle of the Blessed: 'Instead of corn, the fields bring forth loaves of ready-made bread like mushrooms. There are three hundred and sixty-five fountains of water round the city, as many of honey, and five hundred, rather smaller, of sweet-scented oil, besides seven rivers of milk and eight of wine.'

Kirwan the Holy, as founded by the Companion of the Prophet, is said to have been three hundred and sixty paces in circuit.

Modern Bokhara is said to have a mosque for every day, so also Cairo.

Nushirwan fortified a great wall with this number of towers. In the Talmud, it is written that there are three hundred and sixty-five crowned heads in Rome, and the same number of dukes in Babylon. 'Rabbi Samlai explains that six hundred and thirteen commandments were communicated to Moses; three hundred and sixty-five negative, according to the number of days in the year; and two hundred and forty-eight positive, according to the number of members in the human body.'

The mediæval writer of the 'Stations of Rome ' says that the eternal city was surrounded by forty-two walls, with 'grete toweres thre hundred and sixty;' the twelfth century Mirabilia says three hundred three score and one.

William of Malmesbury writes of the church of St Sylvester, in Rome, 'and there too the three hundred and sixty-five martyrs rest in one sepulchre.' There is a legend of St Patrick visiting Rome magically, and bringing back three hundred and sixty-five relics to Ireland (Stokes).

'In the Great City (of Rome) there were three hundred and sixty-five streets, and in each street there were three hundred and sixty-five palaces, and in every one of these there were three hundred and sixty five steps; each of which palaces contained sufficient store to maintain the whole world ' (Talmud, Hershon).

The persistence of this story in regard to Rome is remarkable. It is said to-day that there are three hundred and sixty-five churches in the city (Miss Edwards, Nile).

But it is not in Rome only; all over Europe the number is current; in Cyprus the town of Kuklia (Paphos) is reported to have possessed three hundred and sixty-five churches, there are actual traces of six! (Journal of Hellenic Society, 1888.) In Greece, Athens and other towns claim to have had this number of churches.

The old Arab temple at Meccah had three hundred and sixty statues surrounding that of Hobal the sun god. Sale in his notes to the Koran, quoting an Arab author, says 'there were no less than three hundred and sixty idols, equalling in number the days of the year.' Dupuis mentions three hundred and sixty chapels built around the superb mosque of Balk, erected by the chief of the family of the Barmecides, each for one of the same number of genii: also the same number of temples built upon the mountain Lowham in China, and of idols in a palace of the Mikado (du Dalri) in Japan. Pliny describes the wonderful erection of Scaurus, who 'executed the greatest work that has ever been made by man, even when intended to be of everlasting duration, his theatre I mean: this building consisted of three storeys supported on three hundred and sixty columns.'

The Jew Benjamin of Tudela was at Constantinople in the second half of the twelfth century. He writes: 'At Constantinople is the place of worship called Sta. Sophia, and the Metropolitan seat of the popes of the Greeks, who are at variance with the Pope of Rome. It contains as many altars as there are days in the year, and possesses innumerable riches. All the other places of worship in the whole world do not equal Sta. Sophia in riches, it is ornamented with pillars of gold and silver, and with innumerable lamps of the same precious materials.' The story is evidently as well known in the folk lore of the East as here in the West. Wheeler, travelling in Greece in 1670, says of Arta, where is a Byzantine church, 'Signior Manno Mannia, a rich merchant of that place, told me that the cathedral church is a great building that hath as many doors and windows as there were days in the year.' A Mohammedan writer, El-Harawi, visited Constantinople in the thirteenth century, and writes: 'In this place are statues of brass and marble pillars, wonderful talismans and other monuments of greatness, to which no equal can be found in the habitable world. Here is also Agia Sophia, the greatest church they have. I was told by Yakub Ibn Abd Allah that he had entered it, and that it was just as I have described it: within it are three hundred and sixty doors, and they say one of the angels resides there. Round about this place they have made fences of gold, and the story they relate of him is very strange.' El Harawi promises to speak in another place 'of the arrangement of the church, its size, height, doors, and the pillars that are in it; also of the wonders of the city, its order, and the sort of fish found in it; the gate of gold, the towers of marble, the brazen elephants, and all its monuments and wonders:' exclaiming in conclusion, 'This city, which is greater than its fame, may God of His bounty and grace make the capital of Islam!

It is very curious to find Professor Piazzi Smyth claiming that the great pyramid was 365.25 sacred cubits on each side; the whole four sides having a hundred 'pyramid inches' for every day in the year.

In the English translation, made in the end of the sixteenth century, of 'Doctor Faustus,' one of the passages added to the German original, in the account of the travels of Faustus, describes the great circular castle of St Angelo in Rome. 'Well, forward he went to Rome, which lay and doth yet lie on the river Tibris, the which divideth the city into two parts. Over the river are four great stone bridges, and upon the one bridge, called Ponte St Angelo, is the castle of St Angelo, wherein are so many great cast pieces as there are days in the year, and such pieces as will shoot seven bullets off with one fire.'

Another instance from an English source is to be found in Hakluyt's collection, in the account given by Miles Phillips, one of the company put ashore in the West Indies by Master John Hawkins in the year 1568. In a town near Mexico, he says, there was built by the Spaniards a very fair church called Our Lady's Church, in which there is an image of Our Lady in silver and gilt, being as high and as large as a tall woman; in which church, and before this image, there are as many lamps of silver as there be days in the year, which upon high days are all lighted.'

In the ancient Greek town of Tarentum, there was said by Athenæus to be a candelabrum which carried lights equal in number to the days in the year. There is an appropriateness in these lights, as also in the windows of the same number (especially if the windows are in a circular building), which will lead us to a suggestion why this number should be so universally applied to buildings.

Diodorus Siculus says of the Remessium at Luxor: — 'Through these chambers we reach the top of the sepulchre (of Rameses II.) where is a golden circle three hundred and sixty-five cubits in circumference, and one cubit thick. On this circle are marked divisions for every day in the year, and in each is noted the rising and setting of the stars, and the influence which the Egyptian astrologers attributed to these constellations.'

The two stories following are from Benjamin of Tudela: 'In Rome you find eighty halls of the eighty eminent kings, who were all called Imperator, from the King Tarquin to the King Pepin, the father of Charles, who first conquered Spain, and wrested it from the Mohammedans. In the outskirts of Rome is the palace of Titus, who was rejected by the three hundred senators in consequence of his having wasted three years in the conquest of Jerusalem, which, according to their will, he ought to have accomplished in two years. There is also the hall of the palace of the King Vespasianus, a very large and strong building; also the hall of King Galba, containing three hundred and sixty windows, equal in number to the days of the year. The circumference of this palace is nearly three miles. A battle was fought here in times of yore, and in the palace fell more than a hundred thousand, whose bones are hung up there even to the present day.'

'Damascus contains a Mohammedan Mosque, called the synagogue of Damascus, a building of unequalled magnificence. They say that it was the palace of Ben-Hadad, and that one wall of it is framed of glass by enchantment. This wall contains *as many openings as there are days in the solar year*, and the sun in gradual succession throws its light into the openings, which are divided into degrees equal in number to the hours of the day, so that by this contrivance everybody may know what time it is. The palace contains vessels richly ornamented with gold and silver, formed like

tubs, and of a size to allow three persons to bathe in them at once. In this building is also preserved the rib of a giant, which measures nine spans in length and two in breadth, and which belonged to an ancient giant named Abchamos, whose name was found engraved upon a stone of his tomb; and it was further stated in the inscription that he reigned over the whole world.' Indeed, it seems likely enough he did if this is his palace, for it can be none other than the crystal dome of the world fabric itself, with the windows in the firmament, through which the sun shines successively for each day of the year. It is here we may see the root of the attribution in story of this number of windows to earthly temples; the story originally told of the dome of the sky, the house of the sun, as a true explanation of the facts of nature, gets applied, at last to famous buildings from the hands of man, as a myth. Once at least, and probably many times, the number has actually ruled in the design of a temple. This instance is the triple circular platform of the altar of Heaven at Pekin. 'The balustrades have nine by eight, or seventy-two pillars and rails, on the upper terrace. On the middle terrace there are one hundred and eight; and in the lower one hundred and eighty. These amount in all to three hundred and sixty—the number of degrees in a circle' (Edkins in Williamson's Journeys in N. China).

The three hundred and sixty windows of heaven described in the *Bundahish*, the old Persian writings collected about the eighth century (Sacred Books of the East), is clearly enough the prototype of the story of the Damascus mosque of Benjamin of Tudela. The whole is quite a scientific treatise, and especially clear in its statement of the many layers of the heavenly Olympus as one embracing the other, sphere beyond sphere. Mount

Alburz is the firmament within which the sun travels and is restrained. 'Of Mount Alburz it is declared that around the world and Mount Terak the revolution of the sun is like a moat around the world; it turns back owing to the enclosure of Mount Alburz around Terak. *For there are a hundred and eighty apertures in the East, and a hundred and eighty in the West* through Alburz; and the sun every day comes in through an aperture and goes out through an aperture; and the whole connection and motion of the moon and constellations and planets is with it. . . . And when it arrives at Verak (Aries) the night and day have again become equal, as when it went forth from Verak. So that when it comes back to Verak in three hundred and sixty days and the five Gatha days, it goes in and comes out of one and the same aperture; the aperture is not mentioned, for if it had been mentioned the demons would have known the secret and been able to introduce disorder.'

The editor adds that for the 'five supplementary days added to the last of the twelve months of thirty days to complete the year, no additional apertures were provided in Alburz, and the sun appears to have the choice of either of the two central apertures out of the one hundred and eighty on each side of the world. This arrangement seems to indicate that the idea of the apertures is earlier than the rectification of the calendar which added the five Gatha days to an original *year of three hundred and sixty days'*

CHAPTER XII

THE SYMBOL OF CREATION

> 'They entered an apartment containing
> nothing except a black painting
> representing a woman. Her legs reached to
> the top of one of the walls; her body
> occupied the entire ceiling; from her navel
> hung suspended, by a thread, an enormous
> egg; and the remainder of her body, her
> head downward descended the other wall to
> the level of the pavement, where her finger
> ends touched'.
>
> —SALAMMBO.

THE late William Burges built for himself a house strange and barbarously splendid: none more than he could be minutely intimate with the thought of old art, or more saturated with a passion for colour, sheen, and mystery. Here were silver and jade, onyx and malachite, bronze and ivory, jewelled casements, rock crystal orbs, marble inlaid with precious metals; lustre, iridescence and colour everywhere; vermilion and black, gold and emerald; everywhere device and symbolism, and a fusion of Eastern feeling with his style.

In his own bedroom the bed and other furniture is vermilion heightened by crimson glazes. Over the mantle a syren combs her long gilt hair, looking-glass in hand—the mirror no make-believe. The ceiling has red beams crossing a black field studded with small convex mirrors, two inches across, surrounded by gilt rays, the mirrors giving back the candle-light like stars in the midnight sky. The hangings are Eastern embroidery, and the pictures Persian miniatures. The ceiling of the next room is even more extraordinary and mysterious; it is divided into four squares by heavy beams, at the middle point of which there is a convex mirror as large as the moon: each of these squares is crossed by diagonal ribs of bright flamingo red, and a circle is drawn around the points of intersection, from which hang emus' eggs—four in all—large, almond-shaped, and matchless green. They vibrate as you enter the room.

Burges had been to Constantinople, and there a few years ago hung from the dome of Sta. Sophia, 'the fairest and noblest church in the world,' a light frame of iron, an octagon, perhaps some sixty feet across, with radii and inner concentric lines; a vast spider's web, suspended, it must have seemed—such is the immensity—from the very vault of heaven. On this frame were artlessly hung an infinity of lamps, tiny glass vases of oil with floating wicks. Here and again amongst them were suspended ostrich eggs, all placed with no more precision than the lights and oranges on a Christmas tree—long, short, straight and awry, and so near the floor as to be almost under the sight of the reader of the 'perspicuous book,' as he ascended the high pulpit of the conquered mosque with the law and a naked sabre, the alternatives of Islam.

It appears from photographs that vulgar gas lights have now taken the place of the original lamp frame, but it is shown in the interior view given in Texier and Pullan's book. These hanging eggs seem of universal use in the East, alike in church, mosque, and tomb. Still at Constantinople, the frames of lights in the mosque of Achmet are decorated with globes of crystal and ostrich eggs. They are usually stained in bright colours, and have small metal mounts at top and bottom, with a pendant or tassel below. Such a frame carrying lamps and eggs may be seen in the wonderful water colour by Lewis at South Kensington.

The drawings of interiors of Arab mosques in Eber's 'Egypt' show, in a number of instances, a long cord, an egg, and then the lamp. Sometimes as many as a dozen are thus suspended here and there, or in a row from a beam. As far up the Nile as Assouan, Miss Edwards describes a mosque as 'cool and clean and spacious, the floor being covered with matting, and some scores of ostrich eggs depending from the ceiling.' In the Coptic churches the custom is equally observed, as may be seen in Butler's 'Coptic Churches of Egypt', from which the following extract is taken; and it is interesting to note how such a seemingly trivial circumstance as the hanging of an egg from the ceiling arrests the attention, and invites inquiry as to the intention of it—

'The ostrich egg is a curious but common ornament in the religious buildings of the Copts, the Greeks, and the Muslims alike. It may be seen in the ancient church of the Greek convent in Kasr-ash Shammah, and in most of the mosques in Cairo, mounted in a metal frame, and hung by a single wire from the roof. In the churches it usually hangs before the altar screen; but at Abu-s-Sifain, an ostrich egg is suspended also from the point of the arches of the baldakyn. Here and there it is placed above a lamp, threaded by the suspending cord, as in the Church of the Nativity at Bethlehem; and sometimes it hangs from a wooden arm fastened on to the pillars of the nave, as in the Nestorian church of At-Tahara, in Mosul. Sometimes, instead of the egg of the ostrich, artificial eggs of beautiful Damascus porcelain, coloured with designs in blue or purple, were employed, but these have almost entirely disappeared; in the churches of the two Cairos there is, I believe, not one left; but a few still remain in the churches of Upper Egypt, and in the mosques. The tomb mosque of Kait Bey, without the walls of Cairo, contains some fine specimens. These porcelain eggs are considerably smaller than an ostrich egg, but larger than a hen's egg. In the British Museum there is a porcelain egg from Abyssinia, with cherubim rudely painted under the glaze. It clearly belonged once to a Christian place of worship. The "Griffin's egg" was a common ornament in our own mediaeval churches. In the inventory of 1383 A.D., no less than nine are mentioned as belonging to Durham Cathedral; and Pennant speaks of two as still remaining in 1780.... From the fact that marble eggs are said to have been discovered in some early martyrs' tombs at Rome, and that in all Christian lands eggs are associated with Easter-time, some think that the egg was regarded as emblematic of the Resurrection.' Another explanation was given to the author here quoted, by the Copts themselves. An ostrich is proverbially vigilant, therefore

the egg becomes a type of watchfulness. 'This explanation seems
rational,' he adds, 'for the devotion of the ostrich to its brood is,
I believe, in accordance with the facts of natural history, and the
use of the egg may well have arisen in Africa, where the habits
of the bird are better known. At any rate, it is the best solution
of the question.'

From the conclusion we must dissent, for the custom is
universal, and of ancient origin, handed down from a time before Christianity, and all evidence points to the former explanation being the true one—resurrection, or rather, life. The egg is
the typical germ, and therefore the natural symbol of creation.
That the Copts may see in it a symbol of vigilance we need not
at all dispute, nor even contend that it is now used with definite
symbolical meaning. For centuries —millenniums—they have
been suspended from the ceilings of temples and tombs, and
may now be accepted in many instances as merely ornamental
trappings, but even thus accounted of good and sacred omen,
from the importance of the points from which they are suspended; for not only are they hung in sacred buildings, but in
places of honour and of ritual importance. In the churches in
Athens numbers of ostrich eggs hang before the pictures of the
Iconastasis.

The 'Griffin's eggs' were not necessarily ostrich eggs; in one
instance they are described as having a brown and hairy exterior, the inside white, with a clear liquid yelk. We can buy them
now for fourpence, as cocoa-nuts.

In portraits of Eastern kings an egg is sometimes shown
suspended from the centre of the tester of the throne, and this
is quite a traditional observance, which we find followed in Italian art; unless, indeed, a crown is suspended there, like that
Benjamin of Tudela saw at Constantinople, glittering with jewels. Something pendant and freely swinging there must be to
satisfy the Eastern taste; a means of beauty to which we rarely
resort except for lamps, which have had to give way to the rigid
pipe of gas. Cardinals' hats hang with splendid effect from the
dim height of the vaults of foreign cathedrals, drooping and
faded from age. But of all these things, a large jewel swinging
from a cord would be the most mysterious and magnificent, like
that over the Great Mogul's Peacock throne, as seen by

Tavernier: 'When the king sets himself upon the throne, there is a transparent jewel with a diamond appendant of eighty or ninety carats, encompassed with rubies and emeralds, so hung that it is always in his eye.' Another pendant was a green parrot in one emerald. Suspended votive crowns were frequent in earlier days. Constantine is said to have devoted his to the sepulchre of our Lord; and in England, Canute dedicated his to Winchester. In the Cluny Museum are several of these crowns; a treasure-trove at Toledo. They are of about the eighth century, and there are hardly now in the world objects more strangely fas-

cinating, with their pendant strings of jewels—circlets of blazing splendour, in barbaric gold. In a former chapter we have seen that these insignia and orbs were suspended from the ceilings in Persia and in Assyria We meet, too, in several places with a tradition of suspended chains of gold—in the porch of the Temple of Herod, in India, and in Scandinavia.

Pendant ostrich eggs are found in festoons at Jerusalem and at Mount Athos, and may be seen in the west at Toledo and Marseilles. In India, Miss Gordon Cumming saw ostrich eggs suspended from the gorgeous canopy of one of the great tombs of Delhi. At Tunis, they continue to be brought to the tombs, where they are suspended as *ex votos*. The Moorish mosques and tombs in Algiers are crowded with them, and at Kirwan, the holy city inland, they are hung over the tomb of 'The Companion,' with gilded balls of earth from Mecca. At Damascus, Lady Burton describes the tomb of St John as 'hung over with lamps and ostrich eggs; these latter are the ornaments of all holy places, and are supposed to bring good fortune.' It is the same over the tomb of the holy Hasan and his brother. Enough has been said to show that the practice of hanging these eggs is, or was recently, followed in Europe, Asia, and Africa, by all Christians—Catholic, Greek, Coptic, Nestorian Abyssinian, Armenian; and by all Mohammedans in Turkey, Persia, India, Syria, Egypt, and Algeria. Let us follow up the tradition historically.

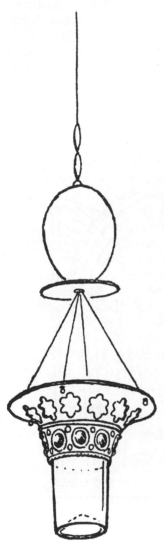

In a picture of the fifteenth century, in the National Gallery, by Marco Marziale, he shows an apse designed after that in St Mark's, Venice, and intended for part of the interior of the Temple. From the centre of this apse hangs a beautiful lamp, threaded on the cord of which is an ostrich egg, directly over the Christ. A picture of Mantegna's has a similar lamp (see next page). Hung over the tomb, as we have seen in several instances, or as here, over our Lord, they are emblems of resurrection, and it is in this sense that they are so universally used in the early spring as 'Easter eggs,' not only in London and Paris, but widely over the world. Walcott's 'Dictionary of Archaeology' says: 'The egg was the symbol of creation in Egypt, and of hope and the resurrection among the early Christians; the custom of giving coloured pasch eggs on Easter morning is found in the East, in the Tyrol, in Russia, in Greece, and many parts of England, where it may be traced back to the time of Edward I., and was observed at Gray's Inn in the reign of Elizabeth. In France, the pasch egg is eaten before any other nourishment on Easter day. Paul II. issued a form of benediction of eggs for England, Scotland, and Ireland; Henry VIII. received a paschal egg in a case of 'silver filagree from the Pope.' And an interesting point follows: 'De Moleon says that at Angers, on Easter day, two chaplains, standing behind the altar, addressed two cubiculars or corbeliers, as they advanced, "Whom seek ye ?" and to the reply, "Jesus of Nazareth, the crucified," answered, "He is risen; He is not here." Then those who personated the Maries took from the altar two ostrich eggs wrapped in silk, and descended singing, "Alleluia, the Lord is risen." '

In the account of Muscovy in 1567, in Hakluyt, it is told how the people prepared eggs against Easter, dyed red with basil, 'and gentlemen and gentlewomen have eggs gilded, which they carry in like manner. They use it, as they say, for a great love, and in token of the resurrection, whereof they rejoice; for when two friends meet during the Easter holidays they come and take one another by the hand; the one of them saith: 'The Lord or Christ is risen;' the other answereth: 'It is so, of a truth,' and then they kiss and exchange their eggs (both men and women), continuing in kissing for days together.' Waterton tells us that where he was at school, in the North of England, they had pasch eggs dyed purple on Easter morning.

The custom of hanging an egg from a dome appears in the story of the lamp, where Aladdin is made to ask for the roc's egg itself to adorn his palace. It was a roc's egg that Sinbad saw, half buried in the sands of Serindib, like a dome fifty feet in diameter. The story of the roc is linked to that of other immense mythical birds. In Japan the appearance of a vast bird is accounted, with earthquake and flood, as one of the 'seven calamities.' 'The Garuda of the Hindus, the Simurgh of the old Persians, the Angka of the Arabs, the Bar-Yuchre of the Rabbinical legends, the Gryps of the Greeks, were probably all versions of the same original fable' (Col. Yule's 'Marco Polo'). Then there are *Amru and Chamru* of the Avesta, which, like the eagle of the Norse and the phoenix of the 'Romance of Alexander,' are perched aloft on the 'tree of all seeds.' The prowess of this mythical bird is one of the story subjects in the world's lore—how it flies with elephants in its grasp, or carries off the strong hero Rustem; or in the Talmud: 'An egg once dropped out of the nest of a bird called Bar-Yuchnei, which deluged *sixty cities* and swept away *three hundred cedars*. The question therefore arose: "Does the bird generally throw out its eggs?" Rav Ashi answered: "No; that was a rotten one"' (Hershon). Already, in the clay writings, there is the mighty Zu bird, on a high mountain, alone.

In Egypt it was the golden egg hatched by the goose that produced the mundane matter; and the bird is only framed on a scale suitable, or even perhaps hardly adequate, to the work it has to do! Nearly all systems giving an account of a genesis agree in this, that as the second or third step there was produced from chaos a gigantic egg. The Egyptian, Phoenician, Assyrian, Hindu, and Greek systems are here at one. 'From Desire and Vapour proceeded primitive Matter. It was a muddy water-black, icy, profound—encompassing insensible monsters, incoherent parts of forms to be born. Then Matter condensed and became an egg. It broke; one half formed the earth, the other half the firmament. The sun, the moon, the winds, and the clouds appeared, and a crash of thunder awakened the sentient animals.' The Orphic fragments and Aristophanes preserve a Greek tradition to the same effect. When only Chaos and Night existed—

> 'At length, in the dreary chaotical closet
> Of Erebus old, was a privy deposit;
> By night the primaeval in secresy laid
> A Mystical Egg, thae in silence and shade
> Was brooded and hatched.'—*The Birds*.

And we may complete the scheme from quite another source—the northern Kalevala:—

> 'From one half of the egg, the lower,
> Grows the nether vault of Terra;
> From the upper half remaining
> Grows the upper vault of Heaven.'

The Hindu code of Manu gives an account entirely similar. The Eternal, willing to create, made by thought the humid principle and in it deposited matter. This primitive germ floated on the waters; soon the mass condensed itself into an egg, brilliant as gold and full of light. From this mysterious envelope was born Brahma, father of all spirits. At the end of a year the egg opened of itself; the upper half formed the sky, the lower part the earth, the air is between, with the eight regions and the reservoir of waters. Another account says the egg contained the five elements, and was enclosed in seven envelopes, like the wrappings of an onion; the seven envelopes falling off became the seven heavens, and the seven worlds of the Brahman world scheme.

M. Dognée, in *Les Symbols Antiques, l'OEuf*, has traced the symbolic use of the egg as it appears on the monuments or in literature, but only in a footnote is the suspended ostrich egg mentioned, as it is found in Temple, Tomb, Church, and Mosque.

'In Japan, in the Pagoda of Miaco,' he says, 'upon a large square altar is placed a bull of massive gold on a block of rock; the animal is ornamented by a rich collar, and pushes with its horns an egg floating in the water contained in a cavity of the rock. To explain this image, the following is told by the Priests. At the time of chaos, before the creation, the world was concealed and inert in an egg which floated on the surface of the waters. . . The divine bull image of creative force broke the egg by a stroke of its horns, and from the egg issued the terrestrial globe.'

The earth itself was considered by several mediaeval writers to be oviform. Bede likened the world to an egg, as did also Edrisi the Arabian geographer: it half floated in water in an upright position, Jerusalem being at the top.

The egg symbol was especially made use of by the Egyptians: it is shown on the monuments and referred to in the texts as a symbol of the embryo creation (Ra in the Egg). Wilkinson, writing of the ostrich, says 'even its eggs were required for some ornamental or religious use, and these with the plumes formed part of the tribute imposed by the Egyptians on the conquered countries where it abounded. The purpose to which the eggs were applied is unknown; but we may infer, from a religious prejudice in their favour among the Christians of Egypt, that some superstition was connected with them, and that they were suspended in the temples of the ancient Egyptians, as they still are in the churches of the Copts.

They consider them the emblems of watchfulness: sometimes they use them with a different view; the rope of their lamps is passed through an ostrich egg shell in order to prevent rats coming down and drinking the oil, as we were assured by the monks of Dayr Antonios.'

When the primordial egg was a part of the cosmological legend of a people, it is easy to see that not only was any egg a symbol of the origin of life, but an especially large egg would be preserved as sacred, and suspended in the temple an image of the world floating in the void: and there does seem something inherently mysterious in the structure and perfect form of a very large egg. One, for instance, in the Museum of Natural History is some thirteen inches long, thirty inches in girth; it will hold two and one-third gallons.

Although there is no incontrovertible evidence of eggs having been suspended in Egyptian temples, of Greece we have the clearest contemporary testimony by Pausanias. 'And hard by (Boonita in Laconia) is the temple of Hilaira and Phoebe, who, the writer of the Cyprian poems says, were the daughters of Apollo; and their priestesses are maidens, called also Leucippides as well as the goddesses. One of their statues was touched up by a priestess of the goddesses, who, with an art not unknown in our days, put a new face on the old statue; but a dream prevented her treating the other statue in the same way.

Here is hung up an egg, fastened to the roof by fillets; they say it is the egg which Leda is said to have laid' (iii. I6). The story of Leda and the parallel one of Latona are but distorted cosmic myths of Night and Chaos, from which is formed the egg mundane.

The egg, firmly and widely accepted as a symbol of life and creation, becomes an emblem of resurrection and new life; and thus the widely-spread observance of Easter egg customs, and the association with the tomb. 'Marble eggs are said to have been discovered in some early martyr's tomb at Rome' (Butler). 'Admitted to the funeral ceremonies, the egg was also deposited in the tomb with the cinders of the dead. Eggs have been found in many tombs at Nola' (Dognee). In the British Museum are six large ostrich eggs, decorated with carvings in low relief, of Archaic style, which were found in one tomb at Vulci, in Etruria. Perrot, who illustrates them, says they are of Phoenician origin. The holes-one large in the centre with three smaller ones round it, and one hole only at the other end—show that they were certainly mounted, probably with a metal cap, for suspension, like the modern ones in the East.

Mr Dennis (Etruria) says: 'The eggs have holes in them as if for suspension, and bring to mind the great roc's egg of the Arabian Nights; or rather, recall the fact of ostrich eggs being suspended in mosques at the present day. Imitations of ostrich eggs in terra cotta (as though the supply of real ones was not sufficient) have been found in the tombs of Vulci. Hens' eggs are often found not only in Etruria but in Greece and her colonies, and are sometimes enclosed in vases. Many museums of Italy contain specimens of this singular sepulchral furniture, probably in this case an emblem of resurrection.' Instances of all these are in the British Museum. In a tomb at Bologna an Etruscan was exhumed with an egg in his hands (Sir F. Burton).

Of the Latin races Dognée says 'it was by following the empire of the same idea that they affected the ovoid form for funeral vases,' an example of the reaction of thought and custom on design which, if true here, is certainly as well founded in the case of Egyptian funeral vases, some of which in the British museum are of the form of an egg: and on the tables of offerings shown in the reliefs there are almost invariably egg-shaped vessels.

Maurice, in his 'Antiquities of India,' says of a serpent coiled around an egg used as a symbol on coins: 'The Phoenecians adorned the lofty temples of Tyre with this emblem, which was

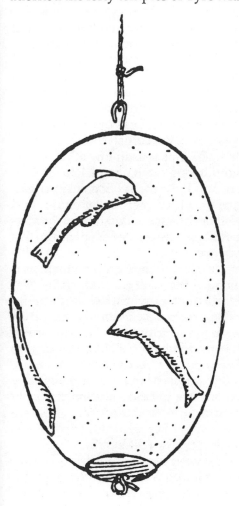

there seen suspended on high, and encircling in its genial folds the mundane

egg or symbol of the universe.' This is entirely parallel on the one side to the account of Pausanias quoted above of the egg suspended in memory of that laid by Leda, and on the other to Chaldian myth. Not only was it a symbol of the earth's first birth to the Phoenicians, but to the Assyrians as well. 'The Chaos serpent,' says Mr Boscawen, 'lay coiled round the earth until slain by Merodach the Lord of Light.' The serpent is represented with the body of a woman, and 'it was this Queen of Chaos who ruled while the earth lay like the cosmic egg in her coils, in the time when as yet none of the gods had come forth.'

Of its early votive use by the Semites, Mr Robertson Smith tells us that the people of Mecca annually visited a tree where they suspended weapons, garments, and ostrich eggs.

In the British Museum is an ovoid stone from Chaldea which has an inscription of Sargon I. (to whose name is attached the earliest date in monumental history) dedicating it to the temple of Sippara: it is of beautiful veined alabaster, about three inches long, and pierced for suspension. Schliemann found several eggs of oriental alabaster at 'Troy' and Mycenae which he considered *ex votos*.

There is a beautiful specimen in the Museum at Athens of an ostrich egg, the surface of which is decorated with swimming dolphins of blue vitreous material probably of Egyptian origin. This was found in a tomb at Mycenae, and would seem to be earlier than the sixth century; it is pierced for a cord, and is an object of singular beauty (see next page). In the South Kensington Museum there are two or three ostrich eggs for hanging, elaborately carved, of Persian work; and many of porcelain, from the churches of Anatolia, painted with cherubim.

It is curious to notice how the hanging lamp affects the form of the egg with which it is so often associated in the East. The Jewish seven-light brass synagogue lamp of several pieces hanging one to the other, has at the bottom an egg-shaped pendant. Many of the Italian renaissance lamps are ovoid: and a very splendid enamelled Russian lamp in South Kensington Museum is of the same form itself, with a pendant separate piece the size and shape of an ostrich egg. It may be that the shape is aesthetically the best for suspension, the form of every drop of water as it falls. It is sufficient for us that the egg was used as an architectural symbol of the origin of the world, suspended from the sky-like dome, record of a genesis, an emblem of the mystery of life, and a hope of resurrection.

Now when we recall the egg which Aladdin desired to suspend from the dome of his palace, we can feel with him that even that room with the twenty-four jewelled lattices was not perfect without it. The mistake was to ask the Genie for the roc's egg itself, and not to be content with its symbol. The adventure is the third and last peril of Aladdin, and the termination of the story: when the younger brother of the African Magician, disguised as the Holy Woman Fatima, is taken to the palace by the Princess Badroulboudour:—'My good mother,' said the princess, 'I am delighted to enjoy the company of such a holy woman as your-

self, who will by your presence bring down blessings upon the
whole palace. And now I mention this palace, pray tell me what
you think of it. But before I show you the other apartments, tell
me how you like this hall?'

'Pardon my freedom of speech, gracious lady,' replied the dis-
sembling magician. 'My opinion, if it can be of any value, is that
if the egg of a roc were suspended from the centre of the dome,
this hall would not have its equal in any of the four quarters of
the world, and your palace would be the wonder of the whole
universe.'

'My good mother,' returned the princess, 'tell me what kind
of bird a roc is, and where the egg of one could be found ?' 'Princess,' answered the feigned Fatima, 'the roc is a bird of prodigious size which inhabits the summit of Mount Caucasus; and
the architect who designed your palace can procure you a roc's
egg.'

Aladdin returned late on the same evening, when the false
Fatima had taken leave of the princess, and had retired to the
apartment allotted to her. As soon as he entered the palace, he
went to the apartment of the princess. He saluted and embraced
her; but she seemed to him to receive him with less than her
usual welcome. 'I do not find you, my princess, in your usual
good spirits,' said Aladdin. 'Has anything happened during my
absence that has displeased or vexed you? Do not, in the name
of heaven, conceal it from me; for there is nothing in my power
that I will not do to attempt to dispel it.' 'I have been disturbed
by a mere trifle,' replied the princess, 'and it really gives me so
little anxiety that I did not suppose that my discomposure would
be so apparent in my face and manner that you could have perceived it. But since you have observed some alteration in me,
which I by no means intended, I will not conceal the cause, inconsiderable as it is. I thought as you did yourself,' the princess
continued, 'that our palace was the most superb, the most beautiful, and the most completely decorated of all the buildings in
the whole world. I will tell you, however, what has come into
my head on thoroughly examining the hall of the twenty-four
windows. Do not you think with me that if a roc's egg were
suspended from the centre of the dome, it would greatly improve
the effect?' 'It is enough, my princess,' replied Aladdin, 'that: you

think the absence of a roc's egg a defect. You shall find by the diligence with which I am going to repair this omission, that there is nothing I will not do for the love of you.'

Aladdin instantly left the princess and went up to the hall of the twenty-four windows; and then taking out of his bosom the lamp, which he always carried about with him since the distress he had undergone from the neglect of that precaution, he rubbed it to summon the genie, who immediately appeared before him. 'O Genie!' said Aladdin, 'a roc's egg should be suspended from the centre of the dome in order to make it perfect; I command you in the name of the lamp which I hold to get this defect rectified.'

Aladdin had scarcely pronounced these words when the genie uttered so loud and dreadful a scream that the very room shook, and Aladdin could not refrain from trembling violently. 'How thou wretch!' exclaimed the genie in a voice that would have made the most courageous man shake with dread, 'is it not enough that I and my companions have done everything thou hast chosen to command? Wouldst thou repay our services by such unparalleled ingratitude as to command me to bring thee my master, and hang him up in the midst of this vaulted dome? For this crime thou dost deserve to be instantly torn to atoms, and thy wife and palace should perish with thee. But thou art fortunate that the request did not originate with thee,and that the command is not in any way thine.'

THE END